MULTICUL

JAMES A. BANKS, *Series Editor*

(continued)

—ENGAGING—
THE
"Race Question"
Accountability and Equity in U.S. Higher Education

ALICIA C. DOWD and ESTELA MARA BENSIMON

Teachers College
Columbia University
New York and London

Published by Teachers College Press, 1234 Amsterdam Avenue, New York, NY 10027

Library of Congress Cataloging-in-Publication Data can be obtained at www.loc. gov

ISBN 978-0-8077-5609-6 (paper)
ISBN 978-0-8077-5611-9 (hardcover)
ISBN 978-0-8077-7346-8 (ebook)

Printed on acid-free paper
Manufactured in the United States of America

22 21 20 19 18 17 16 15   8 7 6 5 4 3 2 1

This book is dedicated to
Ms. Arlease Woods, for her many years of dedicated service
and her important contributions to CUE's mission,
and to
the hundreds of Equity Scorecard evidence team members and
higher education system leaders at colleges and universities
across the United States who have acted as institutional agents
in pursuit of racial equity.

Contents

Series Foreword

Racial segregation as well as race and class inequality are salient characteristics of schools in the United States 60 years after the *Brown v. Board of Education* decision declared racial segregation unconstitutional (Orfield, Frankenberg et al., 2014). We learn in this needed, timely, and illuminating book that the intractable race and class inequality in the elementary and high schools also exists in higher education. Dowd and Bensimon describe ways in which racial and class inequality is institutionalized within higher education and is often not recognized, questioned, or challenged. They point out, for example, that there is a tremendous college completion gap between Whites and African Americans and Latinos. Thirty percent of White students do not attend or complete college; the percentage for African Americans and Latinos is almost 50.

Although access to higher education for African Americans and Latinos has improved significantly since the 1950s and 1960s, most of them attend open-access institutions while most middle-class White students attend selective colleges and universities. Students who attend selective colleges and universities have higher graduation rates because most of these institutions have sufficient resources and provide students with ample learning opportunities and experiences. Many African American and Latino students who have the academic abilities and skills required to attend selective colleges and universities enroll in open-access institutions for many reasons, including close family ties, inadequate counseling, little information about financial aid, and insufficient knowledge about higher education options.

The goal of this incisive and informative book is to provide faculty and administrators in higher education with the theoretical, conceptual, and practical knowledge and tools needed to increase equity and access in higher education for minoritized and low-income students. Castles (2004) identifies two pivotal dimensions of multiculturalism: (1) *recognition of cultural diversity*—in which a nation publicly proclaims that it consists of diverse cultural, racial, ethnic, linguistic, and religious groups; and (2) *social equality*—in which a nation takes action to ensure that diverse groups have equal opportunities to participate in its institutions. Dowd and Bensimon view "diversity initiatives" as part of the recognition dimension, and their work as situated within the social equality dimension, which they conceptualize as attaining equity in higher education by "reversing the college education gap for" minoritized groups such as African Americans, Latinos, and Native Americans.

Dowd and Bensimon—after nearly two decades of innovative and creative work to increase equity in higher education using their ingenious *Equity Scorecard* process as a vehicle—have concluded that institutionalized racism is a major barrier to attaining equity in higher education and that colorblindness is a significant factor that obscures White privilege. An important goal of the Equity Scorecard intervention process is to make institutionalized racism explicit. Another goal is to help faculty and administrators who participate in the process to identify ways in which they can initiate changes within their institutions that will increase equity for marginalized students and create environments in which all students will experience democracy, justice, and cultural recognition.

Dowd and Bensimon—unlike school reformers who focus primarily on academic achievement and test scores as indices of educational attainment—have a broad and inclusive view of educational excellence, which includes creating and sustaining an educational environment in which students can not only achieve academically but will "experience a sense of attention, self-respect, and recognition of personhood." The transformative and caring vision that Dowd and Bensimon articulate for higher education is especially timely and appropriate because of the growing population of students from diverse racial, ethnic, cultural, linguistic, and religious groups who are attending schools in the United States. Hopefully, a significant percentage of these students will matriculate at colleges and universities.

American classrooms are experiencing the largest influx of immigrant students since the beginning of the 20th century. Almost 14 million new immigrants—documented and undocumented—settled in the United States in the years from 2000 to 2010. Less than 10% came from nations in Europe. Most came from Mexico, nations in Asia, and nations in Latin America, the Caribbean, and Central America (Camarota, 2011). The influence of an increasingly diverse population on U.S. schools, colleges, and universities is and will continue to be enormous.

Schools in the United States are more diverse today than they have been since the early 1900s, when a multitude of immigrants entered the United States from Southern, Central, and Eastern Europe. In the 20-year period between 1989 and 2009, the percentage of students of color in U. S. public schools increased from 32% to 45% (Aud, Hussar, Kena, Bianco, Frohlich, Kemp, & Tahan, 2011). If current trends continue, students of color will equal or exceed the percentage of White students in U.S. public schools within one or two decades. In 2010–2011, students of color exceeded the number of White students in the District of Columbia and in 13 states (listed in descending order of the percentage of ethnic minority students therein): Hawaii, California, New Mexico, Texas, Nevada, Arizona, Florida, Maryland, Mississippi, Georgia, Louisiana, Delaware, and New York (Aud, Hussar, Johnson, Kena, Roth, Manning, Wang, & Zhang, 2012).

Language and religious diversity is also increasing in the U.S. student population. The 2012 American Community Survey estimated that 21% of Americans aged 5 and above (61.9 million) spoke a language other than English at home (U. S. Census Bureau, 2012). Harvard professor Diana L. Eck (2001) calls the United States the "most religiously diverse nation on earth" (p. 4). Islam is now the fastest-growing religion in the United States, as well as in several European nations such as France, the United Kingdom, and The Netherlands (Banks, 2009; Cesari, 2004).

The major purpose of the Multicultural Education Series is to provide preservice educators, practicing educators, graduate students, scholars, and policymakers with an interrelated and comprehensive set of books that summarizes and analyzes important research, theory, and practice related to the education of ethnic, racial, cultural, and linguistic groups in the United States and the education of mainstream students about diversity. The dimensions of multicultural education, developed by Banks (2004) and described in the *Handbook of Research on Multicultural Education* and in the *Encyclopedia of Diversity in Education* (Banks, 2012), provide the conceptual framework for the development of the publications in the Series. The dimensions are content integration, the knowledge construction process, prejudice reduction, equity pedagogy, and an empowering institutional culture and social structure.

The books in the Multicultural Education Series provide research, theoretical, and practical knowledge about the behaviors and learning characteristics of students of color, language-minority students, low-income students, and other minoritized population groups, such as LGBT youth (Mayo, 2014). This is the fourth book in the Series that focuses on higher education, which is a significant topic in the Series. The other higher education titles describe issues related to Asian Americans (Teranishi, 2010), undocumented Latino students (Pérez, 2012), and equity for Latino students (Contreras, 2011).

This insightful book is not only theoretically rich and engaging; it is also a helpful resource. It blends theory, research, and practice by providing rich descriptions of a five-phase Equity Scorecard Process that teams of administrators and faculty can use to research their own policies and practices that perpetuate inequality. This process also enables teams to design and implement organizational change that will facilitate movement toward increased equity for all students. The voices of Dowd and Bensimon are authentic because of their original, extensive, and valuable work with colleges and universities. Their message is compelling because of the urgent need to increase equity in our polarized and increasingly unequal society (Stiglitz, 2012). I hope their voices and message will soar and their work to increase equity in higher education will become boundless.

James A. Banks

REFERENCES

Aud, S., Hussar, W., Johnson, F., Kena, G., Roth, E., Manning, E., Wang, X., & Zhang, J. (2012). *The condition of education 2012* (NCES 2012-045). Washington, DC: U.S. Department of Education, National Center for Education Statistics. Retrieved from http://nces.ed.gov/pubsearch.

Aud, S., Hussar, W., Kena, G., Bianco, K., Frohlich, L., Kemp, J., & Tahan, K. (2011). *The condition of education 2011* (NCES 2011-033). U.S. Department of Education, National Center for Education Statistics. Washington, DC: U.S. Department of Education, National Center for Education Statistics Retrieved from http://nces.ed.gov/programs/coe/pdf/coe_1er.pdf

Banks, J. A. (2004). Multicultural education: Historical development, dimensions, and practice. In J. A. Banks & C. A. M. Banks (Eds.). *Handbook of research on multicultural education* (2nd ed., pp. 3–29). San Francisco: Jossey-Bass.

Banks, J. A. (Ed.). (2009). *The Routledge international companion to multicultural education.* New York and London: Routledge.

Banks, J. A. (2012). Multicultural education: Dimensions of. In J. A. Banks (Ed.), *Encyclopedia of diversity in education* (vol. 3, pp. 1538–1547). Thousand Oaks, CA: Sage Publications.

Castles, S. (2004). Migration, citizenship, and education. In J. A. Banks (Ed.), *Diversity and citizenship education: Global perspectives* (pp. 17–48). San Francisco: Jossey-Bass.

Camarota, S. A. (2011, October). *A record-setting decade of immigration: 2000 to 2010.* Washintgton, DC: Center for Immigration Studies. Retrieved from http://cis.org/2000-2010-record-setting-decade-of-immigration

Cesari, J. (2004). *When Islam and democracy meet: Muslims in Europe and the United States.* New York: Pelgrave Macmillan.

Contreras, F. (2011). *Achieving equity for Latino students: Expanding the pathway to higher education through public policy.* New York: Teachers College Press.

Eck, D. L. (2001). *A new religious America: How a "Christian country" has become the world's most religiously diverse nation.* New York: HarperSanFrancisco.

Mayo, C. (2014). *LGBTQ youth and education: Policies and practices.* New York: Teachers College Press.

Orfield, G. & Frankenberg, E. with Ee, J. & Kuscera, J. (2014, May 15). *Brown at 60: Great progress, a long retreat and an uncertain future.* Los Angeles, CA: University of California, The Civil Rights Project (Proyecto Derechos Civi-

les). Retrieved from http://civilrightsproject.ucla.edu/research/k-12-education/
integration-and-diversity/brown-at-60-great-progress-a-long-retreat-and-an-
uncertain-future/Brown-at-60-051814.pdf

Pérez, W. (2012). *Americans by heart: Undocumented Latino students and the
promise of higher education.* New York: Teachers College Press.

Stiglitz, J. E. (2012). *The price of inequality: How today's divided society endan-
gers our future.* New York: Norton.

Teranishi, R. T. (2010). *Asians in the ivory tower: Dilemmas of racial inequality in
American higher education.* New York: Teachers College Press.

U.S. Census Bureau (2012). *Selected social characteristics in the United States: 2012
American Community Survey 1-year estimates.* Retrieved from http://factfinder2.
census.gov/faces/tableservices/jsf/pages/productview.xhtml?pid=ACS_12_1YR_
DP02&prodType=table

Preface

It seems to me that before we can begin to speak of minority rights in this country, we've got to make some attempt to isolate or to define the majority.

— James Baldwin, "In Search of a Majority" (an address delivered February 1960 at Kalamazoo College; 1964b, p. 108)

In writing this book, we have taken "sustenance and perspective by drawing on the humanities" (Ayers, 2006, p. 81), particularly James Baldwin's civil-rights-era essays, which are still highly—and, unfortunately—relevant today. We say "unfortunately" because by 1963 Baldwin was already observing with frustration:

White Americans have contented themselves with gestures that are now described as "tokenism." For example, white Americans congratulate themselves on the 1954 Supreme Court decision outlawing segregation in schools; they suppose, in spite of the mountains of evidence that has since accumulated to the contrary, that this was proof of a change of heart—or, as they like to say, progress. Perhaps. It all depends on how one reads the word "progress." (1964a, p. 75)

In 2013–2014, when this book was written, White and Black Americans were observing the 50th Anniversaries of the March on Washington and the Civil Rights Act with mixed and conflicting assessments of "progress." Commentators such as the *New York Times* op-ed columnist Charles Blow (2013)—who like Baldwin is African American—acknowledged that while "explicitly codified discrimination" had diminished, "the more sinister issues of implicit biases and . . . structural and systematic racial inequality" linger. Nevertheless, White Americans who have tired of attending to issues of racial equality are content with the "tokenism" of landmark celebrations. "In this moment," Blow observed, much as Baldwin had 60 years previously, "Blacks and whites see the racial progress so differently that it feels as if we are living in two separate Americas."

"Mountains of evidence," to use Baldwin's term, that a "change of heart" has not taken place are available for those who care to examine statistics about poverty, school segregation, and incarceration in America. Yet, "centuries of majority privilege and minority disenfranchisement are being overlooked in puddle-deep discussions about race and inequality, personal responsibility and societal inhibitors" (Blow, 2013). To define the *majority* requires recollection of the processes by which minority groups became "minoritized" and willingness to examine how the effects of enslavement, colonization, disenfranchisement, and other forms of subjugation live on today. The majority is reluctant to define itself in relation to "minorities" in ways that motivate sustained and transformative attention to "structural and systematic racial inequality." And many, including educators, administrators, and teachers in training, dispute that structural racism exists or that they hold responsibility to take action to address racism (Grant, 2009).

As we discuss in this book, the call to equity and to "equity mindedness" in our action research (Bensimon & Malcom, 2012) is a call for collaborators, variously positioned as researchers and practitioners, to address structural racialized inequities in education by taking action on their own campuses and in their own higher education systems. Baldwin's observation that "we've got to make some attempt to isolate or to define the majority" before we can address "minority rights" resonates with us. Too often college and university practitioners undertake equity and diversity work with deficit views of students and communities of color. They see themselves as helping the disadvantaged rather than as freeing themselves from unjust social structures (Kemmis & McTaggart, 2005). In many quarters the culture of poverty perspective (Gutierrez, Morales, & Martinez, 2009) has not been displaced by introspection about the causes of the American failure to "achieve our country" (Baldwin, 1964a, p. 89), to live up to the nation's ideals of democratic equality and freedom.

In this book and in our work more generally, we take it as a "personal question," as Baldwin expressed it (1964b, p. 11), to look for solutions to the persistent problems of racial inequity in education. We write this book with the aim of supporting professional accountability among college and university practitioners for reducing racism in all its forms. In our work, we argue against color-blind perspectives and ask teams of practitioners engaged in action research using the Center for Urban Education's Equity Scorecard to adopt a critical perspective and become "race-conscious" in a positive way (Bensimon & Malcom, 2012). In keeping with this stance and to articulate our positionality (Milner, 2007) as researchers, we share our personal stories of growing up in a racialized society. Again we turn to James Baldwin's words as a sounding board for our reflections on our racial and ethnic identities.

ALICIA DOWD'S REFLECTIONS

Although born in 1963, one year before the Civil Rights Act was enacted, I had not read James Baldwin's work until 2012 while on sabbatical in Australia. As Baldwin explains in his essay "The Discovery of What It Means to Be an American," he left America because "I doubted my ability to survive the fury of the colour problem here" (1964b, p. 17). Self-exiled in Paris and later Switzerland, he arrived at the "reconciliation" (p. 18) that he was, indeed, American, despite the torments that had been and were still being unleashed on the "American Negro" (p. 19).

With first dates of publication in America and Europe spanning the end of the 1950s and the beginning of the 1960s, Baldwin's essays provide a personal, intellectual, and historical series of reflections on the "color problem" as the civil rights era was beginning. He looks to the past and to the future. "Alas, Poor Richard" reflects on the life and death (in 1960) of "Negro" cultural icon Richard Wright, whose writings first opened the eyes of White America to the depravations of the Jim Crow South. "A Fly in Buttermilk" provides an account of the painful clashes of court-ordered school integration, which had just begun in the Southern states and which struggle on today. Baldwin visits the mother of a boy who was the first and only "Negro" to attend an "integrated" school (p. 78). He asks her why she would send her son to face such hostility. She describes the terrible quality of education at her son's previous school, the "colored" school. Even now these decades later, her response has an enduring, universal quality. She replies that she wanted her son, who had always done well in school but was getting into mischief as he reached adolescence, to get a decent education: "My boy's a good boy and I wanted him to have a chance" (p. 81). Baldwin punctuates her statement by observing that 18 of the boy's former classmates had recently been sentenced to the chain gang.

The rhetoric and media coverage surrounding the reelection of President Barack Obama in 2012 showed that the problem of the "color line" is a contemporary problem. America's first Black president rarely spoke about Black America. Despite this silence, the question of minority rights and the definition of the majority were very much on stage, through political campaigns and advertising meant to divide voters into haves and have-nots, true Americans and others. The "new majority" prevailed in the election, with African American, Latino, and Asian voters combining with gay and lesbian voters, urban voters, and single White women to carry the day for the Democratic Party.

On sabbatical, I watched the election from afar and reflected. Like Baldwin, I was at a great distance from America, but in contrast to him I never doubted my Americanness. I was, after all, in the majority: a White, middle-class, native English speaker. And perhaps that—that very lack of doubt, that lack of a sense of "otherness" or "double consciousness," in W.E.B. DuBois' famous phrase—provides the definition of the majority that Baldwin was seeking. For the majority very clearly does not rely on numbers. The new majority may have carried the election, yet its diverse members are not truly a coalition and its non-White members, though growing in numbers, are still "minoritized" by their lack of political and economic power and spoken of as "minorities." Latinos are the majority of the young adult population in many states, but the wealth of White Americans is 18 times greater than that of Latinos. Though the day of the chain gang may be gone, harsh sentencing laws and uneven, racialized enforcement have put a burgeoning number of young Black men in jail or on parole, withering their chances of obtaining employment or federal financial aid for college.

While legal action and education are the two main avenues for upward mobility in the United States, the courts are assisting social progress for gays and lesbians today much more assertively than for racial/ethnic minority groups. The recent Supreme Court case *Fisher v. University of Texas*, which upheld affirmative action, was decided on the thinnest of margins and on merits that were badly battered by the dissenting judges. The notion of a compensatory obligation to counter the history and legacy of racism was barely part of the discussion.

Baldwin's essays in *Nobody Knows My Name: More Notes of a Native Son* (Baldwin, 1964b) portray America's majority as willingly blind to the racism inherent in segregated schools, a portrait still too accurate today. My formative years in a "White flight" neighborhood of Queens, New York City, and my current view of the differences in educational resources on the University of Southern California (USC) campus and at our neighboring community colleges in Los Angeles lead me to view a willingness toward indifference, combined with the ongoing fear of the racialized "other," as still very much the underlying issue.

I never heard my parents use racist language or slurs, but I gleaned a sense of wariness of the neighborhood being taken over, as African Americans, Puerto Ricans, Jamaicans, and other Caribbean families moved in and White families moved out. Observing the changes, my father invoked the metaphor of the "British square," a military formation from the 17th century in which musketeers ("red coats") stood in a square back to back ready to defend each other from attack from any direction. For some reason, when our neighborhood changed from White to Black, the houses on the four corners of the street, ours being one, remained White. My father, who was always an armchair sociologist despite his day job as a construction worker, would scratch his head, look at me, and say, "We have a British square." Then he would laugh with a squint of his eyes and shrug his shoulders with resignation.

I went to a grammar school on the White side of a park dividing my neighborhood and to a high school a bus and subway ride away, both parochial schools. My commute to the affluent neighborhood of my high school on the other side of Queens was a journey through demographic change. The bus took me past a housing project on Jamaica Avenue, where the residents were nearly all Black. I would look out the window at a world that was foreign to me, with its brick buildings and harshly paved plazas, and wonder what it would be like to live there. Over time the world became clearly divided between White and Black, the latter being the group on which the fears of difference, crime, and "otherness" were uniformly projected. I did not learn until much later of the hand of real estate agents, banks, federal urban renewal policy, and the federal housing administration in creating incentives for "White flight," as they corralled Black families into certain blocks and pushed highways through where communities once were.

These are my reflections on how I first learned about race and otherness. I chose to quote James Baldwin because I know that I cannot voice the experiences of the Black man or the Black woman in America, or the experiences of others who have lived with racial or ethnic discrimination. I can, however, actively learn about race and racism and find ways of countering it. Doing that, as Baldwin suggests, depends on understanding my place in the majority.

ESTELA MARA BENSIMON'S REFLECTIONS

In America, the colour of my skin had stood between myself and me; in Europe, that barrier was down.

—James Baldwin, *Nobody Knows My Name* (1964b, p. 11)

My first conscious realization of race as a basis of differentiating between people came on my arrival, as an immigrant, to the United States at the age of 12. It was 1962, just one year after Baldwin's *Nobody Knows My Name* was first published. Until then my life had revolved around my neighborhood in Neuquen, a very small and remote town in the southern part of Argentina. My experience of moving between countries and contexts was in many ways the opposite of Baldwin's. When my parents decided to abandon Argentina and start a new life in the United States, we left a life of relative privilege for one where "the color of my skin," or perhaps more important, the language I spoke, began to matter in new ways. I first became conscious of "the barriers" of race once I acquired the new identity of immigrant and foreigner. My life in Neuquen was almost idyllic. I went to a public school, wearing a starched, pleated white uniform and carrying a gigantic briefcase. I was part of a nucleus of friends whose parents, like mine, were well-educated, cosmopolitan, and affluent. We lived in large homes that had separate living quarters for *"las muchachas"* (maids), owned cars, took winter vacations in Buenos Aires and summer vacations on Argentina's silky Atlantic ocean beaches.

Although I did not become conscious of race until I arrived in the United States, in fact I had been surrounded by racial separation all my life. I experienced segregation as the natural order of things. *"Las muchachas"* who made my bed in the morning, cleaned my room, washed and ironed my white uniform, cooked my meals, and walked to the grocery store, the baker, and the butcher, purchasing the items in my mother's neatly written *"mandados"* list, were dark-skinned. They were not of "European" ancestry like us and everyone with whom we associated. No one, at the time, and to a large extent today in contemporary Argentina, questions the separate and unequal world of *"las muchachas"* and their employers.

In preparation for our immigration, my parents went on a serious diet and my father shaved his mustache. Our orientation to the United States was based on the one or two American movies we saw just about every week in Neuquen. The lesson we learned was that Americans are blond and blue-eyed, thin, and men did not have mustaches. Black people did not figure very prominently in these movies. My parents changed their physical appearance to make their foreignness less noticeable.

We arrived in the United States in May 1962, just as the civil rights movement was getting under way. The vestiges of Jim Crow were still very much in evidence. We travelled through the South by bus and I can still recall the separate water fountains and bathrooms for Blacks and Whites at the bus stations. My parents did not give up speaking Spanish. Nor did they seem particularly self-conscious about being Spanish speakers. I, on the other hand, avoided speaking Spanish as much as I could. I do not recall exactly how this happened, but somehow I must have gotten the message that it would be better to fit in.

My parents settled in Cherry Hill, New Jersey, a very White and middle-class suburb of Philadelphia with a large concentration of upwardly mobile Jews who had moved from nearby Camden, a city with a rapidly growing Black population. My high school had a very small number of Black students, and no Latinos. The only other foreign students were my best friend, a blond French-speaking Egyptian with considerable élan, and a girl from Pakistan. All my other friends were White Americans, the "majority." I thought of myself as White, but I also knew that as a foreigner who spoke English with an accent I was an outsider.

In 1966 I went off from my parents' home to a state college in New Jersey. Here my peers were much more likely to be working class. Many were White, but for the first time my circle of friends included Blacks, Cubans, and Puerto Ricans. Unlike me, most were first-generation college students. It was in college, in a course on urban education, that I developed an interest in working in urban schools. I was admitted into the Teacher Corps program where the majority of my peers were Black. In my senior year I was placed as an intern at Broadway Junior High School in Newark, a city that was undergoing a racial and political transformation. Around this time I first began to grapple with my mixed feelings about speaking Spanish and speaking English with an accent. I met other Spanish speakers, many Puerto Ricans who were active in the Young Lords Movement and community organizing. I began to discover myself as a "Latina," an identity that was both affirming and marginalizing at the same time, as I remembered my parents' great efforts to belong.

In the early 1970s I worked for Aspira, a nonprofit organization dedicated to improving educational opportunities for Puerto Ricans in New Jersey. By the end of the decade I was the director of Bilingual Education in New Jersey's Department of Higher Education, a position that to a great extent dealt with issues of access to higher education for students with limited proficiency in English. Around that time, my boss told me I should go to graduate school. With that push, I enrolled full-time in a doctoral program. My studies gave me the opportunity to again travel around America, as I interviewed college presidents and other executive administrators as part of a study on leadership teams and teamwork.

In the early 1990s I codirected a project on organizational change that was part of the National Center for the Improvement of Teaching, Learning, and Assessment, which was funded by the Office of Educational Research and Implementation (OERI). This project took me to campuses that were embroiled in the "curriculum war" debates about whether diversity courses should be required of all undergraduates. On one campus, a bitter conflict erupted, and was featured on the national news, between African American and Jewish faculty and staff. I saw firsthand the futility of dealing with diversity exclusively as a matter of human relations when the issues that fueled the conflict were as much about power and politics as they were about racism and anti-Semitism. Another study I led in the mid-1990s revealed to me the very different perceptions individuals have of race relations, depending on their racial and ethnic backgrounds. I interviewed tenure-track faculty who were Latino, African American, Native American, and Asian American, as well as department chairs, on predominantly White campuses. The experience of being "minority" was often quite stark for these junior professors. Yet, for the most part, the department chairs had little perception of the experiences of minority faculty or the myriad ways their own practices and that of their peers were experienced as marginalizing and oppressive.

My views about diversity are based on the impressions I have formed in the 30 years that I have been involved in higher education. As we describe in Chapter 1, by 2000, with funding from the James Irvine Foundation, I started an action research project that involved 14 public and private, 2-and 4-year campuses in Southern California. We dubbed them "opportunity colleges," because these institutions enrolled very high percentages of African American and Latino students. They and other institutions like them were and still are the main avenues to higher education for students of color. The goal of this project, which was called the Diversity Scorecard, was to work collaboratively with institutional teams on the use of data to identify and document inequities in educational outcomes for African American and Latino students, and to develop strategies to eliminate them.

Being in a long-term collaborative relationship with these 14 campuses gave me the opportunity to view the work of "diversity" in real time. I heard how faculty and staff talk about diversity, the interpretations they come up with to explain away "bad news," and the frequency with which anecdotal information trumped evidence, even when the very data that were the source of that evidence was in their hands. I was also in the unique position to observe how Diversity Scorecard participants' assumptions about diversity and diverse students changed over time, as they became more "equity-minded." Soon afterwards, I renamed the Diversity Scorecard the Equity Scorecard, because it was clear to me that the meanings of diversity and equity were quite distinct. As we observe the 50th anniversary of the Civil Rights Act in 2014, I feel now more than ever that there is a need to assert a commitment to equity. Despite the gains in access to higher education over the last 50 years and the many contributions of diversity scholars and practitioners of multiculturalism, the playing field for African Americans, Latinos, and Native Americans is not yet level. To quote Lyndon Johnson's famous speech at Howard University's commencement ceremony in 1965 (LBJ Presidential Library), we have not yet achieved "equality as a fact, equality as a result," but the need is as pressing as it was then:

> You do not wipe away the scars of centuries by saying: "now, you are free to go where you want, do as you desire, and choose the leaders you please." You do not take a man who for years has been hobbled by chains, liberate him, bring him to the starting line of a race, saying, "you are free to compete with all the others," and still justly believe you have been completely fair. . . . This is the next and more profound stage of the battle for civil rights. We seek not just freedom but opportunity—not just legal equity but human ability—not just equality as a right and a theory, but equality as a fact and as a result.

ADVANCING THE CAUSE OF EQUITY

We ask ourselves, as university researchers, what can we do and what should other practitioners be asked to do to bring about "equality as a fact, equality as a result" for people of color on college campuses and in the broader American society. This book presents the intellectual journey we have been on to answer those questions. The Center for Urban Education's (CUE) Equity Scorecard is intended to evoke contradictions between our espoused purpose and the racial inequities that are more than evident at our front doors, in our classrooms, and in our auditoriums and amphitheaters come graduation day. The pages that follow present what we have learned, how we have changed our approach to our research as a result of our experiences, and the challenges we have encountered along the way. The text integrates our insights with those of other scholars of race, equity, and organizational change in the American context and identifies what we view as the most important strategies for advancing the cause of accountability for equity.

THE ORGANIZATION OF THIS BOOK

This book consists of an introduction, four core chapters, and a concluding chapter with recommendations for institutional action. The introduction poses the challenge of accountability for racial equity in higher education, calling on the field to collectively ask the "race question" with wisdom. Higher education is having a muddled conversation about race and equity. Therefore, we describe the standards of equity based on three theories of justice: justice as care, justice as fairness, and justice as transformation. The chapter introduces the action research design, tools, and theory of change for CUE's Equity Scorecard, which has been developed to address issues of racial equity in higher education.

The core chapters—Chapters 2–5—present case studies. Our objective throughout in presenting these is to theorize organizational learning and change toward racial equity, drawing on our experiences with Equity Scorecard evidence teams to provide models for those who wish to design similar tools and processes.

Chapter 2, "Remediating 'Race Talk,'" draws on a case study of a CUE partner institution. Here, and throughout the book, we use pseudonyms to refer to field sites and Equity Scorecard participants. Chapter 2 features "Las Flores Community College" (LFCC). Equity Scorecard evidence team members at LFCC, which is located in California, collaborated with us and our colleagues at CUE over a number of years through several cycles of practitioner inquiry using Equity Scorecard tools. This chapter highlights the steps we take to center issues of racial equity in the inquiry process. It shows how cultural–historical activity theory can be used to design tools and processes for participatory critical action research. Focusing on an Equity Scorecard evidence team meeting where race talk surfaced a critical disturbance in the organizational culture, Chapter 2 concludes with a discussion of the relevance of critical race theory in the design of just accountability policies. It argues for a shift from diversity to critically conscious equity policies as the basis for deeper institutional commitments to justice.

Chapter 3, "Enacting Justice as Care," provides examples of changes in practitioner agency and educational practice that occurred through inquiry using Scorecard tools. Again set in California, it shows how faculty members who engaged in inquiry used CUE's Equity-Minded Syllabus Review Protocol to gain insight on their pedagogical relationships with minoritized students. Faculty members were moved by an ethic of care to make changes in their pedagogical relationship with students. We viewed these changes as a sign of the transformative potential of practitioner inquiry to bring about change in educational practice. However, it was also clear that the faculty members lacked the full extent of knowledge, expertise, and authority necessary to enact justice as care in a manner that would significantly change the organizational culture.

Chapter 4, "Enacting Justice as Fairness," moves east to Wisconsin, a state that has been an important nurturing ground for the Equity Scorecard. Here we report on the inquiry process and outcomes of several evidence teams that were convened at University of Wisconsin campuses. It demonstrates the actions of team members who were motivated by the Equity Scorecard process to experiment with changes in programs, institutional policies, and other organizational structures to improve racial equity in student participation and outcomes. This chapter provides examples where evidence team members identified inequitable policies and practices on their campus and took steps to change them. They were motivated by a deepening commitment to their role in addressing equity issues. Their beliefs shifted, in many cases, from "weak" to "strong" conceptions of equity. The findings presented in this chapter demonstrate the potential of action research and inquiry to shake practitioners from a passive position where racial inequities are somebody else's business to a position of agency as institutional change agents.

Chapter 5, "Enacting Justice as Transformation," is set in both California and Wisconsin. It focuses on racial equity issues in developmental education and access to bachelor's degrees through transfer from community and technical colleges. The first part of the chapter presents our experiences collaborating on the Wisconsin Transfer Equity Study. The second part revolves around the California community colleges' Basic Skills Initiative, which we studied as part of CUE's California Benchmarking Project. Both the Wisconsin Transfer Equity Study and the Basic Skills Initiative present cases where educational and system leaders were engaged in thoroughly coordinated and well-supported inquiry projects that nevertheless "hit a wall" when it came to enacting transformative changes. The potential that these projects had to produce meaningful changes in policy and practice was dampened by political considerations and limitations of political organization. The design of our tools was inadequate to address these expertise gaps. Thus the chapter raises challenges to relying on individual practitioners to enact justice as transformation, which requires changes in the systemic policies and practices that create structural racism.

Following the four core chapters with their case studies, Chapter 6, "Designing Equitable Institutions," serves as a conclusion to the book and offers recommendations for action. We believe that colleges and universities should engage more directly with the relationship between race and place in their institutional histories and in their current priorities. We recommend that the equity-enhancing potential of the "college completion agenda" be strengthened by adopting data practices designed to identify equity gaps and organizational routines that commit to achieving institutional equity goals.

Acknowledgments

We wish to acknowledge the contributions of colleagues at colleges and universities across the country who have collaborated with us in developing the Equity Scorecard by engaging in practitioner inquiry as Equity Scorecard evidence team members, team leaders, and system leaders. To our benefit, they have continually challenged us to refine our action research design and tools.

We also wish to express our appreciation to the philanthropic foundations that have provided funding throughout the development and implementation of the Equity Scorecard. This support has enabled us and CUE colleagues to conduct the research that is the basis for this book. Many foundation officers gave generously of their ideas, positively influencing the direction of our work. We are grateful to Gregory Anderson, Jeannie Oakes, and Doug Woods (Ford Foundation); Pamela Burdman (William and Flora Hewlett Foundation); Sam Cargile, Gerry Davis, Tina Gridiron-Smith, Derek Price, and Heather Wathington (Lumina Foundation for Education); Barbara Gombach and Michele Cahill (Carnegie Corporation of New York); Donna Heilman (Teagle Foundation); Elise Miller (Bill and Melinda Gates Foundation); and Hilda Hernandez-Gravelle and Robert Shireman (The James Irvine Foundation).

CUE's policy work has also evolved over time through our partnership with the Western Interstate Commission on Higher Education (WICHE). We have greatly valued the collaborative support of David Longanecker, WICHE's president, and are thankful to have been able to draw on his extensive experience and expertise in the policy arena.

Action research is a truly collaborative enterprise. We could not have engaged in it all these years without the many contributions of dedicated and talented staff members at the Center for Urban Education. Over time, many of CUE's project specialists and program directors have contributed intellectual capital and tremendous design talents to the materials and tools of the Equity Scorecard. We are grateful to Georgia Lorenz Bauman, Edna Chavarry, Lee Ann Cornell, Marcy Drummond, Frank Harris III, Laura Lord, Elsa Macias, Debbie Peterson Hanson, Rosita Ramirez, Marta Soto, and Tara Watford. Don Polkinghorne and Robert Rueda were among our USC Rossier School of Education colleagues who provided research expertise at key points in the development of the Scorecard. We are thankful for their contributions and regularly take note of the many insights their work introduced into our ways of thinking about action research.

All of us were supported by an administrative team anchored by the indomitable Arlease Woods and headed for many years by Dominic Alpuche, who was also instrumental in developing the Benchmarking Equity and Student Success Tool (BESST). Maricela Rodriquez kept us in order with her true love of accounting and Emily Ogle has assumed managerial responsibility with such aplomb that she almost makes it look easy (almost). We express our most sincere appreciation to everyone at CUE for their contributions to the center's mission and research. Without them, the research on which this book is based would not have been possible.

Deanna Cherry of Deanna Cherry Consulting has been CUE's go-to facilitator for nearly 5 years. We call on her to provide professional facilitation for our most important and high-profile meetings with such regularity that we can scarcely imagine holding one without her. She contributed her considerable energy and talents in the facilitation of "difficult dialogues" about race in numerous settings and also contributed many valuable action research design ideas, drawing on her experience in interpersonal relations.

Many doctoral students studying at USC's Rossier School of Education have been integral to CUE's research. They assisted us in designing action research protocols, provided data coaching to practitioners, interviewed Scorecard evidence team members, and conducted observations and critical policy analyses of transfer policy in six states (in addition to Wisconsin).

Dissertation studies are of particular value to study long-term patterns and prospects for change, because doctoral students often spend longer in the field than more established researchers and have time to collect observational data. Such data tend to be lacking because most studies of data use and organizational change tend to rely on retrospective practitioner accounts provided through interviews or surveys (Little, 2012). We have drawn on these studies, and other doctoral research, as secondary data to synthesize our insights. This tradition of doctoral student research continues at CUE, producing rich case studies of individual agency for racial equity and organizational learning through action research.

Case studies and equity gap analyses completed under Estela Bensimon's guidance, many of which used interpretive methods, generated new insights about the lived experience of practitioner inquiry by evidence team members and leaders (Bauman, 2002; Bishop, 2014; Bruning, 2006; Bustillos, 2007; Chase, 2013; Hao, 2006; James, 2008; Jones, 2013; Mmeje, 2012; Peña, 2007; Pickens, 2012; Post, 2007; Rivas, 2008). Case studies and developmental evaluation studies completed under Alicia Dowd's guidance have informed our understanding of what is working and what is not in the Equity Scorecard's action research design to bring about practitioner agency and praxis (Aguirre, 2012; R. Z. Brown, 2012; Cornell, 2012; Enciso, 2009; Gaur, 2009; R. Gonzalez, 2009; Javier, 2009; Levonisova, 2012; Patton, 2014; Salazar-Romo, 2009; Smith, 2012; Subramaniam, 2012; Tschetter, 2009; Vines, 2012; Woerner, 2013). We are grateful to have had the opportunity to work with and learn from these practitioner-scholars. They have made substantial contributions to the knowledge base about critical action research for equity in postsecondary settings, and their insights have informed our ongoing redesign of the Equity Scorecard tools and processes. We would like to express particular appreciation for the research conducted in Wisconsin by Robin Bishop, Megan Chase, and Loni Bordoloi Pazich.

As we wrote this book, Alicia Dowd was on sabbatical and affiliated as a visiting scholar at the Center for the Study of Higher Education (CSHE) at the University of Melbourne, Australia. She extends her appreciation to CSHE colleagues Sophie Arkoudis, Richard James, Gabriele Lakomski, and Simon Marginson for welcoming her so graciously and providing her with a wonderful research home away from home. We received helpful comments on a draft of the preface from Boston College professor Ana Martínez-Alemán, for which we thank her.

As Executive Acquisitions Editor at Teachers College Press, Brian Ellerbeck shepherded our prospectus and was kindly patient as we wrote past our deadline for submitting our manuscript. We are thankful for this additional time, as it allowed us to deepen our thinking in a number of areas of the text. Finally, and leaving "best for last," we would like to thank series editor Professor James Banks. He believed in our work and encouraged us to write this book. His faith in us was tremendously important to both of us through the inevitable ups and downs. We express our deep appreciation to him for being an inspiration and a leader in our field.

CHAPTER 1

Introduction

The beginning of wisdom is calling things by their right name.

—Chinese proverb, attributed to Confucius

The proverb above is a popular one. A quick Internet search reveals its appearance on numerous websites, where it is put to use in various contexts and quests for enlightenment. And no wonder, because the proverb seems to hold a promise that if we can just name something properly, we will understand it and perhaps even know what to do about it. This book is titled *Engaging the "Race Question": Accountability and Equity in U.S. Higher Education. Accountability* in this case refers to the responsibility of educators and policymakers to hold themselves and one another responsible for creating and sustaining just, caring, equitable, and effective postsecondary learning environments in America's colleges and universities. Over 50 years after the signing of the Civil Rights Act in 1964, racism in education is still a pressing and difficult problem. The *race question* refers to the challenge of gaining wisdom about how to name, talk about, and do something about racism in educational contexts and the racialization of educational opportunity. *Racialization* "is the process by which skin color, or any other physical attribute, becomes imbued, over time, with social, cultural, psychological, socioeconomic, and/or political significance" (Teranishi & Briscoe, 2006, p. 593). In postsecondary education in the United States, the core educational concepts of college, college student, and education are racialized by the ideological values of merit and equal opportunity.

The challenge of engaging issues of race and racism constructively is not unique to higher education settings, where our work is centered. However, it has particular salience because colleges and universities have played and continue to play a role in sorting people based on racial characteristics. Historically, this role was based on legal discrimination in college admissions, enrollment, and resource distribution. Currently, discriminatory sorting occurs through structures and practices that are so thoroughly institutional-

1

ized that they seem normal (to many) until we ask why racial inequities in outcomes are occurring so routinely and prevalently.

The field of higher education scholarship and policy has not yet acquired the language and tools to collectively engage the race question with wisdom and apply that wisdom to hold ourselves accountable for equity in education. As stated previously by Estela Bensimon and Robin Bishop (2012):

> Simply put, the scholarship and policy frames that are familiar to decision-makers and practitioners too often fail to ask the "race" question critically and knowledgeably. Race, understood critically, focuses on structural racism: the systematic but often invisible way in which routine practices, traditions, values, and structures perpetuate racial inequity in higher education. (p. 2)

This book describes the ways we have faced the challenge of "critically and knowledgeably" asking the race question as we engaged practitioners at colleges and universities and policymakers in higher education systems in the Center for Urban Education's (CUE) action research process known as the Equity Scorecard. It is about the ways practitioners make sense of equity and accountability when they are participating in constructive attempts to address higher education's legacy of racism and contemporary role in sustaining discriminatory practices. It is about the steps college leaders, faculty, and student affairs professionals can take to play the role of "institutional" and "empowerment" agents (Stanton-Salazar, 1997, 2011) enacting changes geared at attaining racial equity.

That said, this book also acknowledges the challenges that often stop well-intentioned practitioners in their tracks and keep them from gaining a sense of agency and efficacy in pursuit of equity goals. These challenges include the unquestioning acceptance by many college and university practitioners of liberal ideology, most prominently the values of equal opportunity, color blindness, and meritocracy, which block awareness of structural racism (Haney-López, 2010; Laughter, 2013). As Taylor (2009b) observes:

> Merit and colorblindness claims have an insidious effect that has been difficult to counter with traditional forms of research, statistics and legal procedures. By insisting on a rhetoric that disallows reference to race, groups affected by racism cannot name their reality or point out racism without invoking denial and offense. Colorblindness also has the perilous effect of rendering White privilege invisible, and thus reinforcing its preeminence. (p. 8)

ACCOUNTABILITY FOR RACIAL EQUITY

Structural racism is difficult to address because it is incorporated into core practices and organizational features of higher education such as admissions and student assessment. As Chesler and Crowfoot (1989) have argued, "our history of racial injustice is maintained through contemporary policies and practices, and is reflected in the dramatic differentials . . . in opportunity and other outcomes that still exist between people of color and white persons" (p. 436). Yet White Americans often view such dramatic differentials with historical "amnesia" (Taylor, 2009b, p. 7). Consequently, White students and practitioners are much less likely than their peers of color to see occurrences of racial discrimination on their campuses (Harper & Hurtado, 2011) or to acknowledge that educational practices can cause "social harm" (Kleinman & Copp, 2009). Racism is such a "normal fact of daily life in U.S. society" that the "assumptions of White superiority are so ingrained in political, legal, and educational structures that they are almost unrecognizable" (Taylor, 2009b, p. 4).

Further, many White Americans do not acknowledge that educational practices can be discriminatory in the absence of conscious, overt, interpersonal acts of racial discrimination (Haney-López, 2010). They do not realize that racism can be embedded within organizational structures and routine operations. The notion of structural racism calls attention to the ways institutional structures and policies "operate to pass on and reinforce historic patterns of privilege and disadvantage," such as deciding which groups gain access to the baccalaureate and which do not (Chesler & Crowfoot, 1989, p. 441). Developing awareness among practitioners that educational practices are rooted in culture and history, including racist practices, is necessary to address issues of racial inequities (Bartolomé, 2008; Dowd, Sawatzky, & Korn, 2011; Grant, 2009; Harper, 2012; Harper & Hurtado, 2011; Howard, 2006; Ladson-Billings, 2009). Accountability policy can support practitioner knowledge and agency to dismantle structural racism, but the current state of affairs in postsecondary accountability practice and policy is characterized by historical amnesia about higher education's role in the racialization of educational opportunities and outcomes.

Colleges and universities in the United States are institutions operating in a society where "the racist virus in the American bloodstream still afflicts us" (Moynihan, quoted in Bobo & Charles, 2009, p. 244). To understand how this "virus" lives on in educational practice and policy, the higher education community of scholars and policymakers must take up a concerted humanistic and social scientific endeavor to counter racism in its interpersonal, institutional, and structural forms. We see a central role for action research in that endeavor.

Our purpose in writing this book is to share what we have learned, by doing action research focused on racial equity, about promoting accountability in higher education to address the race question with wisdom. Here the term *accountability* refers both to *public accountability*, as it exists in state and federal postsecondary policies and bureaucratic procedures, and to *practitioner accountability*, as it exists in professional norms and standards (Martínez-Alemán, 2012). The audiences for this book include college and university policymakers and practitioners who wish to act as institutional agents (Stanton-Salazar, 2011). As many scholars argue, practitioners must play a role to remediate the educational practices that are resulting in inequitable educational experiences and outcomes among racial and ethnic groups in the United States (Gutierrez et al., 2009; Gutierrez & Vossoughi, 2010; Nasir & Hand, 2006; Roth & Lee, 2007).

We acknowledge that structural racism in educational systems and the racialization of educational opportunities are not the only causes of educational inequities. Disparities in economic and political power are also important and interrelated factors. However, in our experience, racism is the one factor contributing to unequal educational participation and outcomes that is most often unstated or avoided in public conversations, particularly in professional settings.

This is not surprising because race continues to be a highly divisive topic in the United States. We believe that most higher education practitioners, if asked, would say that racial discrimination has no place in American higher education and they fully support equal opportunity. Yet most are not actively involved in taking steps to end racial inequities in student outcomes. Some may feel that the movements toward diversity, multiculturalism, and inclusiveness are making significant headway and that higher education is contributing in effective ways to right past wrongs. We offer a mixed assessment on that score. Important work has been done, is under way, and should continue. But more needs to happen, and at a higher level of coordination and urgency.

Racial Segregation in Higher Education

Equity goals today must focus on equalizing the quality of opportunity and closing the college completion gap that is both an outcome and a contributor to ongoing segregation in U.S. society. Unless the national diversity project commits to these goals we can expect increasing economic and social polarization along racial lines. In contrast to diversity initiatives that focus on intercultural understanding, equity initiatives focus on reversing the college education gap for American Indians, African Americans, Latinos, and other subordinated racial/ethnic groups to reduce racial polarization.

A shift from a diversity focus to an equity focus is necessary because despite growing acceptance of diversity and difference in some quarters of American society, neighborhoods and schools are as much or more segregated than they were in 1964 when the Civil Rights Act was passed (Orfield, Bachmeier, James, & Eitle, 1997; A. Wells, 2014). Higher education is no different.

First-generation Latino and African American college students are disproportionately enrolling in open-access institutions, while their White counterparts with equivalent scores on standardized tests choose selective institutions (Carnevale & Strohl, 2013). In *Separate & Unequal*, Carnevale and Strohl conclude that racial stratification "permeates the two- and four-year college and university system" to such a degree that "the American postsecondary system is a dual system of racially separate and unequal institutions," marked by "polarization by race and ethnicity" (p. 7). The report's findings forcefully highlight the failure of the decades-long diversity agenda to realize the liberal American ideal of equal opportunity in education. The playing field is not yet equal, and this is due both to the personal consumption and investment choices of White families and to institutional practices in higher education.

Carnevale and Strohl observe that racial polarization of postsecondary education evident in their findings is due to "complex economic and social mechanisms." They offer several insights as to the nature of those mechanisms, including the following: White parents have higher levels of college completion than their African American and Hispanic counterparts; they capitalize on the greater assets of largely segregated public schools or private schools "to pass their educational advantages on to their children" (p. 7); Whites have, on average, six times the wealth of African Americans and Hispanics (p. 39); and Whites segregate themselves in affluent neighborhoods, leaving African Americans and Hispanics in "geographic isolation" (p. 37). In addition, differences in per-student funding are stark, with selective private, not-for-profit institutions having 30 times the level of resources as open-access colleges. Colleges and universities do not by themselves cause racial segregation, but their efforts to address the social problem of segregation and the status quo of institutional and structural racism have been insufficient.

Racial segregation occurs within and between colleges and universities of different institutional types. Over time, selective colleges have, with varying intensity and commitment, used affirmative action, institutional financial aid, and targeted recruitment strategies to enroll students of color. Yet most selective colleges remain disproportionately White. The majority of students of color are enrolled in open-access and for-profit colleges. Approximately half of community colleges in the United States are racially segregated, with the college enrollments largely mirroring segregation in the communities they serve. About a quarter are predominantly White and a quarter are predominantly African American or Latino (Goldrick-Rab & Kinsley, 2013, p. 119). Those colleges that predominantly enroll students of color tend to have larger enrollments. Their per-student revenues are half of what is available on a per capita basis in predominantly White colleges (p. 124). Urban community colleges face a funding deficit relative to rural and suburban colleges (Dowd, 2004). These lower levels of funding are associated with lower levels of student success (Melguizo & Kosiewicz, 2013). Similarly, 4-year institutions with higher levels of resources are likely to have higher graduation rates (Titus, 2006).

In addition, tracking occurs within open-access colleges through standardized testing and placement into degree-credit–bearing and non-degree-credit–bearing courses; through greater use of transfer pathways by higher-income students (Dowd, Cheslock, & Melguizo, 2008; Dowd & Melguizo, 2008); by limited access to bachelor's degrees for students in technical colleges; and by differential participation in the "high-impact practices" (Kuh & Vesper, 1997) believed to foster student engagement and success. Community college students are easily tripped up by college entry tests that have not even been validated as relevant measures of a student's capacity to succeed in college (R. S. Brown & Niemi, 2007). Remedial placements consign many students of color to academic pathways with overall degree completion rates of less than 10%.

Segregated enrollment patterns are not entirely due to academic preparation. Students of different racial and ethnic groups who are apparently equally well prepared for college opt to enroll in community colleges at different rates, with "more than 30% of African Americans and Hispanics with a high school grade point average (GPA) higher than 3.5 going to community colleges compared with 22% of Whites with the same GPA" (Carnevale & Strohl, 2013, p. 8). Comparisons of academic preparation and college outcomes based on standardized test (SAT/ACT) scores show that high-scoring African American and Hispanic college students are much less likely than their White peers to complete any college credential (Carnevale & Strohl, 2013). These disparities in enrollment by institutional type contribute to racial inequities in outcomes. Those African Americans and Latinos who are do attend a selective institution see a degree completion boost, graduating "at a rate of 73 percent compared with a rate of 40 percent for equally qualified minorities who attend open-access colleges" (p. 12).

While community college students have only limited access to college advisors to help them understand the importance of the placement test (Grubb, 2006), students at private nonprofit institutions benefit from access to advisors who provide them with academic and emotional support to complete college. In addition, remedial testing regimes can often be avoided altogether by students whose families can afford private institutions (Attewell, Lavin, Domina, & Levey, 2006).

An Imperative Focus

The focus of this book on postsecondary accountability for racial equity in higher education is imperative because, despite progress in improving access for subordinated racial/ethnic groups, sizeable racial/ethnic gaps in college participation and degree completion remain (Perna & Finney, 2014). Whereas only 30% of White students either do not attend or do not complete college, the comparable figures for African Americans and Latinos are near 50% (Carnevale & Strohl, 2013, p. 11). Over half a century after the Supreme Court's landmark *Brown v. Board of Education* decision ordering an end to segregation in schooling, racial segregation in U.S. higher education is entrenched and growing (Carnevale & Strohl, 2013; Goldrick-Rab & Kinsley, 2013).

While access to college has improved, as shown by increasing enrollments of Latinos and African Americans in college, new entrants to postsecondary education who are students of color are enrolling primarily in open-access institutions. Their White counterparts, however, are enrolling in selective institutions (Carnevale & Strohl, 2013), which have much greater resources at their disposal to expend on each student (Baum & Kurose, 2013; Carnevale & Strohl, 2013; Melguizo & Kosiewicz, 2013; Titus, 2006). The second-chance, open-access institutions that are intended to create equality of opportunity are not doing so effectively, in large part because they are not funded adequately to do the job of producing equitable outcomes in a society with such a high degree of social and economic inequality. Racial segregation in college enrollments traces directly to selective university admissions policies and segregation in the communities surrounding colleges (Olivas, 2005a, 2005b).

Consistent with their overrepresentation in 4-year universities and selective institutions and underrepresentation in community colleges, White students are also much less likely than their Latino and African American peers to conclude their postsecondary schooling with a certificate or associate's degree. Among students who enroll in 4-year institutions, White students also have higher rates of bachelor's degree completion than Latino and African American students: 41% who started at 4-year institutions in 2004 completed their degrees. The comparative figures for Latinos and African Americans are 28% and 20%, respectively (Melguizo & Kosiewicz, 2013). The racial gap in bachelor's degree completion is even greater when the comparison is made in the broader group of potential college students in the college-age population. In this case, the completion rates are 57% for White students and only 36% and 37% for Hispanic and African American students, respectively (Carnevale & Strohl, 2013, p. 11).

A Growing Disjuncture

In saying that the race question is not being addressed "with wisdom" in U.S. postsecondary accountability, we are not saying that issues of equity are not being addressed at all or that the ways they are being addressed are not of consequence to Native Americans, African Americans, Latinos, Southeast Asians, Pacific Islanders, undocumented immigrants, and other traditionally subordinated groups, whom we refer to as "minoritized" rather than "minority" groups. We use the term *minoritized* instead of *minority* to amplify the fact that certain groups acquire minority status through the beliefs and social processes enacted by other groups who place them in a position of the "minority," the "other." From this point of view, the status of minoritized groups is defined by their lack of power and more limited access to economic and social assets, rather than by numerical underrepresentation in society or educational institutions (Gillborn, 2005).

Equity is a word that appears in reports and conversations about accountability policies and responses to accountability. In fact, Gregory Anderson (2012), who had served as a program officer at the Ford Foundation, observed:

> Despite the work that still needs to be done regarding equity, the term itself has been more or less universally embraced by policy centers/institutes, major foundations interested in reform, and the higher education field. This growing congruence with respect to the use of "equity" in higher education stems in large part from the reality that demographic trends in the United States have altered the higher education landscape forever. (p. 135)

But despite the emergence of equity as a common point of discussion, "a significant and growing disjuncture exist[s]" among the policy, practitioner, and research communities whose involvement is "critical to ensuring equity and access for historically underrepresented students" (Anderson, 2012, p. 134).

In this disjuncture, the race question is muted or referred to euphemistically as the problem of the "achievement gap." The concerns and methods advanced by critical race scholars in response to or in attempts to shape educational policy are not aired. The liberal ideological commitment to equal opportunity and meritocracy is evident—and, we venture to say, quite authentic—in diversity initiatives, multicultural curricula, and the widespread calls of organizations involved in forwarding the "college completion agenda," a broad public discourse calling for institutions to produce more college graduates. But liberalism's adherents are too often closed, for intellectual or political reasons, to critiques from scholars of color who draw on more critical perspectives. From these quarters, liberalism's self-congratulatory and incremental approach does not do enough to "envision the personal responsibility and the potential sacrifice inherent in [the] conclusion that true equality for blacks [and other racialized groups] will require the surrender of racism-granted privileges for whites" (Bell, 2009a, p. 75).

Unlike the term *equity*, terms such as *racialized, subordinated, oppressed, minoritized*, and *White privilege* (Gillborn, 2005)—which are used in critical policy analysis—are not often heard in mainstream policy circles. In these circles the focus today tilts more toward the technical aspects of student persistence and degree completion databases, metrics, scorecards, and accountability design. This is because the root cause of racism is not being addressed in public accountability initiatives, which are more concerned with efficiency and productivity (Dowd, 2003; Dowd & Shieh, 2013; Dowd & Tong, 2007; Pusser, 2011). Some postsecondary educators (of different races and ethnicities) certainly practice professional accountability with an explicit recognition of racism as a root cause of inequalities in schooling. However, it is difficult for these race-conscious practitioners to achieve a broader impact when the very language they use to communicate their knowledge is disallowed as too politically volatile or lacking in objectivity. As a result, accountability environments and communities are largely segregated by language, place, and methodology.

NEGOTIATING MEANINGS OF JUSTICE AND EQUITY

Thus far we have used the expressions *educational equity* and *racial equity* without specifying their meaning. Equity means different things to different people. In some ways, the abstractness and pliability of the term *equity* is advantageous when one wants to open a dialogue about race and racism in the United States. The expression *equity* does not elicit the fear and defensiveness evoked by the word *racism*. It is open to interpretation, and people have an intuitive sense that when we are speaking about equity we are speaking about fairness. In a general sense, this intuition is correct. Equity is a standard for judging whether a state of affairs is just or unjust. To say that a policy or practice is inequitable is to say that it is unjust. However, many college and university practitioners quickly interpret equity as referring to equality of opportunity, which is only one aspect of most formal definitions of equity. This narrowing of the meaning of equity shuts out more nuanced principles that we believe should also be guiding accountability policy.

In this book we draw on several standards of justice and argue that accountability policy must draw more explicitly on these standards. To begin to lay the foundation for the interpretations and arguments that will be carried throughout the book, this section provides an introduction to ethical reasoning on the standards of justice, which we group as stemming from theories of justice as fairness, justice as care, and justice as transformation (the term *transformation* encapsulating concepts derived from critical race theory). The notion of transformative justice is muted in the postsecondary accountability agenda today. We utilize it to conceptualize a social scientific endeavor promoting change toward "a decent society," as Taylor, Gillborn, and Ladson-Billings so plainly and accurately stated in their forward to the *Foundations of Critical Race Theory in Education* (2009), an edited volume that reproduces foundational works in this field of study.

Justice as Fairness

Standards of justice are intended to guide the distribution of society's benefits, including the recognition of human rights (Noddings, 1999). A major impediment to meaningful reform of educational policies and practices that produce racial inequities is a lack of shared understanding of what equity means. The theory of justice as fairness is dominant in educational policy-making today, with thinking about postsecondary educational policy heavily influenced by the work of philosopher John Rawls (DesJardins, 2003; Lucas, 1980; Paulsen & Toutkoushian, 2008; St. John, 2013). In terms directly relevant to postsecondary policy issues such as affirmative action, remedial education, and college admissions, Rawls's principles of justice state that "offices and positions" are to be "open to all under conditions of fair equality of opportunity." However, "social and economic inequalities," such as they are introduced through policy, for example, through differential taxation or need-based financial aid, "are to be arranged . . . to the greatest benefit of the least advantaged" (Rawls, 1971, p. 302).

Rawls's principles of equal rights provide the foundations for the concepts of horizontal and vertical equity, which feature in scholarship on K–12 educational policy, particularly in consideration of school finance reform and litigation (Clune, 1994; Levin, 1994; Odden & Picus, 2008; Satz, 2007; Verstegen, 1998) and to a lesser extent in discussions of equity in community college financing and accountability (Century Foundation Task Force, 2013; Dowd, 2003; Dowd & Shieh, 2013). The standard of *horizontal equity* asserts that those with equal needs deserve equal educational resources. *Verti-

cal equity, which is more often the point of contention, states that those with greater needs should receive greater resources.

In some formulations of the vertical equity principle, it has become the basis for educational policy in support of outcome equity and adequacy. *Outcome equity* judges equality based on educational outcomes rather than human, material, and financial inputs. The principle of *adequacy* asserts that society is obliged to provide adequate resources to educate all students to a minimum threshold level. That threshold of schooling is where one can function as a full member of a democratic society and experience the benefits of social and economic well-being. Not surprisingly, what that threshold should be, and who should pay to finance the educational system necessary to obtain it, is a point of conflict.

Although the formal language of Rawls's social contract theory and concepts of "distributive justice" are not "heard in everyday discussions of justice, the points of emphasis are familiar," as philosopher Nel Noddings (1999) points out:

> People have *rights*; people are to be regarded as *individuals*; everyone should have a fair chance at securing desirable positions (*equal opportunity*); and if the rules cannot remove inequalities, they should at least be designed so that inequities favor the least advantaged. All of these are familiar (if controversial) notions in contemporary political conversation. . . . [Yet,] they are notoriously difficult to encode without a discussion of the goods people seek, and these goods cannot be limited to material welfare. (p. 9)

In other words, creation of a fair educational system demands something besides the equitable distribution of material and financial resources. It requires the equitable distribution of other "social primary goods," which include liberty and self-respect (Rawls, 1971, p. 303).

Rawls's first principle of justice, standing ahead of and operating in conjunction with the principles of equal opportunity and the provision of unequal (greater) benefit to the least advantaged, addresses this other, nonmaterial dimension of a just system. The first principle states that "each person is to have equal right to the most extensive total system of equal basic liberties compatible with a similar system of liberty for all" (Rawls, 1971, p. 302). In this statement, it is clear that the liberties of individuals depend on a society's "total system" of liberties. But what should this "total system" look like and what steps are necessary to provide the "least advantaged" with an equal right to equal basic liberties? Noddings (1999), arguing that Rawls's principles are "notoriously difficult to encode" in educational policy, urges that an ethic of care should be applied in educational policy (p. 9).

The notion of care provides a different standard for judging whether a state of affairs is just or unjust. From the care perspective, school settings should be places where students not only get a fair chance and equal material resources, but also, and equally important, where they experience a sense of attention, self-respect, and recognition of their personhood.

Justice as Care

Based on Rawls's (1971) principle of equal basic liberties and an individual's fundamental right to self-respect, current applications of his theory of justice as fairness, based narrowly on an individual's right to equal opportunity and resources, are insufficient to bring about racial equity in education.

Noddings, the author of *The Challenge to Care in Schools* (1992), offers a different set of principles to guide educational policy. Noting that often "injustice lies not only in whatever inequalities result [from educational policies], but even more deeply in the lack of consent of those concerned," Noddings (1999) argues that it is necessary to move beyond the current focus on the rights of individuals to benefit from equitable distribution of material resources. In addition, educational policies must grant individuals and communities a right to experience self-respect as a primary social good (Rawls, 1971) in educational settings. The right to self-respect is neglected in educational policy today due to overreliance on "scientific processes" and standardized "one-size-fits-all" standards that prevail over humanistic thinking (Noddings, 1999, p. 18). Offering care as an ethical concept to guide educational policy, care theorists elevate attention to the experiences of students and communities that are most forcefully subject to policy implementation, for example, the experiences of students of color who were bused to primarily White schools under desegregation policies. Care theorists ask, "Do the cared-fors *feel* cared for under [educational] policies? Are their legitimate goods considered? Are relations of care enhanced or weakened?" (Noddings, 1999, p. 16).

Without dismissing that a "just government" must at times "prod action through law," Noddings (1999) emphasizes the importance of attending to the needs and experiences of local communities. She gives priority to the question—one that must be asked to fully assess whether a policy is just—"What happens to the quality of experience for those who will undergo the consequences of our [policy] decisions?" Noddings argues it is not acceptable to "pronounce" a problem "theoretically solved" based on universal tenets of individual rights and then fail to reckon with the consequences of policy decisions for specific communities (p. 12). Among the dangers of scientifically applied theorizations of universal rights are "losses of identity, group respect, and community feeling" (p. 12), which we refer to as a "self-worth tax." Heeding these dangers leads to the conclusion that "nothing could be as unjust as an attempt to achieve equity through sameness" (p. 13). Advocates of justice based in care "seek an equity that [takes] account of differences" and places importance on the relationship between the caregiver and the "cared-for" (p. 13).

Instituting an ethic of care in educational policy will require adherence to the "participatory ideal," which is based on principles of nondiscrimination and nonoppression. Creating nondiscriminatory and nonoppressive educational settings requires a presumption of "equal worth" of students and communities (Howe, 1997, p. 70). Recognizing that "differences in group power and group privilege are real and rooted in group membership" (p. 77), the participatory ideal calls for full recognition and participation of groups that have experienced "cultural imperialism," which is "the imposition of the cultural meanings of the dominant group on all groups" (p. 70). Educational settings that undermine students' sense of self-worth through cultural imperialism or through inadequate provision of material resources provide only "bare" opportunities to education. To provide "real" rather than "bare" opportunities, educational programs, curricula, and systems must be designed with awareness of the meaning students assign to their interactions with the institution. These interactions "function to increase or diminish the worth of formal educational opportunities" (p. 28).

The participatory ideal has two dimensions: the personal and the political. The personal dimension calls on educational institutions to avoid imposing social harm—a "self-worth tax"—on students. The political dimension prioritizes democratic values and insists on adherence to principles of nonoppression (Howe, 1997, p. 105). In higher education scholarship, these ideals are articulated in validation theory and theories of institutional and empowerment agents (Stanton-Salazar, 1997, 2011). As introduced by Laura Rendón (1994) and subsequently incorporated in student affairs practice and higher education scholarship (Rendón, Jalomo, & Nora, 2000), "validation refers to the intentional, proactive affirmation of students by in- and out-of-class agents (i.e., faculty, student, and academic affairs staff, family members, peers) in order to: 1) validate students as creators of knowledge and as valuable members of the college learning community and 2) foster personal development and social adjustment" (Rendón Linares & Muñoz, 2011, p. 12).

Validation theory applies the concept of justice as care to theorize improvements in the relationship between college and university faculty members and students who have experienced subordination based on their racial or ethnic characteristics. Drawing on Freire's liberatory pedagogy, the practice of validation "honors diverse ways of knowing, invites all to participate in knowledge production, allows both teachers and students to be holders and beneficiaries of knowledge, promotes an ethic of care, helps students find voice and self-worth, and works with a curriculum that is democratic, inclusive, and reflective of student backgrounds" (Rendón Linares & Muñoz, 2011, p. 20). In our work, we have drawn on Stanton-Salazar's (1997, 2011) conceptualization of institutional agents to describe the ways that college and university practitioners can develop validating relationships with minoritized students (Bensimon, 2007; Bensimon & Dowd, 2012; Bensimon, Dowd, Chase, et al., 2012; Dowd, Pak, & Bensimon, 2013).

Through their interactions with students, college authorities with high status can create a secure base, in a psychological sense, for learners from minoritized groups to develop their identities as college students. Having a secure psychological base and attachment to an authority figure increases students' capacity to receive and act on pertinent information, resources, and opportunities that are available to them in the college environment, but which they may fail to access absent a sense of validation (Dowd, Pak, & Bensimon, 2013). Validating relationships foster the democratic participation and social agency of the caregiver and the cared-for.

Justice as Transformation

To explicate the mechanisms of oppression in schooling, critical race theorists working in the field of education, such as Gloria Ladson-Billings and William Tate (1995, 2006), extended the work of legal scholars Derrick Bell, Richard Delgado, and others into educational research. Their work centers issues of race and foregrounds how racism is institutionalized and is reproduced through structures of education (Taylor et al., 2009). In the critical race tradition of scholarship, educational equity is often referred to as *racial equity*, a term that invokes broader social phenomena beyond schooling and that maintains the focus on racism in education. The term *critical* refers to scholarship that is, "at its center, an effort to join empirical investigation, the task of interpretation, and a critique of . . . reality" (McClaren & Giarelli, 1995, p. 4).

Critical race theorists in education critique the reality of the condition of education for minoritized students of color. They highlight institutional and structural racism as the ongoing source of the problem of racial equity gaps in education. Liberalism's failure to effectively counter racial discrimination in educational practice and policy indicates that a broader, more racially inclusive political frame is needed. Higher education scholars who adopt critical perspectives (Bergerson, 2003; Espino, 2012; Harper, 2012; Harper & Patton, 2007; Harper, Patton, & Wooden, 2009; Peña, 2012; Yosso, Parker, Solórzano, & Lynn, 2004; Yosso, Smith, Ceja, & Solórzano, 2009) argue that the key themes of liberal egalitarianism mask racial inequities in schooling. The dominant themes of democratic equality, social efficiency, and social mobility (Labaree, 1997) are so ideologically embedded in education policy discourse that they function as "majoritarian" master narratives. Practitioners who have a majoritarian worldview do not see evidence of racial injustice in racial equity gaps because they believe that existing educational structures provide equal opportunity and social mobility. They tend to attribute unequal participation and achievement in education to the cultural pathologies and deficits of minoritized groups, or to the failure of individuals from those groups to do what is necessary for academic success (Carter-Andrews & Tuitt, 2013; Gutierrez et al., 2009; Haney-López, 2010; Nasir & Hand, 2006).

Critical race scholars view persistent racial inequalities in educational participation and outcomes as evidence of institutional and structural racism. Sociologists refer to the systematic sorting of the stratified educational system as "effectively maintained inequality" (Minor, 2008; Posselt, Jacquet, Bielby, & Bastedo, 2012). Even as the poor and racially minoritized make gains in their educational preparation and attainment, more affluent families acquire greater levels of preparation, consequently leaving equity gaps essentially unchanged. Institutional and structural racism exist independent of specific acts of racial discrimination by individuals. Yet "critical agency" (Baez, 2000) on the part of higher education practitioners will be required to change institutional practices and structures that are discriminatory (Bensimon, 2007; Bensimon & Bishop, 2012; Bensimon & Dowd, 2012).When institutional agents adopt a critical consciousness and use their positional authority, resources, and networks to reduce stratification, they take on the role of "empowerment agents" (Stanton-Salazar, 2011). Like justice as care, justice as transformation operates on the principles of nondiscrimination and nonoppression. In addition, justice as transformation calls on educational practitioners, leaders, and policymakers to act as empowerment agents to dismantle institutional and structural racism.

In this book we delineate institutional racism as a phenomenon within the control of institutional actors and structural racism as a broader social phenomenon requiring coordination among institutional actors from multiple sectors, policymakers, and politicians. In making this distinction, *institutional racism* refers to seemingly objective standards of academic life that are racialized, because they take their existing form due to historical racial discrimination and contemporary amnesia about race policy. These include institutional policies and practices such as recruitment and admissions, student assessment and placement, faculty and staff hiring and promotion, pedagogy and curricular content, and degree qualifications. *Structural racism* refers to the stratification of educational opportunity among members of different racial and ethnic groups produced by formal systems and structures of education. Tracking in secondary schools and the lack of alignment of many associate's and baccalaureate degree programs provide examples of the types of structures that function in discriminatory ways.

Action Research for Praxis

After surveying the negative consequences of educational policy implementation in the post–civil rights era, Noddings (1999) argued that the time had come to assess the policy accomplishments of the liberal-egalitarian tradition. Critical race scholars would also like to recast the master narratives of educational equity, as well as the policy solutions, but point out that dominant group members tend to view their perspectives on reality as "the truth." Knowledge construction and deconstruction are central to scholarship in the critical race tradition, which "began with the recognition of the relationship between knowledge construction, naming, and power" (Taylor, 2009b, p. 4).

The accountability field of higher education is beginning to call issues of racial segregation to the attention of mainstream policy audiences and presenting them as a sign of liberal policy failure (Carnevale & Strohl, 2013; Century Foundation Task Force, 2013; Goldrick-Rab & Kinsley, 2013; Melguizo & Kosiewicz, 2013). Yet the field is ill-equipped to critique its own roots and incorporate critical race perspectives. It does not yet have the capacity to address the complexities of racial segregation because it is largely segregated itself in terms of epistemological beliefs, methodological preferences, and the racial diversity of its members. As Gregory Anderson (2012) observed, based on his years as a program officer at the Ford Foundation with responsibility for its higher education portfolio of funding, "scholars/ researchers trained in specific disciplines such as economics" hold a position of dominance "when it comes to policy analysis in higher education." Mainstream policy analysts are often reluctant to tackle "more uncomfortable" topics such as racism and income inequality (p. 135).

The dominant position of rational policy analysts is problematic because the scholarship of critical scholars provides analytical tools to more deeply understand the complex social and economic forces that have created and now sustain unequal education (Bell, 2009a, 2009b; Delgado, 2009; Ladson-Billings, 2009; Taylor, 2009a, 2009b). Critical scholars pose a critique of liberal egalitarianism that must be seriously engaged to effectively address racial inequities. To bridge the experiences and beliefs of diverse practitioners and policymakers, language and conceptual tools are needed to open a constructive change process aimed at reducing racial inequities.

In our experience, action research tools and processes involving practitioner inquiry (Bensimon & Malcom, 2012; Bragg & Durham, 2012; Cochran-

Smith & Lytle, 2009; Kemmis & McTaggart, 2005) provide a viable approach to deconstruct and reconstruct knowledge about racial equity. For educators who derive a sense of identity from and embrace *praxis*—the goal of "doing the good" (Polkinghorne, 2004) through collective action—the notion that we educators are part of a system of social harm built on past and present discrimination based on skin color, language, and national origin can be quite "distressing" (Taylor, 2009a). Our choice of action research methodology and our development of the Center for Urban Education's Equity Scorecard action research process reflects our interest in doing more than developing a better language to productively discuss race and racism in educational settings. In this we echo Bartolomé (2008), who, observing the "insidious invisibility" of dominant ideologies that subordinate students based on their racial, ethnic, and immigrant status, observed:

> It is not enough to struggle to name and critique these discriminatory ideologies and practices; there is also an urgent need to identify effective counter-hegemonic orientations and pedagogical interventions that work to neutralize unequal material conditions and biased beliefs. (p. ix)

The Equity Scorecard was developed in the action research tradition of practitioner inquiry, which engages educational practitioners in research into their own policies and practices (Cochran-Smith & Lytle, 2009; Greenwood & Levin, 2005; Groundwater-Smith, 2009; Kemmis & McTaggart, 2000, 2005; McTaggart, 1997; Noffke, 1997, 2009; Noffke & Somekh, 2009; Reason, 1994; Rodgers, 2002a, 2002b; St. John, 2013; G. Wells, 2009; Witham & Bensimon, 2012).

In our experience, practitioner inquiry is a good strategy with which to address racial equity issues. When the inquiry process is of high quality, practitioners gain expertise to support their capacity to act as change agents and develop a commitment to "inquiry as stance" (Cochran-Smith & Lytle, 2009). As stance, inquiry is not about the steps in what is commonly formulated in a "cycle of inquiry," involving data use, reflective practice, experimentation, and evaluation. Cochran-Smith and Lytle explain: "Working from and with an inquiry stance involves a continual process of making current arrangements problematic; questioning the ways knowledge and practice are constructed, evaluated, and used; and assuming that part of the work of practitioners individually and collectively is to participate in educational and social change" (p. 121). Practitioners will engage in such questioning, deconstructing, and reconstructing of practice to address racialized equity issues when they observe their own educational practices (and those of their peers) functioning as part of the architecture of institutional and structural racism.

Inquiry does not always or easily lead practitioners to create more equitable learning opportunities and environments for racially minoritized groups, such as Native Americans, African Americans, Latinos, and Southeast Asians. Practitioners, whether they are in positions of leadership, classroom faculty members, or student affairs professionals, can find it difficult to see their own practices implicated in racial discrimination.

When such recognition does occur, practitioners are often not able to act as empowerment agents because they are immersed in the culture and political economy of their own institutions. They face the challenge of producing organizational change from within, which is known as the problem of "embedded agency" (Battilana, 2006; Seo & Creed, 2002). Yet social actors are not caught in a cultural web from which they cannot escape. Under certain conditions, they can and will act to change their own culture and cultural practices (Seo & Creed, 2002). These conditions include the recognition that one's practices are implicated in producing an unjust society.

Through action research using the Equity Scorecard tools and processes, we and our colleagues at the Center for Urban Education (CUE) collaborate with college and university practitioners and leaders to change organizational culture in ways that will facilitate movement toward racial equity in postsecondary education. Our objectives are similar to that of critical action researchers more generally. As Kemmis and McTaggart (2005) explain, "Participatory action research aims to help people recover, and release themselves from, the constraints embedded in the social media through which they interact—their language (discourses), their modes of work, and the social relationships of power" (p. 567). The participation of faculty, administrators, and student affairs professionals as knowledge producers is essential to enable these practitioners to function as the empowerment agents who will create more equitable educational systems.

THE EQUITY SCORECARD

The Equity Scorecard was developed because it was clear by 2000 when the Scorecard was first introduced that the majority of diversity initiatives are based on the assumption that "contact" with and among people who are different from others would attenuate racial tensions, increase tolerance, prepare individuals to work effectively in a more diverse workforce, and generally make them more aware of and concerned with the connection between diversity and democratic ideals. But "contact," without a strategy for achieving equity, has not taken us very far in eliminating educational and economic stratification along racial lines.

Figure 1.1. The Phases of the Equity Scorecard

EQUITY SCORECARD

| Laying the Groundwork | Defining the Problem | Assessing Interventions | Implementing Solutions | Evaluating Results |

The mission of the Center for Urban Education is to create the tools needed for institutions of higher education to bring about racial equity in educational outcomes. We pursue that mission by designing action research tools and processes, which are collectively referred to as the Equity Scorecard. The Scorecard is used by college practitioners as part of a practitioner inquiry process intended to promote equity. Figure 1.1 represents the inquiry process as it occurs through the five phases of the Scorecard process: Laying the Groundwork, Defining the Problem, Assessing Interventions, Implementing Solutions, and Evaluating Results.

The Evidence Team

On a college campus, practitioner inquiry using the action research tools of the Equity Scorecard is carried out by a group of administrators, faculty, and student affairs professionals invited by their president or chief academic officer to participate on an "evidence team," which typically has about 10 members. We provide the senior leaders with a team selection protocol, which describes how to identify individuals from different functional areas whose responsibilities and experience position them as potentially influential change agents. The team member protocol identifies roles such as team leader, boundary spanner, data interpreter, and friendly skeptic, all of which are necessary to assemble "high-functioning teams" (Bauman, 2005; Neumann, 1991). Team members are oriented to these roles through an activity called "roles we play on an evidence team."

Evidence teams typically hold monthly team meetings led by one or two team leaders over a period of 18 months or so. Institutional researchers provide access for teams to campus data systems and help them interpret what the data mean based on campus-specific coding of student success indicators. CUE staff members in the role of Equity Scorecard project specialists hold monthly phone calls and occasional webinars to coach team leaders and team members on the use of CUE's inquiry protocols. The project specialists provide tools and advice designed to make the technical aspects of the inquiry process, such as data use and reporting inquiry findings, proceed smoothly. The evidence teams engage in various forms of data collection, interpretation, and strategic planning during and between meetings. Evidence teams produce customized Equity Scorecard Reports, using a template we provide. The Scorecard Report documents the team's inquiry findings and presents recommendations to the senior administration for actions that should be taken to reduce equity gaps observed through the inquiry process. Equity gaps are those variations in student participation and outcomes that reflect a systematic difference in the college experience among students of different racial and ethnic backgrounds.

A variety of group gatherings, such as "kickoff" workshops, institutes, and retreats, provide opportunities for interactions among evidence teams from different campuses, institutional and system leaders, and CUE staff and researchers. Major meetings are facilitated by a professional facilitator, most often Deanna Cherry of Deanna Cherry Consulting, who has been an important member of CUE's Scorecard implementation team since 2007.

The Scorecard tools and step-by-step protocols are intended to provide instrumental steps that realistically structure a joint productive activity. If the tools work well, they can keep the focus on the inquiry tasks while at the same time allowing for meaningful conversations about the existence and causes of racial inequities. Team leaders are provided by CUE with leadership training and tools for leading conversations about racial inequities. "Tools" in this sense refer to a wide array of cultural artifacts, such as data, language, and interaction scripts that are designed to "remediate" practice (Bensimon & Malcom, 2012; Bustillos, Rueda, & Bensimon, 2011; Dowd, Bishop, Bensimon, & Witham, 2012; Peña, 2012; Peña, Bensimon, & Coylar, 2006; Witham & Bensimon, 2012). We and our CUE colleagues introduce a variety of action research tools to infuse practitioner inquiry with an equity perspective.

Evidence teams produce an Equity Scorecard Report using a template we provide. The Scorecard Report documents the team's inquiry findings and presents recommendations to the senior administration for actions that should be taken to reduce equity gaps observed through the inquiry process. The Equity Scorecard evidence team members are also asked to share their knowledge and express their willingness to engage in dialogue about issues of racial equity to others on their campus.

Language Tools, Interaction Protocols, and Data Tools

When we convene an evidence team, we typically start out with in-person institutes or workshops. The Scorecard materials, our presentation of them, and the way we ask team members to engage with the tools are characterized by particular language tools that constitute the Scorecard as a set of cultural practices.

The concept "equity-minded" is a language tool for questioning cultural assumptions. Equity-mindedness is contrasted with the notion of "deficit-mindedness" to provide a language artifact to surface underlying assumptions about what causes the exclusion or loss of minoritized students from colleges and universities. Evidence team members are asked to actively use the concept of equity-mindedness in conversation or to slow themselves down in their own thought processes to identify stereotyped assumptions about student deficits. Cultural assumptions about the motivation, preparedness, and collegiate aspirations of students from minoritized groups often come up in conversations about equity issues. In the activity settings of the Equity Scorecard, race talk is sanctioned and elicited through the language tools, as well as through the use of numerical data disaggregated by race and ethnicity and the prompts of the inquiry protocols that guide qualitative data collection. The objective is to catalyze organizational learning and positive change in the way college practitioners engage the race question.

Terms such as the *leadership team, team leader,* and *evidence team member* refer to particular team roles. Interactions among participants are structured in a particular arrangement of activities, such as the planning meeting and evidence team meeting, while the use of ground rules calls attention to habits of interaction based on social status. Evidence team members are asked to attend to the division of labor and exercise of power among participants with different levels of authority and racial characteristics.

CUE's data tools include the Vital Signs data, the Benchmarking Equity and Student Success Tool (BESST), the Scorecard Report, and a series of quantitative and qualitative data analysis worksheets and data display templates. The Vital Signs, displaying raw numbers, rates, and shares disaggregated by race and ethnicity, have been a mainstay since the 1st year of the Scorecard's development. The first evidence team meetings have always centered on review and discussion of Vital Signs, which are organized on four perspectives of institutional performance in producing racial equity: *access, retention, excellence,* and *completion.*

The Vital Signs include core indicators selected by CUE and system, institutional, or team leaders. Access indicators typically include, for example, application, enrollment, course placement, and financial aid data. The retention perspective is focused on student progress through courses, persistence from year to year, and credit accumulation. The retention perspective leads to the completion perspective, which is focused on degree and certification completion. The excellence perspective refers to participation in high-reward educational programs, such as honors programs, undergraduate research, and science majors, which are often reserved for "top" students and provide greater resources to help students succeed.

The numerical data typically already exist in college databases. The data are not "self-acting" (Raudenbush, 2005). Once disaggregated, as the Vital Signs and the BESST are, data users can pose questions about the experiences and outcomes of students of color. At that juncture, qualitative accountability indicators that assess the quality of educational practices from a race-conscious equity perspective are needed. The qualitative data are collected through observations, document analysis, and interviews conducted by evidence team members. The content of inquiry protocols calls attention to racial equity by prompting practitioners to observe practices and interactions through a race-conscious lens. The inquiry protocols ask practitioners to become researchers of their own practices (Bensimon, Polkinghorne, Bauman, & Vallejo, 2004) and to exercise equity-minded race consciousness in their interpretation of the data (Bensimon & Malcom, 2012).

Drawing on practitioner inquiry as a strategy to bring about organizational change, the Equity Scorecard uses data to prompt reflection—the "aha moments"—among practitioners about the relationship between their own educational practices and racial inequities observed in the data. They ask what's working, what's not, and why. The practitioner inquiry model is based on the belief that practitioner expertise is necessary to address equity issues. Expertise is acquired through inquiry, which supports the acquisition of new knowledge, beliefs, cultural practices, and experiences.

THEORY OF CHANGE

Data tools and interaction scripts are the instrumental methods of the Equity Scorecard for using data and managing intercultural group dynamics surrounding racial equity issues. Whether these instrumental processes lead to changes that have an impact on equity issues depends on the quality of reflective practice, critical race consciousness, and individual and collective agency that emerges through the inquiry process. As a process that holds the potential of organizational change, the Equity Scorecard is a cycle of inquiry

Figure 1.2. Practitioner Inquiry as a Driver of Change

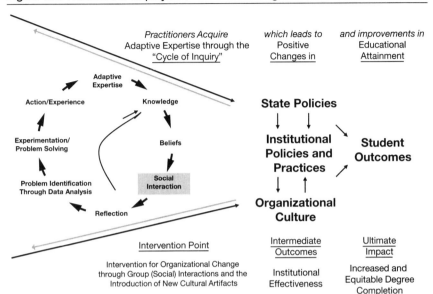

in which practitioners' knowledge, beliefs, and expertise change as they engage in problem framing and problem solving informed by data analysis, experimentation, and evaluation.

Inquiry as a Driver of Change

Anyone interested in bringing about changes in organizations like schools and colleges needs to consider what insights and incentives will lead insiders to want to change their own settings. This is particularly important when it comes to asking those insiders who hold social position and power within the status quo to use their authority to enact changes (Battilana, 2006; Seo & Creed, 2002).

Our theory of change relies on the power of practitioner inquiry that is structured using critical action research protocols as a driver of change. This is illustrated in Figure 1.2, with the cycle of inquiry on the left side of the diagram and the intermediate and ultimate desired outcomes on the right side. The intermediate outcomes include changes in state policies, institutional policies and practices, and organizational culture in a manner that will produce more equitable student outcomes.

Inquiry is a knowledge production process that, when occurring in a cyclical manner and informed by systematic use of data, generates the expertise practitioners need to bring about changes in institutional policies, practices, and organizational structures to address inequities in student experiences and outcomes. Through inquiry, practitioners are expected to attain a higher level of adaptive expertise, which is necessary in dynamic, educational settings. Expert practitioners are those who can adapt to changing conditions and the individual needs of learners to educate their students effectively, whether their role in educating takes place in the classroom, in counseling sessions, or behind a desk in administrative offices. Becoming conscious of the relationship among beliefs, behaviors, and organizational routines is particularly important in an inquiry process. The ideological belief systems of individual practitioners and communities of practice strongly influence the students' educational experiences.

As highlighted by the box around the term social interaction on the lower right side of the cycle of inquiry in Figure 1.2, a crucial point of intervention in the Equity Scorecard occurs when action research tools designed with critical race consciousness are adopted for use by a group of practitioners during inquiry. These equity-minded tools are intended to disrupt social interaction scripts that uphold color blindness as the standard for social interactions in professional settings.

Speaking more theoretically, we draw on sociocultural theories of learning (Nasir & Hand, 2006; Rogoff, Baker-Sennett, Lacasa, & Goldsmith, 1995; Säljö, 2003; Tharp, 1993; Tharp & Gallimore, 1988) and cultural–historical activity theory (CHAT) (Ellis, 2011; Engeström, 2001, 2008; Lee & Roth, 2007; Ogawa, Crain, Loomis, & Ball, 2008; Roth & Lee, 2007; G. Wells, 2011) to design remediating artifacts and joint productive activities centered on remediating institutional and structural racism.

The activity settings created by the action research design of the Equity Scorecard are intended to bring about expansive learning by making the contradictions among practitioners' sense of purpose (Engeström, 2001, 2008) and the impact of their practices on racial equity more evident. Contradictions are motivating when educators embrace praxis as a core aspect of their professional identity. Educators who strive for praxis have an interest in "doing the good." As a particular form of life task, praxis requires a particular form of knowledge sometimes referred to as "practical wisdom" *(phronesis)*, which is contrasted with epistemic knowledge and the *techne* knowledge needed to build and reproduce effectively functioning systems (Greenwood & Levin, 2005; Polkinghorne, 2004). Praxis is pursued experientially through reflective practice and collective action toward producing just social arrangements (Seo & Creed, 2002). Organizational learning theorists posit that "contradictions" and "critical disturbances" (Argyris, 1977; Engeström, 2008; Seo & Creed, 2002) lead practitioners to see and act on the "gaps" between their espoused theories of action and their actual practice (Argyris & Schön, 1996). Being able to see those gaps and gain practical wisdom to close them is the desired outcome of practitioner inquiry using the Equity Scorecard. Therefore, disturbances are valued in our research methods as catalysts of individual and organizational learning.

Action researchers and organizational learning theorists view the experience of contradictions and disturbances as necessary and important motivators of organizational innovation (Kemmis & McTaggart, 2000; Sco & Creed, 2002). They are necessary to bring about the critical reenvisioning of educational practice necessary for transformative justice. Engeström (2008) defines *disturbances* as "deviations from the normal scripted course of events in the work process, normal being defined by plans, explicit rules and instructions, or tacitly assumed traditions" (p. 24). Some disturbances exist at a technical level and can be addressed through technical solutions, that is, through "single loop" learning (Argyris, 1977; Argyris & Schon, 1971). Others are *critical disturbances*, which "reveal substantive disagreements, fears, or other strong indicators of systemic contradictions" (Engeström, 2008, p. 38). Critical disturbances must be addressed at the level of values and meaning making about purpose, that is, through "double loop" learning. Reflective practitioners eschew single-loop solutions and engage at a deeper level with critical disturbances to improve their practices (Argyris, 1977; Argyris & Schon, 1971; Schon, 1983, 1987, 2010).

Organizational Change Agents

As shown on the left side of the cycle of inquiry in Figure 1.2, ideally, reflective practice about critical disturbances leads to problem identification through data analysis. In turn, this leads to experimentation and problem solving that engage practitioners in new actions and experiences that generate adaptive expertise to address racial inequities. This is important because institutional agents (Stanton-Salazar, 1997, 2011) acting as "entrepreneurs" (Battilana, 2006) can bring about organizational change by changing the institutional "logics" of educational practice in their institutions. Changes in institutional logics and organizational routines are the source of cultural change in organizations (Spillane, 2012).

Although Figure 1.2 suggests that reflection and problem framing precede problem solving, it is important to note that actions themselves are a source of learning that leads to new conceptualizations of the nature of the problem (McLaughlin & Mitra, 2001). The notion of a cycle of inquiry reflects that dynamic relationship between actions and beliefs. Action research methodology that relies on action as a source of cultural change is challenged by the fact that different actors attach different meanings to the same actions. Divergent understandings emerge from differences in racial, gender, ethnic, and language attributes. Racialized power imbalances can hamper productive knowledge construction through action research if the research design does not accommodate critical perspectives on power, voice, and authority.

The strategy of the Scorecard is not to persuade participants with strongly divergent views through didactic instruction, but rather to involve them in ongoing inquiry along with their colleagues who may hold a range of beliefs about the meaning of equity. Activity theory indicates that introducing new artifacts of educational practice, whether in the form of data or policy or language, can remediate community norms and initiate cultural change. The Scorecard theory of change is premised on the tenet that cultural artifacts can act as remediating artifacts (Bensimon & Malcom, 2012; Bustillos et al., 2011; Dowd, Bishop, et al., 2012; Dowd, Bishop, & Bensimon, in press; Witham & Bensimon, 2012). Our strategy, therefore, is to design activity settings and tools that create repeated exposures for participants to equity concepts based in critical race consciousness.

We design "equity-minded" artifacts and new forms of social interaction using those artifacts in order to stimulate, first, awareness of the differential impacts of institutional practices on students of color, and second, the belief that practitioners bear some responsibility for changing institutional practices. The Equity Scorecard process is designed to introduce cultural artifacts in activity settings to prompt awareness of contradictions and to motivate reflective practice and changes in practice. The Equity Scorecard includes tools designed to change the social media of data use and of race talk surrounding equity issues, and the social interactions through which problems of practice are framed and acted on. They invite active adoption of new cognitive frames about the purposes of educational practice. These frames support a shift from deficit- to equity-minded thinking about institutional responsibilities for students of color (Bensimon, 2005a, 2005b, 2006; Bensimon & Malcom, 2012; Bensimon, Rueda, Dowd, & Harris, 2007). In order to change the culture of an organization, it is necessary to change the organizational routines that make up daily work practices (Spillane, 2012). Equity Scorecard tools invite equity-enhancing changes in the core organizational routines of institutional research and assessment, admissions and student placement, curriculum and instruction, student services, and administration.

COLLABORATORS, PARTNERS, AND SETTINGS

As codirectors of the Center for Urban Education (CUE), we, as well as numerous research assistants, doctoral students enrolled in the Rossier School of Education's Ed.D. and Ph.D. doctoral programs, and professional staff members of our Center, have collaborated with hundreds of college admin-istrators, faculty, and staff across the country to conduct the Equity Score-card. As of Fall 2013, CUE's tools have been utilized as part of a long-term Equity Scorecard process (spanning one or more years) in over 40 colleges and universities. Portions of the Equity Scorecard process have been intro-duced and activities conducted using Scorecard tools in daylong or half-day workshops at over 40 additional postsecondary institutions. The settings for this work have included community and technical colleges, research uni-versities, comprehensive state universities, liberal arts colleges, and higher education system offices. In addition, a K–12 focused Scorecard was pilot-tested in two Boston Public Schools (Jones et al., 2011).

Figure 1.3 provides an at-a-glance summary of the development and implementation of the Equity Scorecard. In 1999 the Center for Urban Edu-cation was founded by Estela Bensimon with generous seed funding from USC's Urban Initiative. The Scorecard was introduced a year later, in 2000. Since that time it has evolved considerably through redesign periods de-picted on Figure 1.3 as The Early Years, the 2nd Generation, and the Cur-rent Design (see also Bensimon & Malcom, 2012). The figure indicates the names of key milestone projects, higher education systems, and colleges in five states that brought together partner institutions, educational leaders, and educators in significantly new ways, using new tools and strategies of the Equity Scorecard. In addition to the campuses listed, the Equity Score-card was also conducted at numerous other individual colleges and universi-ties that are not indicated on the figure. Examples include Trinity College in Connecticut and Purdue University in Indiana. (For a full listing of insti-tutions that have used Equity Scorecard tools, see the Partners section of CUE's website at cue.usc.edu/).

In California and in Wisconsin, the settings featured in this book, the Equity Scorecard has been utilized in many inquiry projects in community colleges and universities. The first implementation took place at 14 Califor-nia institutions of higher education, including 3 state universities, 6 private not-for profit colleges and universities, and 5 community colleges. (Bensi-mon, Polkinghorne, et al., 2004). This was followed quickly by the Equity for All project (Bauman, 2005; Bensimon, Hao, & Bustillos, 2006; Ben-simon & Malcom, 2012; Bensimon, Rueda, et al., 2007; Bustillos et al., 2011), which involved nine California community colleges.

From the early years of the Equity Scorecard to the present day, Wis-consin—particularly the University of Wisconsin (UW) system—has been an important site for Scorecard development and implementation. In 2005 the UW Board of Regents and system leaders determined that the decades-old diversity plan for the university system was not achieving its goal of in-creasing diversity. Therefore, beginning in 2005, UW leaders decided to try something new. The system leaders invited campus chancellors to convene Equity Scorecard evidence teams on their campuses, which they did, in three waves referred to on Figure 1.3 as UWI, UWII, and UWIII. By 2012, all the universities and associate's degree–granting (2-year) colleges ("the Colleges") of the UW system, with the exception of the University of Wisconsin at Madison, had conducted the Equity Scorecard process with support from CUE and the UW system office.

A number of these projects have been focused specifically on inequities in transfer access from 2-year public colleges (community and technical colleges) to 4-year universities. The "Missing 87" study was conducted at a California community college in spring 2006. A team of faculty, administrators, and counselors at Long Beach City College (LBCC) collected data through interviews, observations and data analysis to investigate why students who had become "transfer ready" at LBCC had not transferred (Bensimon, Dowd, Alford, & Trapp, 2007). In a second study, from fall 2008 to fall 2010, a team of system-level administrators conducted inquiry into the vertical transfer pathways existing among the University of Wisconsin associate's and bachelor's degree–granting institutions and the Wisconsin Technical College System (WTCS), which enrolls the majority of African American and Latino students in the state's public colleges.

Policymakers in two states, Nevada and Colorado, asked us at CUE and our colleagues at the Western Interstate Commission on Higher Education (WICHE) to develop campus-based inquiry projects to complement state-level goals adopted as part of the national college completion agenda. In Nevada, leaders of the Nevada System of Higher Education (NSHE) were involved in a national initiative called Complete College America (CCA), which was designed to mobilize political will at the state level to prioritize attention to the issue of college completion. NSHE leaders saw that through CCA the system and its campuses would soon have easier access to a large amount of student access and success data. The question arose, how would the campuses make sense of the newly available data and make plans to act on it? To address this concern, NSHE asked CUE and WICHE to facilitate inquiry on three campuses using a number of the tools and action research processes of the Equity Scorecard and to provide recommendations for next steps (see Bensimon, Dowd, Longanecker, & Witham, 2012).

During the past 2 years, Colorado's policymakers have established a broad foundation for reform of the state's higher education system. These efforts, including a new strategic plan and renewed performance contracts with each of the state's college and universities, are aimed at increasing the numbers of degrees and certificates of value awarded annually and closing gaps in postsecondary access and success for the rapidly growing population of underrepresented minority students. These policy efforts are forward-

		CALIFORNIA	WISCONSIN	NEVADA	PENNSYLVANIA	COLORADO
The Early Years	1999	Center for Urban Education's founding				
	2000					
	2001	The Diversity Scorecard (14 colleges and universities)				
	2002					
2nd Generation	2003		University of Wisconsin System Equity Scorecard Implementation (UW I) (5 universities and the 2-year colleges)			
	2004	Equity for All (9 community colleges)				
	2005					
	2006	"The Missing 87" (1 community college) Benchmarking Equity and Effectiveness	Transfer Equity & Accountability Study (UW and WTCS system leaders) UW Equity Scorecard Implementation (UW II) (5 universities)			
	2007			Nevada System of Higher Education (NSHE) Equity Benchmarking Project (2 universities and 1 community college)		
	2008	(3 "lead" community colleges and 24 affiliated community colleges)				
	2009		UW Equity Scorecard Implementation (UW III) (3 universities)			
Current Design	2010	Equity Scorecard Implementation (3 community colleges)			Pennsylvania State System of Higher Education (PASSHE) Equity Scorecard Implementation (14 state universities)	Equity and Excellence in Colorado Higher Education (2 universities and 1 community college)
	2011					
	2012	Expanding Transfer Pathways into Private Institutions (2 liberal arts institutions)				
	2013				→	→

thinking and show the state's commitment to increasing access and success for students from across Colorado's diverse communities. But policy changes alone are not enough—the commitment and collaboration of college leaders, faculty, and staff are critical to the success of these ambitious goals. Thus in partnership with WICHE, CUE launched Equity in Excellence, a project that involved a customized yearlong inquiry, goal-setting, and action-planning process using the Equity Scorecard. Equity Scorecard evidence teams at Community College of Aurora, University of Colorado Denver, and Metropolitan State University examined data, set goals, conducted deep inquiry into campus policies and practices, and crafted concrete action plans around areas of focus that are explicitly tied to policy goals delineated in the master plan for higher education (Colorado Competes).

Similarly, leaders of the Pennsylvania State System of Higher Education (PASSHE), a confederation of 14 master's degree–granting universities, each with its own president and governing board, were involved in Complete College America (CCA) as well as the Education Delivery Institute and Access to Success (A2S) (all national initiatives with an express focus on using data to improve college access and success). The chief academic officers of the PASSHE universities adopted the Equity Scorecard as an integral part of the system's commitment to institutional improvement. In 2012–2013, PASSHE invested resources to build capacity for data use through practitioner inquiry using the Scorecard at the same time that it instituted a new performance-based funding system. "Scaling up" the Scorecard in PASSHE provided a rich setting for our design efforts to integrate a grassroots and system-level focus. PASSHE's statewide commitment to a sustained equity focus during a period of demographic and economic change in their state was particularly forward-looking. Their vision provides a model for other state leaders, and we are proud to have played a part.

CHAPTER 2

Remediating "Race Talk"

It's okay to move forward, I get it.

—Participant in an Equity Scorecard kickoff meeting (Vines, 2012, p. 86)

As critical race theorists have emphasized in critiquing liberal views of the educational policies needed to produce educational equity, participants in educational settings do not have equal power or voice. The voices of people of color, particularly on the subject and experience of racism, are devalued (Taylor et al., 2009b). Through the tenets of *historicity* and *multivoicedness*, activity theory highlights that:

> An activity system is always a community of multiple points of view, traditions, and interests. The division of labor in an activity creates different positions for the participants, the participants carry their own diverse histories, and the activity system itself carries multiple layers and strands of history engraved in its artifacts, rules and conventions. . . . It is a source of trouble and a source of innovation, demanding actions of translation and negotiation. (Engeström, 2001, p. 136)

Any equity work that depends on transformative change in educational institutions will require a "translation and negotiation" of ideals. As we emphasized in Chapter 1, the meaning of equity is not singular. Equity advocates may articulate their values based on social contract theory and view justice in terms of fairness, equal opportunity, and merit. They may draw on an ethic of care and emphasize an equal quality of education for all students, regardless of where any individual falls on measures of "student quality." Or, informed by critical studies, they may view nothing short of a transformation of democratic institutions, including the law and public policies that govern education, as what is required to bring about a just society.

Grant (2009) observes that historical lessons about race and multicultural education are marginalized because "they are situated within a struggle between the democratic ideals of the country and the United States

31

Constitution and the affirmation of those ideals" (p. 159). For that reason, the United States is having difficulty moving from a plural to a pluralistic society. Though diverse, the *plural society* is segregated, resists multiculturalism, and "does not actively facilitate communication and cooperation across racial and ethnic groups." A *pluralistic society*, in contrast, has "multiple voices and perspectives drawn into one culture and community" (pp. 158–159).

Discussions about race and racism can be uncomfortable, for ideological or cultural reasons, for Equity Scorecard team members. This discomfort is often expressed as a desire to broaden the focus of inquiry to other types of "diversities." This tendency to want to change the conversation from equity to diversity is consistent with Pollock's (2001) observation that "the question we ask most about race in education is the very question we most suppress"(p. 2), namely, the question of the role of race in producing inequities. Many college practitioners have grown up and been educated in settings where diversity is its own ideal. As Ladson-Billings (2009) observed,

> Although scholars such as James Banks, Carl Grant, and Geneva Gay began on a scholarly path designed to challenge schools as institutions so that students might be prepared to reconstruct the society, in its current practice iteration, multicultural education is but a shadow of its conceptual self. Rather than engage students in provocative thinking about the contradictions of U.S. ideals and lived realities, teachers often find themselves encouraging students to sing "ethnic" songs, eat ethnic foods, and do ethnic dances. Consistently, manifestations of multicultural education in the classroom are superficial and trivial "celebrations of diversity." (p. 33)

The tensions between diversity discourse and race talk that occur in Scorecard meetings present opportunities for constructive renegotiation of the meanings college and university practitioners attach to race and to their role in addressing institutional racism in higher education.

OVERVIEW OF THE CHAPTER

In this chapter we present an extended case study and analyze a "critical disturbance" (Engeström, 2008) that occurred during an Equity Scorecard meeting at a California community college. Our analysis illustrates that the negotiation between dominant and critical ideals about justice in a pluralistic democracy will be both emotional and incremental. However, the nature and course of such disturbances can be anticipated, allowing activity settings to be designed to capitalize on the shift from "business as usual" to a collective understanding of the work that needs to be done to address racial equity issues.

In this chapter (and in Chapter 3) activity system theory provides the lens for case analysis. Therefore, the first section presents the tenets and analytical methods of activity systems analysis. The second section explains the setting, data, and inquiry activities of the Equity Scorecard evidence team at Las Flores Community College (LFCC), a pseudonym for one of the dozens of California community colleges that have participated in CUE's Scorecard workshops and institutes. Among those, LFCC is one of several colleges that have used the Equity Scorecard tools and action research process over the course of several years.

The third section presents the extended LFCC case analysis. It describes the concerns of Equity Scorecard team leaders about the quality of teamwork that they had experienced interacting in previous inquiry activities and how we, in response, redesigned tools that function as interaction scripts, giving more attention to the "division of labor" in racial equity work. The case then focuses on the critical disturbance that occurred after the evidence team viewed a cartoon that illustrates the meaning of structural racism. This section presents and reanalyzes excerpts from a dissertation study by Vines (2012), who collected observational, documentary, survey, and interview data at LFCC to study organizational learning about equity during this time of transition for the team.

We conclude by arguing that college and university leaders should provide time and resources for practitioners on their campuses to engage in facilitated discussions of racism in order to move past celebrations of diversity under an "umbrella of inclusiveness" to an organizational commitment to racial equity.

Before presenting the LFCC case in the remainder of this chapter, one additional note is in order. Although we are discussing the importance of allowing talk about race and racism in everyday work practice at colleges and universities, we do not reference the race or gender of the participants in the LFCC setting. This is due to the fact that although LFCC is a pseudonym, the number of practitioners represented in the case is small and individuals could be identified by others familiar with our work at this campus. Therefore, we face a trade-off among conflicting values. On the one hand, we would like to provide a richly detailed analysis that attends to racialized interactions. On the other, we want to protect the anonymity of collaborators who participated in our research with the expectation of anonymity. We have chosen to resolve this trade-off here by not directly referencing the racial or ethnic characteristics of the participants. We hope to avoid such trade-offs in the future by using human subject research protocols where Scorecard participants are not anonymous. Then we will be able to invite team members to coauthor analyses with us or produce their own analyses, to interpret the meaning of critical incidents of the type we discuss below.

ACTIVITY SYSTEMS ANALYSIS

Organizational learning theorists posit that contradictions and disturbances (Argyris, 1977; Engeström, 2008; Seo & Creed, 2002) lead practitioners to see and act on the gaps between their espoused theories of action and their actual practice (Argyris & Schön, 1996). Being able to see and act on those gaps to close them is the desired outcome of practitioner inquiry using the Equity Scorecard. Therefore, disturbances are valued in our research methods as catalysts of individual and organizational learning.

Engeström (2008) defines *disturbances* as "deviations from the normal scripted course of events in the work process, normal being defined by plans, explicit rules and instructions, or tacitly assumed traditions" (p. 24). Some disturbances exist at a technical level and can be addressed through technical solutions (i.e., through single-loop learning, in Argyris and Schon's terms; see Argyris, 1977; Argyris & Schon, 1971). Others are critical disturbances, which "reveal substantive disagreements, fears, or other strong indicators of systemic contradictions" (Engeström, 2008, p. 38). Critical disturbances must be addressed at the level of values and meaning-making about purpose (i.e., through double-loop learning); they cannot be addressed by technical solutions.

Activity theorists and action researchers share common ground in their development of Vygotsky's activity triangle to represent activity systems as theoretical and empirical units of analysis (Ellis, 2011; Lee, 2011; Lee & Roth, 2007; Roth & Lee, 2007; Saunders & Somekh, 2009; Somekh & Nissen, 2011; G. Wells, 2009; Yamagata-Lynch, 2007). The interlocking triangular shapes that appear in the diagrams later in this chapter have been used by Engeström (2001, 2008) and other activity system analysts. The interlocking triangular shapes have an upper triangle representing *subject*, *object*, and *instrument* and a lower triangle representing the *community* in which objects take on particular meaning and motivate action by the subjects, or actors, in the activity system. The two other points on the base are labeled *rules* and *division of labor*. The term *rules* encompasses functional roles, organizational structures, and the norms governing actors and their roles. The term *division of labor* refers to who typically does what, both informally and when acting in formal settings or as a member of formally constituted groups.

The *instruments* of an activity system are also referred to, and understood in cultural terms, as artifacts, tools, and signs (Engeström, 2001, 2008). A change in the instruments in use in an organizational setting has the capacity to catalyze organizational change through "expansive learning." According to Engeström's formulation of expansive learning, "an expansive transformation is accomplished when the object and motive of the activity are re-conceptualized to embrace a radically wider horizon of possibilities than in the previous mode of the activity" (2001, p. 137). This means that through expansive learning the actors in a setting assign a new meaning to the object (the motivating objective or goal) of their activities and the ultimate outcomes of those activities. A change at any point of the activity system triangle is also theorized to bring about cultural change in the whole system. The culturally remediating power of instruments follows from their ability to reshape a subject's perception of the object of activity, which can also be understood as the "reason for doing something," in effect, motivation (Engeström, 2008).

Engeström (2001) explains that objects are not "raw material," but "collectively meaningful" and "collaboratively constructed" understandings of organizational purpose (p. 136). From this point of view, objects are not physical artifacts, but culturally situated motivations that shape cognition and activity. They are cultural entities that provide the "cultural means" for human agency (Engeström, 2001, p. 134). This perspective helps address a theoretically confusing aspect of asking individuals to learn "on behalf" of their organizations: If motivation and agency reside in individuals and not in organizations, how can organizations "learn"? Based on activity theory, Lee and Roth (2007) emphasize that learning among individuals has a dialectical (mutually constituting) relationship with learning in organizations. They explain that "in their actions individuals concretely reproduce the organization and, when actions vary, realize it in novel forms; organizations therefore presuppose individuals that concretely produce them" (p. 92).

INQUIRY INTO EQUITY GAPS AT LFCC

Among the first steps of inquiry into equity gaps at Las Flores Community College, CUE's project specialist and LFCC's institutional researcher developed Vital Signs and a longitudinal cohort analysis of student progress through the basic skills curriculum, which is also known as developmental education. Basic skills courses do not carry college degree credit. Students must sometimes complete more than one course before they begin taking courses that would count toward an associate's degree or transfer toward a bachelor's degree.

Figure 2.1 is reproduced from materials CUE project specialists used in 2011 during a series of benchmarking workshops that we offered to community colleges as part of CUE's California Benchmarking Project to help colleges identify equity gaps in the basic skills curriculum. The curriculum

Figure 2.1. Mapping the Basic Skills Curriculum

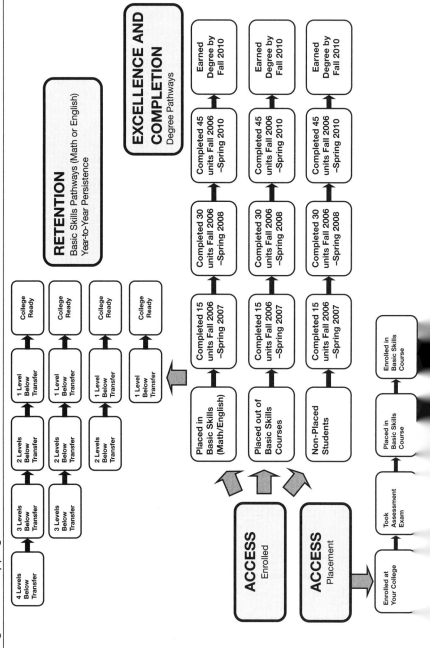

map is organized by the four perspectives of the Scorecard: access, retention, excellence, and completion. It illustrates the complexity of obtaining clear indicators of student success in the basic skills curriculum, which has many entry and exit points. Students can begin as many as four levels below the transfer-level courses that students are allowed to take when they are "college-ready." Cohort analyses, therefore, need to distinguish between groups of students who were placed in basic skills at different levels and also take into account the fact that even if students were placed through assessment testing in basic skills courses, the students may nevertheless have opted out of these courses. Once these different pathways are sorted out, a college can determine whether there are equity gaps in timely student progress in accumulating the units needed to earn a degree or transfer.

Seeing Equity Gaps

When LFCC's data was organized for the evidence team, they were able to see that among a cohort of students aged 17–19 years old who had enrolled in the college for the first time several years prior, only 7% had made progress sufficient to enroll in transfer-level math courses and only 13% had progressed to transfer-level English. Within these overall low rates of student progression, equity gaps were observed for Latinos (who were one-third of the student body) and African Americans (who were one-sixth of the student body), mainly due to differences in year-to-year persistence. The situation was particularly acute for the 200 African American students who were in the selected cohort, only three of whom had begun their studies enrolled in a degree-credit course. The data also revealed that African American students were opting out of the basic skills courses that they had been referred to based on assessment test scores. Inquiry using the numerical Vital Signs and cohort analysis highlighted for the LFCC Equity Scorecard team that the college was not serving as a gateway to associate's or bachelor's degrees for Latino or African American students.

The evidence team members questioned what institutional practices and policies might be creating inequities in basic skills. For example, they asked how well the college's enrollment procedures were working and whether African Americans and Latinos were registering too late or having difficulty for other reasons in getting into the courses they needed. They questioned whether the college could advise students better, or if something going on inside classrooms was deterring students from enrolling in the next class. Team members began to consider the cultural aspects of the student experience of basic skills assessments and placements, particularly for African Americans and Latinos. The team realized that placement in a basic skills class might be perceived by students as placement in the "dummy" class, which would be a particularly stigmatizing experience for students of color. For those who were recent high school graduates, the realization that they were ineligible to take college degree–credit classes could well elicit a sense of betrayal, having earned a diploma yet still being "unprepared."

Inquiry Activities

With these hunches in mind, the LFCC evidence team engaged in several inquiry activities to become "practitioner researchers" (Bensimon, Polking-horne, et al., 2004) into their own practices. Figure 2.2 summarizes the menu of inquiry activities CUE supports by providing data collection protocols, worked examples, and instruction on how to summarize the data.

LFCC elected to do observations and to analyze a number of different documents. They "took a walk in students' shoes" to experience the matriculation process from the student point of view, getting a firsthand experience of what it means to complete an application to the college, take assessment tests, receive a course placement, and register for courses. They collected qualitative data through document analysis of enrollment information on the college website. And they took time to sit and observe the comings and goings of staff and counselors at campus advising centers. The team also inquired into curricular and pedagogical practices inside the classroom by reviewing syllabi for basic skills English courses.

The inquiry findings highlighted issues of institutional effectiveness such as poor signage and a confusing web-based application system. It also stimulated conversation at evidence team meetings about whether it was sufficient for the college to simply enroll new students without doing more to help them succeed. Some team members argued the college should engage students at the outset in creating an educational and life plan. The team delved more deeply into questions of fairness and equity, discussing how priority in course enrollments should be assigned.

The recommendations the team generated from their inquiry findings ranged from student policy mandates (e.g., mandated preparation for assessment testing and mandatory assessments) to improved communication with students (e.g., creating clear steps and an easy path for new students to apply). In this way, the inquiry process engaged team members at LFCC in identifying how the very structures of the college could be contributing to overall low rates of student success.

The inquiry findings from the syllabus review shed light on the quality of pedagogical relationships students were encountering. Many syllabi adopted a stern tone emphasizing classroom and college policies and warning about sanctions for noncompliance. The team asked what conditions led to such a stern tone. They considered that it revealed a lack of knowledge or efficacy

Figure 2.2. A Menu of Inquiry Activities

Developmental Education

Self-Assessment Opportunities in Instruction	Document Analysis	Syllabi reviews Test/assessment reviews
	Observation Guides	Classroom observations
	Interview Protocols	Faculty interviews on classroom practices
	Surveys	Faculty awareness of transfer of underrepresented students in their classes and support service resources "Getting to know you," "I learn best," and "My progress"
Self-Assessment Opportunities for Administration	Data Analysis	Faculty hiring pool, representation, and retention by race/ethnicity Campus climate reports
	Document Analysis	Analysis of faculty development resources (website and handouts) Analysis of questions posed in course evaluations
	Observation Guides	Observation of faculty and TA training Observation of faculty development sessions
	Interview Protocols	Administrator interview on recruitment, hiring, and retention strategies and priorities Faculty interviews on experiences with recruitment, hiring, and retention Faculty and TA interviews on training experience
	Mapping Activity	Curriculum mapping Mapping course objectives/lesson plans with the progress of the curriculum
Process Benchmarking	Campus Visits	Visiting campuses with existing, effective developmental course practices
	Literature Review	Research existing best practices in developmental education

on the part of faculty to address issues of classroom behavior and respect on a one-on-one basis with students. It seemed that the syllabi communicated a sense of frustration with students, an attempt to elicit control and compliance, and a lack of willingness to engage in an authentic caring relationship with the students as learners.

This led the team members to question what type of mentoring and support were available to faculty, for example, through their department chairs. The team members also questioned whether faculty should be held to some standard for the content and tone of the syllabus, for example, through department-level evaluations. The team ultimately recommended that a list of questions be developed to prompt reflective practice around syllabus construction. They recommended to faculty and college leaders that teaching workshops of a variety of types (e.g., teaching academy, new faculty orientation) be offered. They felt the standards should encourage greater creativity in communicating the faculty members' expectations for students in the classroom and also be clear about what they wanted students to learn from reading the syllabus. They viewed the impact of changing the syllabus as an impact on the reflective practice of faculty, calling on them to develop a deeper understanding of the needs of students.

Embedded in these recommendations was a sense that faculty lacked the cultural competencies to interact effectively with their students. Some team members felt that unstated, racialized fears were placing African American students, in particular, in the position of "the other." Team members, viewing the emphasis on control and compliance in the syllabi, questioned whether faculty had the cultural competencies to interact in a caring manner with students. Therefore, the team recommended an expansion of faculty training and professional development in the use of culturally relevant pedagogy.

As an outgrowth of these activities, the LFCC evidence team moved in their next steps to involve others in inquiry using Equity Scorecard tools. The team leaders reassembled a new evidence team, with some members carrying over and new members added. It was in this mixed group, where some team members already had spent time with one another negotiating the meanings and status of race and equity at LFCC that the critical disturbance in the activity system of the Scorecard erupted.

CONTRADICTIONS OF RACE, DIVERSITY, AND EQUITY

In this section we use narrative text, excerpted from Vines (2012), and interpretive commentary to illustrate the Equity Scorecard inquiry process and what we learned when attempting to negotiate the ideals of justice as fairness, as articulated in celebrations of diversity in broad forms, and justice as transformation, as articulated in ideals for substantive organizational change to remediate structural racism. The "basic model" for analysis using CHAT is "minimally two interacting activity systems" (Engeström, 2001, p. 136). Further, action research entails a commitment to reflective practice and learning among all research participants, whether they are insiders or outsiders to the focal setting, local practitioners or university researchers (McTaggart, 1997). Therefore, we describe the activity setting of CUE's action research "design team" in addition to the activity setting of the LFCC evidence team.

In regard to formatting in this first narrative section, the narrative text is indented, with verbatim quotations from Vines's (2012) dissertation indicated in italics. Our interpretation of the data appears in plain text.

> The three evidence team leaders, all faculty members at Las Flores Community College (LFCC), were holding a planning meeting to prepare for an Equity Scorecard kickoff workshop that would bring together members of the new evidence team for the first time. One of the team leaders and CUE's facilitator led the 4-hour meeting, which began with a review of some of the issues that had slowed up the inquiry process for the previous evidence team.
>
> CUE's facilitator stood to summarize project information using PowerPoint and to demonstrate a new interactive data tool that CUE had developed, called the Benchmarking Equity and Student Success Tool (BESST), which would be used to present student cohort progression data to the new evidence team members. The team leaders sat in a conference room on campus, arrayed around a small table where they could talk easily while still having a view of the projected images.
>
> *One leadership team member said, "I am excited. However, I do not want to kick-start this work unless we are ready so that it will work." . . . The group discussed potential problems and concerns as they worked to mitigate foreseen issues, which they identified as participants leaving early, not following the agenda, not being prepared, not being committed to ground rules, and not following the process. . . . One statement that seemed to command a lot of discussion was one regarding participants' taking the focus away from where the [evidence] team intended to concentrate.*
>
> *They found that some participants had a difficult time leaving the investigative stage, which delayed action, and others were concentrated on their personal agendas. One team member stated, "I have seen so many people spend so much time trying to find the problem and we do not get anything done. Then, those are the same people who have a pet project that they try to make work any way possible." As the team members reflected on [their experience on the first evidence team], there appeared to be a great fear of this concern being repeated. This led to further dialogue of how to avoid this behavior.*

[At many points in the conversation], the Leadership Team members brought up concerns regarding which data to utilize as they anticipated what the Evidence Team and Critical Friends would say to critique the data. The team members showed a strong desire to use the BESST data in a way that they all could stand by it without any unintentional misleading information. (Vines, 2012, pp. 98–100)

Although expansive learning aims to open "a radically wider horizon of possibilities" (Engeström, 2001, p. 137), it is clear from this text that the starting point for this Equity Scorecard planning meeting is in many ways routine. A small group of professors sit around a conference table and plan a meeting. The presence of an outsider facilitator is somewhat unusual, but the facilitator and team leaders already know one another due to the previous phase of Scorecard work at the college, so the interactions are informal. They have a shared interpersonal history as well as shared knowledge of the college's prior diversity efforts, which had been mapped out as part of an initial planning activity by the previous Scorecard team. The team leaders readily express their concerns with the facilitator and one another. They refer to common points of reference in the college's history of diversity work and use language artifacts from the Scorecard, such as "ground rules," a CUE facilitation tool that had entered their discourse. In this seemingly bounded and routine setting, due to the action research design of the Equity Scorecard the history of racism work is evident and intentionally brought to the surface in the planning process.

The concerns expressed by the team leaders at LFCC as they planned ahead reflected the *historicity* of the evidence team (based on the shared experience of the group), and the history of racial discrimination in the broader community surrounding the college. They did not *"want to kick-start this work unless we are ready so that it will work."* The team leaders at LFCC planned ahead anticipating "multivoicedness," technical and critical problems in a variety of forms, critiques from many corners, and a lack of shared understanding in and outside the evidence team of the goals of the Equity Scorecard process.

For example, based on their prior experiences, they worried that some team members might bring a "pet project" to the table and try to make their own project the focus of the group. They feared that team members might not have a willingness to engage in experimentation with new ideas, spending "so much time trying to find the problem" that the team would not be able to "get anything done." The leaders anticipated a lack of capacity to engage effectively in the inquiry process. Team conversations would ideally be informed by close attention to the data at hand, such as the BESST data the facilitator was reviewing with the LFCC team leaders at the planning meeting. However, experience told them that team members often wandered into conversations that took the focus away from the data at hand, diffusing the focus on equity. Their experience on the first Scorecard evidence team told them that anecdotal storytelling, much of it unsupported or even contradicted by the college's data, might advance deficit views about the causes of equity gaps. Once those views were aired within the collaborative setting of a Scorecard evidence team meeting, they became subjects of discussion. For the team leaders, these types of discussions were old news; they were tired of them and wanted to avoid retreading old ground.

Poor data quality can be so damning that "The team members showed a strong desire to use the BESST data in a way that they all could stand by it without any unintentional misleading information" (Vines, 2012, p. 100). Some of the data that had been presented to the previous LFCC evidence team had not been defined in the college's student data management system properly. The data's lack of credibility had mired the team in data discussions and technical aspects of the Scorecard process, threatening the team's ability even to begin to address equity issues. Data issues and an overemphasis on data quality can easily swamp the communicative aspects of the Scorecard process (Dowd, Malcom, Nakamoto, & Bensimon, 2012).

The hope of reaching conclusions that would allow all the team members to "stand by" the data sounded a fear of inevitable critique. Drawing on the experience on the first LFCC Scorecard team, the team feared that their conclusions would be called into question, that the knowledge produced through the Scorecard process would not be viewed as legitimate.

The Activity System of the Equity Scorecard

The team leaders included "not being committed to the ground rules" in their list of concerns. They knew that simply stating ground rules of mutual respect and collaboration as part of expectations for teamwork is not sufficient. Social norms involving interactions among people with varying degrees of formal, positional status, and ascribed social status based on race, gender, ethnicity, and language are not easily disturbed. All of these concerns, which were not unique to LFCC team members, have impressed on us that the Equity Scorecard action research design must involve both a technically well-designed inquiry process and also activities that tap deeper motivations to evoke what Freire called *conscientizacao*, or "critical consciousness" (Stanton-Salazar, 2011, p. 1089) and what we refer to in the discourse of the Scorecard as "equity-mindedness" (Bensimon & Malcom, 2012).

Figure 2.3 illustrates the setting depicted in the narrative above using the theoretical constructs of activity system analysis, showing the desired *outcome* as expansive learning about how to bring about equity. The *subjects* are college faculty members acting within typical norms of professional decorum (*rules*). The *object* of the planning meeting (in this particular case, though it varies by different types of Scorecard meetings) is to plan the kickoff workshop. The team leaders engage in the discussion with attention to a larger campus *community* of faculty and administrators, already finding that their relationship to some of these members has shifted due to their role as evidence team leaders. They feel a responsibility to lead a meaningful inquiry process. They also do not like wasting their own time or that of others. Their previous experience of evidence team members arriving late to meetings, leaving early, and not coming prepared receives attention as a weakness in their organizational capacity to conduct inquiry.

In order for the Las Flores Community College evidence team to successfully conduct inquiry to address racial disparities in student experiences on their campus, they need to interact in different ways. The *instruments,* or artifacts, of the Equity Scorecard that are designed to help achieve this outcome include the professional facilitator, the structuring of the team leader's role relative to the evidence team members, and the object of planning the kickoff workshop. Our objective in creating these roles is to provide tools to equip the evidence team members to pay attention to social norms, the historicity of equity effort as well as the neglect of those efforts, and ideas about how to remediate the *division of labor* among team members.

Ground rules are an artifact of the Equity Scorecard, a tool for social interaction to remediate cultural norms of interaction based on differential status and privilege. Examples include "no rank in the room," "listen with respect," and "be present at the meeting." Ground rules are introduced at evidence team kickoff workshops to all team members. Team leaders are encouraged to refer to them regularly throughout the Scorecard process, for example, by posting them at evidence team meetings. Ground rules anticipate and are a tool to remediate the concerns expressed by the LFCC team leaders in the narrative above.

Issues such as "leaving early, not following the agenda, not being prepared . . . and not following the process" are common in organizational life. However, in the context of the Scorecard's intended focus on reducing institutional racism, such behaviors take on stronger emotional content. Inattentiveness and disrespectful participation can be experienced by some team members, particularly those who have experienced racial discrimination, as a manifestation of racism: the "same old, same old" of giving lip service to the value of diversity yet not investing deeply in understanding how educa-

Figure 2.3. Remediating Artifacts of Social Interaction

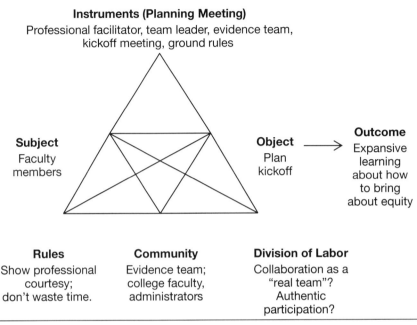

Instruments (Planning Meeting)
Professional facilitator, team leader, evidence team,
kickoff meeting, ground rules

Subject
Faculty
members

Object
Plan
kickoff

Outcome
Expansive
learning
about how
to bring
about equity

Rules
Show professional
courtesy;
don't waste time.

Community
Evidence team;
college faculty,
administrators

Division of Labor
Collaboration as a
"real team"?
Authentic
participation?

Source: Diagram features reproduced from Yrjö Engeström (2001), Expansive learning at work: Toward an activity theoretical reconceptualization. *Journal of Education and Work,* 14(1), 133–156, reprinted by permission of the publisher (Taylor & Francis Ltd, www. tandfonline.com)

tional institutions are implicated in racial discrimination. Behaviors such as "leaving early, not following the agenda, not being prepared" are in many ways the behaviors of busy people with too much to do. But these behaviors also reflect social privilege. Given the social norm of race muteness and the team leaders' experience with the previous evidence team, the team leaders feel they are facing a critical disturbance that is deep-seated in their institutional culture as well as the broader society. The technical and critical disturbances are conjoined because the technical disturbance is imbued by the history of racial discrimination and elicits a more emotional response from people attuned to the manifestations of racism.

Therefore, CUE's action research, and any accountability program concerned with racial equity, must address the routine technical disturbances introduced by discourteous behaviors as well as the critical disturbances of institutional racism.

Remediating the Division of Labor

Figure 2.4 adds two jagged arrow symbols to the previous figure. They represent the two disturbances in the activity system of the Equity Scorecard process at LFCC revealed by the narrative presented above. The jagged line between rules and object represents the problem of competing social norms about time use and interactions among professionals. On the one hand, professional courtesy is expected (e.g., do not arrive late), but on the other, faculty and many administrators and staff have autonomy over their schedules and priorities. If practitioners think their time is being wasted and that the object of an activity is not useful, they will exercise their professional autonomy and restrict their investment in a project. The "ground rules" introduced and then negotiated with evidence team members by CUE's facilitator are intended to marshal the mutual respect necessary to establish shared ownership of the object of conducting inquiry as a team. In addition, the ground rules are intended to garner authentic participation and collaboration as a "real team" (Bensimon & Neumann, 1993), so that the team leaders do not get stuck doing all the work of the Scorecard process of data analysis, interpretation, and action planning.

When the team leaders expressed reluctance to start the work of the Scorecard until they felt the team was ready, it signaled to us that the "ground rules," as previously implemented at LFCC, had not functioned adequately. This disturbance in the Equity Scorecard activity system is represented by the jagged line on Figure 2.4 between the Equity Scorecard instruments and the desired division of labor of an evidence team. As the Equity Scorecard unfolded at LFCC, we could see that a contradiction existed between the intended purpose of the inquiry protocols we created in the CUE "design team" and the object of our action research.

This shortcoming was clearly counterproductive. It was essential that the Equity Scorecard team function to remediate professional norms surrounding the division of labor around racial equity work, which too often leave people of color serving on marginalized diversity committees and experiencing an overburdened sense of "cultural taxation" (Padilla, 1994, p. 26). To address the concerns raised at LFCC's planning meeting depicted above, LFCC's Equity Scorecard facilitator regularly debriefed with us to address the problem of team members not "committing to the ground rules" and "taking the focus away" from equity issues, both of which are recurring challenges to the Scorecard process. A new protocol was designed for use at the upcoming kickoff workshop that would bring the second LFCC evidence team together for the first time. The new tool was a four-page document titled "Roles We Play on an Evidence Team." It lists team member roles initially derived from Estela Bensimon and Anna Neumann's study of Teams and Teamwork in Higher Education (Bensimon & Neumann, 1993;

Figure 2.4. Disturbances in the Activity System

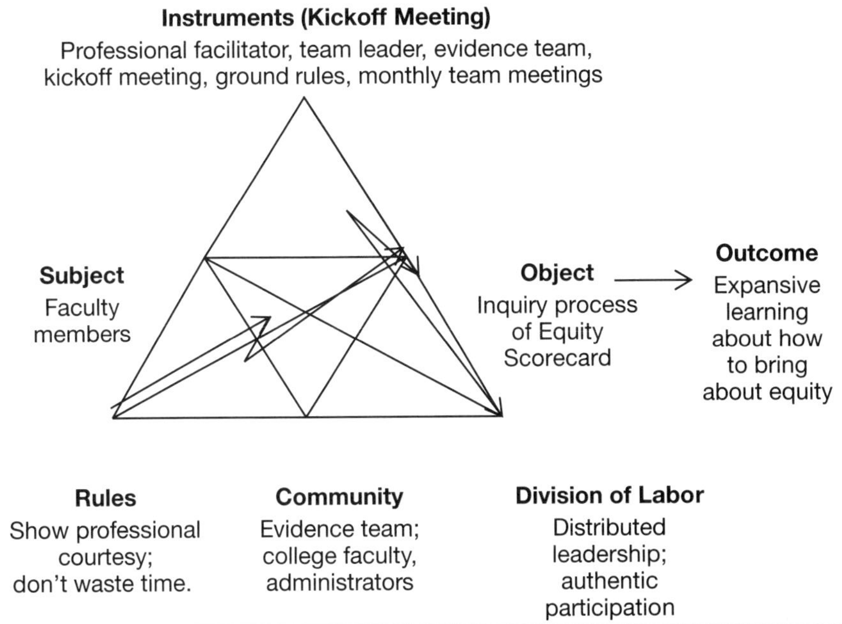

Instruments (Kickoff Meeting)
Professional facilitator, team leader, evidence team, kickoff meeting, ground rules, monthly team meetings

Subject
Faculty members

Object
Inquiry process of Equity Scorecard

Outcome
Expansive learning about how to bring about equity

Rules
Show professional courtesy; don't waste time.

Community
Evidence team; college faculty, administrators

Division of Labor
Distributed leadership; authentic participation

Source: Diagram features reproduced from Yrjö Engeström (2001), Expansive learning at work: Toward an activity theoretical reconceptualization. *Journal of Education and Work,* 14(1), 133–156, reprinted by permission of the publisher (Taylor & Francis Ltd, www. tandfonline.com)

Neumann, 1991) and further developed by CUE staff. These include roles such as "boundary spanner," "critic," and "emotional monitor," 10 in all.

This list of roles was presented in a worksheet format, with instructions asking new evidence team members to jot down notes reflecting on their typical modes of interaction in group work relative to the roles described. It also asks them to consider what role they expect to play or would like to play on the evidence team. As a mediating artifact, the tool was intended to signal to team members that they were being asked to actively attend to the quality of their participation as a team member and to take ownership for the quality of the inquiry process. By listing and defining the various team roles, the tool also provided an initial knowledge base for team members to increase their awareness of team dynamics.

Engaging the "Race Question"

Other tools were needed to evoke an emotional understanding among White team members of what was at stake, to enable collective, pluralistic deliberation about the lived experience of contradictions between democratic ideals and the failures of our educational institutions to function equitably. We view these organizational contradictions as the very place we need to focus our attention to initiate a meaningful change process. Our approach acknowledges, as Engeström (2001) does, that "contradictions generate disturbances and conflicts, but also innovative attempts to change the activity" (p. 137). In effect, critical disturbances caused by institutional racism must be brought to the surface in productive ways to stimulate expansive learning rather than resistance. To develop a sense of collective agency for change among team members, the action research design needed to ask team members to realize how those ideological tensions operated at their institution. This means finding ways to situate current educational practices in historical discrimination, while at the same time generating energy among evidence team members and their colleagues to invent a "historically new form" of educational practice to replace problematic ones currently "embedded in . . . everyday actions" (Engeström, 2001, p. 137, citing Engeström, 1987, p. 174). Action research aimed at remediating structural racism must grapple with the past while also inventing new ways of knowing and doing.

LFCC Kickoff Workshop. The following excerpt from Vines is based on his observational field notes from the kickoff workshop and depicts how the "Roles We Play on an Evidence Team" tool was used. One of the first things we see is that the team leaders act on what they learned from their previous Scorecard team experiences. They begin the meeting by providing information to the assembled group about the "status of those who were not in attendance." This starting point guarded against the chance that what might simply be a superficial disturbance (scheduling difficulties) would mushroom into a critical disturbance if team members were to mistakenly interpret late arrivals as a sign of disrespect for the group and its goals.

> The [evidence team's] lead faculty updated everyone on the status of those who were not in attendance, stating that two participants would be a little late. Specifically, this protocol was helpful and designed to address concerns that emerged during the planning session regarding the campus community's culture when dealing with commitment to meetings. The lead faculty opened the workshop by asking the participants about their understanding of the project. This allowed for clarity of the objective of inquiry. Then, the CUE facilitator welcomed everyone before leading the group into introductions. The facilitator reviewed the agenda before engaging the team in an icebreaker. The icebreaker was an asset-mapping activity, which entailed the CUE

facilitator sharing a Prezi presentation titled "Roles We Play on an Evidence Team." This tool was designed to help subjects understand the roles which they are asked to play throughout the project. The participants wrote their names down on a paper that was posted on a wall next to the roles they believed they would be most interested in contributing. (Vines, 2012, p. 101)

Two key points of action research using the Equity Scorecard are highlighted in this narrative. The first is the attention to the process as an opportunity for professional development and expansive learning. Through the planning meeting, the team leaders had acted purposefully, drawing on what they learned through their experience on the first Scorecard team, to design the kickoff workshop. The second key point is the attention paid to obtaining "clarity of the objective of inquiry" by making time to ask the participants about their understanding of the project. Figure 2.5 represents these iterative aspects of the action research design process by adding an activity system triangle representing CUE on the right-hand side of the previous figure.

The figure shows that the *subjects* of CUE's action research activity system include the two of us as the codirectors of CUE, CUE's project specialists, the professional facilitators who consult with us, and doctoral students who do research on organizational learning and equity. The *object* of our work is to design action research tools and processes that will be useful for educators to engage in expansive learning about equity issues. In addition to the debrief and design team meetings already noted, the physical artifacts of our work, our *instruments*, are written texts, worksheets (such as "the ground rules"), visual images (such as the "racism cartoon"), and data tools for conducting inquiry. Our *rules* include review and revision, experimentation, and viability (i.e., usefulness in professional settings). In addition, we try to deviate from the predominant social norm of "race muteness," though sometimes that is difficult to do without putting people on the defensive or causing discomfort to ourselves, our collaborators, or others. CUE's action research *community* includes past and future Equity Scorecard participants, "critical friends" (college leaders, equity advocates, and friendly skeptics), other academic researchers, and other intermediary organizations that work with colleges and universities, typically as part of accountability initiatives. Our *division of labor* involves horizontal collaboration among us and academic researchers in other settings, as well as vertical collaboration among us and our staff.

After the icebreaker, copies of the cartoon shown in Figure 2.6 by B. Deutsch (of leftycartoons.com), which is titled "The Story of Bob and Race," but which we referred to as the "racism cartoon," were distrib-

Figure 2.5. Inquiry and Action Research Settings

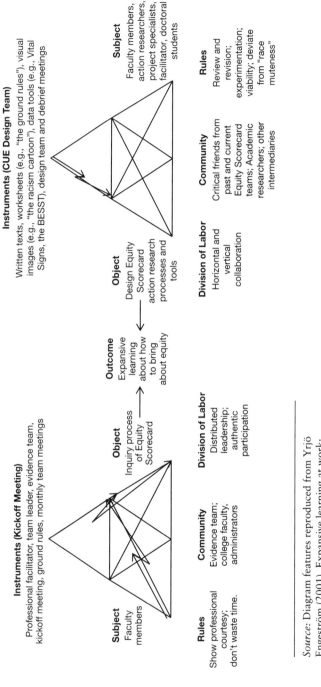

Source: Diagram features reproduced from Yrjö Engeström (2001), Expansive learning at work: Toward an activity theoretical reconceptualization. *Journal of Education and Work, 14*(1), 133–156, reprinted by permission of the publisher (Taylor & Francis Ltd, www.tandfonline.com)

uted to the kickoff workshop participants. Vines (2012), describing each panel (or "slide," as he describes it), explains the relevance of the cartoon to CUE's goal of acknowledging the history of racial discrimination in the United States through the Equity Scorecard's inquiry process:

> After the asset mapping activity to clarify Evidence Team roles, the CUE facilitator introduced a tool to illustrate structural racism and how the historically White dominant culture has benefitted in society and people of color have not. This tool intended to add knowledge on how CUE views inequity in society and provide an opportunity to reflect. The first slide of the cartoon was of a character named "Bob," and it explained how his great-grandparents arrived in the United States. The slide shows what appears to be a politician stating, "Our immigration laws should make it easier for the right kind of people to immigrate." The second slide shows Bob's grandparents becoming homeowners as they are approved for a mortgage loan while a couple of color are being told "sorry we can't help you." The third slide illustrates how Bob's dad began his career as the employer tells him "you seem like one of us. We're offering you a foot in the door." Behind the scene, a person of color is told "sorry, the position is filled" at the very same time. The fourth slide is of [Bob's parents becoming homeowners] as the real estate agent informs Bob that they only show homes in this neighborhood to the "right sort of people." Bob's father comments to his wife on how lucky they were that their parents were able to help with the down payment. The fifth slide tells how Bob got through his teen years. The slide is an illustration of a police officer telling Bob that he is letting him off a drug offense with a warning, and, in the background, the slide illustrates a girl of color being arrested for the same offense. The last slide is of Bob emphatically stating "I have never benefitted from racism." (Vines, 2012, p. 108)

Vines (2012) concludes his description of the cartoon with the observation, "Due to limited time to discuss the cartoon, this tool did not command the type of interaction during the workshop to make it a focus of conversation or reflection" (p. 109). In this statement, Vines is commenting on the lack of explicit reference to the images or content of the cartoon in the ensuing conversation. The discussion did not turn to an exploration of the meaning intended by the final frame in which Bob states, "I have never benefitted from racism." Nor was the relevance of structural racism in housing and employment to racial disparities in education discussed.

Instead, one participant suggested that the focus of the project should be broadened to include other groups that have experienced discrimination. Vines (2012) relates the ensuing discussion:

Figure 2.6. The "Racism Cartoon"

"The Story of Bob and Race," by B. Deutsch (of leftycartoons.com). Used with permission.

[The participant stated,] "We always talk about race and gender; we never talk about socioeconomic levels, students with disabilities, or GLBT." The respondent went on to talk about the importance of focusing on such issues and how focusing on other issues may help participants understand and relate to the race and ethnic issues, stating, "The lesbian and gay issues can help us understand; I know that CUE's purpose is race and ethnicity. . . . We don't have to bring in those issues . . . but we have to talk about it." Some inquiry team members were persistent in making sure that the team stayed focused on race and ethnicity. One participant stated the reason people were having difficulty staying focused on race was because of the level of discomfort talking about race. The respondent stated, "You can muddy the water by the issues of other groups; if we are talking about race and we talk about other stuff, it's because we don't want to talk about race. . . . White people feel safe talking about other stuff." Another team member stated, "My feeling is, when we start talking about race, there is an interest to expand it to other things because people are uncomfortable talking about race and want to talk about other things." (pp. 106–107)

In this exchange, we see a new team member wishing to broaden the Scorecard focus to include multiple forms of diversity. Other participants, including those who had already spent time together talking about equity issues as members of the first LFCC Scorecard team, responded with an insistence that the group must retain its focus on race. For these participants, the new team member's request for a broader focus on diversity carried a great deal of history. That history was local, recalling participants on the first Scorecard team who returned again and again to "pet projects." They did not want to allow this habit of deflecting attention from racial equity. The local history was also an instantiation of the broader history of racial discrimination and indifference to racial inequities.

"I get it." After the more experienced team members argued against a broadened diversity focus, the participant who had raised the idea "appeared to absorb and reflect on the comments made," according to Vines (2012, p. 86). Then, after thanking the more experienced Scorecard team members for their perspectives, the new member said, "It's okay to move forward, I get it" (p. 86). The tone of this conversation (and our subsequent debrief meetings with CUE's facilitator) indicated that this exchange was one that held strong emotional content for the participants.

In Engeström's terms, this emotion indicated the existence of a critical disturbance in the work environment. However, with the words, "It's okay to move forward, I get it," and the group's acceptance of this acquiescence, the phenomenon Engeström refers to as *masking* occurred. Masking represents a return to established norms; it enables work to flow in the typical manner and relies on this restoration to move beyond a critical disturbance. In the weeks following the workshop, interviews conducted by Vines (2012), as well as evaluation survey results that Scorecard team members provided anonymously, confirmed our expectation that masking and acquiescence was not the same as resolution. Several survey respondents felt that the inquiry focus should be broadened to a diversity frame. Others felt just as strongly that multiple diversities should not be the focus.

One respondent indicated that the conversation "overtook the task at hand" (Vines, 2012, p. 107). But another saw that the conversation was relevant to the purpose of constructing knowledge among the workshop participants about structural racism, stating during an interview:

We have such a range of folks on the team; the point was to highlight institutional racism. We have a range of understanding of privilege and oppression. I think there were a number of folks who were like, "yeah, I get it," but my hunch is that it was eye-opening for them, but they didn't say much. There is a huge educational component to action research. For some in the group, it wasn't necessary. There were a number of folks who said, "yeah, I get it," but the concept is central to the work we are doing. (p. 109)

This divergence of views and knowledge about race and racism is typical among Scorecard team members. This division exists in a group of people who are essentially hand-selected to participate in a project focused on racial equity, just the same as it would in a general population of college and university practitioners.

Expansive Learning About Racism

The statement by two LFCC Scorecard team members that White people feel "discomfort" talking about race echoes a key theme of critical race studies concerning the historicity of the diversity movement. Critical scholars are skeptical that racism can be addressed through a liberal agenda because racism has become normalized to the point where it is invisible to many White people. Racism is an everyday phenomenon that must be explicitly addressed before any progress can be made. Discomfort arises for White practitioners who are not attuned to these ideas. They experience a contradiction between liberal democratic ideals and any focus on race that does not occur as part of a celebration of diversity.

In part this is due to miseducation that has occurred under the rubric of multiculturalism. As Ladson-Billings (2009) explained:

> The race-neutral or colorblind perspective, evident in the way the curriculum presents people of color, presumes a homogenized "we" in celebration of diversity. This perspective embraces the so-called multicultural perspective by "misequating the middle passage with Ellis Island" (King, 1992, p. 327). Thus students are taught erroneously that "we are all immigrants," and, as a result, African American, Indigenous, and Chicano students are left with the guilt of failing to rise above their immigrant status like "every other group." (p. 29)

To celebrate the American master narrative of immigration and assimilation denies the reality of African Americans whose ancestors were shipped, through "the middle passage," to North America in chains, as well as the subjugation of Chicanos and American Indians whose lands, language, and culture were colonized.

In many educational settings, these histories are subdued if not forgotten or outright contradicted. When participants in our Scorecard workshops argue, as the new team member at the LFCC meeting did, that a broader diversity framing might "help participants understand and relate to the race and ethnic issues," their view is often informed by beliefs about justice as fairness. Liberal egalitarian beliefs hinge on the existence of a just legal and political system. Liberal ideology endorses the belief that the United States, despite its discriminatory history, will ultimately function to create a more encompassing umbrella of civil rights, and therefore a just society.

As noted above, Engeström (2001) declares that "an expansive transformation is accomplished when the object and motive of the activity are reconceptualized to embrace a radically wider horizon of possibilities than in the previous mode of the activity" (p. 137). For some participants at LFCC, the Equity Scorecard kickoff workshop was an opportunity to engage in expansive learning. These participants were not about to let that opportunity slip away. They acted with a sense of "agency for equity" (Bishop, 2014) to try to insist on positive race consciousness as the focus of the Equity Scorecard. The critical disturbance that occurred at LFCC, though initially masked, evolved over time to a constructive redesign of the Equity Scorecard and to a broadening of perspectives among LFCC's evidence team members.

Action research is fundamentally about producing knowledge about how to act in particular settings to achieve "the good" that motivates action in that setting. Theories of situated action, cognition, and learning emphasize that "learning opportunities occur when people are involved in activities. It is here where the gap between generalities and particulars can be closed" (Säljö, 2003, p. 320). What is important in order to transfer knowledge produced in one setting to other settings is not "task-to-task" transfer, but identification of "patterns of participatory processes across situations" that provide opportunities for knowledge production and application in the new settings (Tuomi-Gröhn & Engeström, 2003, p. 25).

Critical disturbances in a setting, or more theoretically in an activity system, reveal contradictions. As Engeström (2008) emphasizes:

> In activity theory, contradictions play a central role as sources of change and development. Contradictions are not the same as problems or conflicts. Contradictions are historically accumulating structural tensions within and between activity systems. The activity system is constantly working through tensions and contradictions within and between its elements. Contradictions manifest themselves in disturbances and innovative solutions. In this sense, an activity system is a virtual disturbance- and innovation-producing machine. (p. 205)

At LFCC, the contradiction that caught our attention was expressed through an emotional exchange that ensued after one participant stated an interest in pursuing equity through a focus on diversity. We know from the results of evaluation surveys that we routinely collect at the end of each Scorecard workshop that about half of the participants on Equity Score-card teams would prefer or express interest in what they view as a broader framing based on inclusiveness of multiple diversities. This contradiction between diversity and equity is not surprising because over the past few decades the racial equity agenda has been pulled into the diversity agenda. The disturbance in the activity system of the Scorecard at LFCC was an expression of this social, ideological contradiction that is manifest in the organizational life of colleges and universities.

In *Telling Tales*, Denning (2004) distinguishes the types of organiza-tional stories leaders should tell to bring about innovation in their organi-zations. A story that "focuses on mistakes made and shows in some detail how they were corrected" will "solicit alternative—and possibly better—so-lutions" (p. 5). The listener becomes attuned to the nature of the challenge and, if there is buy-in that the challenge must be addressed, then also be-comes a collaborator in innovation.

Prodding the ideological tensions of diversity and equity values is as much an emotional as a thought-provoking endeavor. After we experienced the critical disturbance in the activity system at LFCC, we invested more of our resources in developing tools to mediate the emotional risk participants experience as they engage in inquiry using Equity Scorecard tools.

We decided to develop content about the dynamics of trust and involved a second professional facilitator to help us do so, Dr. Tenny Mickey. Ma-terials such as a PowerPoint presentation and facilitated group discussion were added to the Scorecard toolkit. These materials asked participants to become aware of criteria for building trust (e.g., integrity, reciprocity, and goodwill). They also presented scenarios of "trust busters" and "trust build-ers" that emerged from prior Scorecard team work. An example of a trust-busting scenario evocative of the LFCC case describes "A shift away from equity because it's easier to tackle problems if they address the whole cam-pus: 'I don't think it's fair to focus on one group. Why don't we just look at all groups?'" The trust-building response offered suggests, "Remind the team that while remedies for the entire campus are worthwhile, it is impor-tant to create intentional changes that benefit underrepresented students if equity gaps are going to be effectively addressed."

Using these types of interaction tools also helps us to engage Score-card team members as collaborators in managing risk. In educational and business settings alike, leaders are recognizing the importance of devoting resources to assist organizational members in recognizing where fear of fail-ure or of saying the wrong thing hampers teamwork (Dyer, Gregersen, & Christensen, 2011; Sawyer, 2007). We added questions to the workshop evaluation forms we collect at the end of each day of a Scorecard workshop to gauge affective responses. For example, we ask whether the participants perceive that it is risky to talk about race on their campus. This item, which is not written to draw conclusions about specific sources or contexts of risk, typically returns a bifurcated response. We use the results, for example, by presenting word clouds of the recurring terms expressed in the survey responses, to let Scorecard teams know that about half of their members perceive a sense of risk. We ask them to become emotional monitors of the team's interactions and to explicitly engage with feelings of risk. In addition, doctoral student researchers studying with us are taking up research agendas that will generate a better understanding of the emotional dimensions of race talk and racialized discourses in educational settings.

The activity setting of the Scorecard depicted above provided a venue for developing praxis, which, as Greene (1988) reminds us, refers to the actions we undertake to gain freedom from unjust conditions: "We might think of freedom as an opening of spaces as well as perspectives, with everything depending on the actions we undertake in the course of our quest, the *praxis* we learn to devise" (p. 5). The LFCC case illustrates praxis in the context of the Equity Scorecard. The participatory ideal articulates the responsibility of educational institutions to engage in practices that are not oppressive of the voices and experiences (both historical and contemporary) of racially minoritized groups. The critical disturbance in the narrative above represents for us the potential of action research to produce tools and activity settings where higher education practitioners engage in expansive learning to move beyond color blindness and race muteness. We believe the White privilege that serves to silence discussions of race can be actively deconstructed in a process of expansive learning through action research.

MOVING FROM DIVERSITY TO EQUITY

Critical race theorists argue that it is better to call out the master story of generational progress as a myth. Notwithstanding the abolishment of slavery and other forms of de jure racism, they point out that progress has been too slow and contemporary racial disparities are too great to warrant wholesale reliance on liberal policies. Critical race scholars do not "automatically or uniformly 'trash' liberal ideology and method. . . . Rather, they are highly suspicious of the liberal agenda, distrust its method, and want to retain what they see as a valuable strain of egalitarianism which may exist despite, and not because of, liberalism" (Bell, 2009b, p. 41).

Critical scholars do not aim to encourage or sustain racial conflict. As Bell (2009b) expressed it, critical race theorists "strive for a specific, more egalitarian, state of affairs" and, in contrast to the existing state of affairs, strive to "empower and include traditionally excluded views." The emancipatory and transformative potential of critical studies stems from its belief in a "collective wisdom" (p. 42). That collective wisdom cannot be actualized under the current state of affairs. The key step, Bell argued, is an unremitting critique involving deconstruction (of existing unjust laws and policies) and reconstruction of a society that is truly egalitarian. The work of reconstruction demands "the unapologetic use of creativity" (p. 41), because in critique one must envision what does not yet exist. The work of deconstruction and reconstruction is inherently dialectical because "to see things as they really are, you must imagine them for what they might be" (p. 40).

Developing Organizational Capacity for Race Talk

In the LFCC narrative above, when the team members from the first LFCC evidence team said that White people feel uncomfortable talking about race and spoke against a broader focus on diversity, they were engaged in the work of deconstruction. Because this critique often goes unstated in educational settings, and certainly in postsecondary policy accountability debates, we view organizational capacity to articulate such a critique as a sign of progress. In Chapter 1 we asserted that justice as fairness is the dominant ideology in the United States and in postsecondary accountability policy. We argued that principles of justice as care and justice as transformation must be incorporated in equal standing. This chapter illustrates the type of equity work that must be carried out to enact standards of justice as care and justice as transformation in educational practice and policy.

The majority of diversity initiatives are directed at improving human relations and tolerance, rather than on achieving equity. The goals of diversity efforts are typically to increase minority representation, improve intercultural human relations, incorporate cultural diversity into the curriculum, and make diversity more visible and valued. The strategies to pursue diversity goals include: (1) educating majority faculty and students about the importance and value of diversity, (2) encouraging greater interracial and intercultural contact, and (3) expanding student services and programs to ease racial tensions, provide a safe space for minority students, and help minority students adjust to a predominantly White campus. This typically involves hiring diversity program coordinators and student affairs personnel in specialized roles to support minority students. These efforts represent the enactment of the principles of justice as fairness, particularly the concept of vertical equity, which calls for directing more resources and support toward students who have greater educational needs due to social inequality.

Higher education research documents the benefits of diversity to White students and to students of color who attend college alongside diverse peers of different racial and ethnic groups (Hurtado, Alvarez, Guillermo-Wann, Cuellar, & Arellano, 2012). While the diversity agenda and special programs for students of color have given many students a "leg up" in navigating college, it has not changed the "playing field" to make it more equitable.

Umbrella of Inclusiveness

Despite the successes of the diversity agenda in contributing to a growing acceptance of difference, there are troubling shortcomings in implementation. Most institutions adopted diversity through an umbrella approach celebrating diversity in all its forms and commodifying the human capital benefits of diversity in a global economy (Iverson, 2007; Swain, 2013). The particular discourse that is used in instituted diversity programs matters, because commodified and color-blind "inclusiveness" dissipates the initial thrust of the diversity agenda as a matter of civil rights. Today the concepts of diversity and inclusiveness call for recognition of a wide variety of differences—by religion, sexual orientation, veteran status, physical abilities, to name a few. The modern focus on diversity as an umbrella concept for all students contrasts with the civil rights era focus on expanding access to college for African Americans, Mexican Americans, Cubans, Puerto Ricans, and other Latino groups as well as increasing their representation and voice on campus. Treating these groups in the aggregate, as in the current usage of the term "underrepresented minorities" (URMs), does little to recall differentiated histories. This is problematic because the histories of colonialism, conquest, migration, and immigration are quite varied and the interests of minoritized groups are certainly not always aligned (Thompson, 2013).

When diversity research contributed to the successful defense of affirmative action in the *Grutter* and *Gratz* cases (Hurtado et al., 2012), the success of this important effort was overshadowed by its emphasis on the value of diversity to White students and mainstream society rather than to African Americans, Native Americans, Latinos, and Asian groups that had historically been excluded from college. The need to compensate for past and present racial discrimination was muted as diversity was recast, for purposes of interest convergence, in neoliberal terms focused on the economic and individual benefits of diversity (Yosso et al., 2004).

The celebratory approach of the "umbrella of inclusiveness" commodifies the "homogenized 'we' in celebration of diversity" (Ladson-Billings, 2009, p. 29). Such homogenization is a form of cultural imperialism and oppression. In addition, it causes social harm to members of those groups by damaging their sense of identity and self-worth, both of which are essential to successful participation in schooling and a democratic society (Howe, 1992). Celebrations of diversity are problematic because they lump the different experiences of racial discrimination of people of color under an "umbrella of diversity." While immigrants, native, and enslaved peoples have all been treated as "the other" due to the color of their skin, language, and cultural practices, the immigrant experience differs from the experiences of enslaved and colonized people. Celebrations of diversity will only serve to instill self-worth in all students if we abandon the metanarrative of the "homogenized 'we'" that obfuscates these differences (Ladson-Billings, 2009). The accountability field should make a commitment to educate its own members, higher education practitioners, and students about the differences in those experiences and how they influence educational participation and outcomes. Achieving the goal of nonoppression is currently hampered by color-blind practices.

Practitioners and accountability policymakers must create learning environments, such as those depicted in this chapter, for their own professional development about histories of discrimination and how they contribute to structural racism in higher education today. In order to support a shift away from color-blind educational practices, system and institutional leaders should provide practitioners with financial support to produce knowledge about equity through inquiry. The focus of inquiry must be on those institutional conditions that contribute to racial inequities. Institutional leaders should also provide symbolic support by firmly articulating an institutional commitment to racial equity.

CHAPTER 3

Enacting Justice as Care

A disturbance may occur between people and their instruments or between two or more people.

— Yrjö Engeström, *From Teams to Knots* (2008, p. 24)

Equity is a topic of conversation in many quarters of higher education accountability and practice, but the meanings participants attach to the word *equity* in those conversations are often very different. Miscommunication and bad feelings ensue when people are talking past each other. Not surprisingly under these circumstances, little of substance is achieved to bring the goal of equity closer within reach. The accountability field is having a garbled conversation about equity because speakers and listeners are judging the state of affairs and potential remedies using very different principles of justice. We have identified three perspectives on justice that are evident in the dominant and minor chords of equity discourse: justice as fairness (the dominant ideology), justice as care, and justice as transformation. These "three justices" draw, respectively, on social contract theory concerning individual rights and liberties; a humanistic ethic of care respecting the rights of all learners to a humane, nonoppressive education that does not impose a "self-worth tax"; and critical race perspectives that challenge the efficacy of liberalism and color blindness to enact change toward a more egalitarian society.

The different meanings of equity held by educational practitioners, which are typically smoothed over through masking and race muteness, play out as a contradiction of organizational life in educational settings that are at the same time articulating an embrace of diversity and multiculturalism. In this chapter we provide examples where disruptions between practitioners and their tools led not to masking but to changes in practice made in the interest of enhancing equity. In doing so, we continue our illustration of CUE's Equity Scorecard tools and processes. The cases we feature in this chapter were encouraging to us as a sign that the Scorecard's inquiry process was creating an environment in which practitioners felt a sense of agency to promote racial equity.

Here, as in earlier publications, we illustrate the value of action research to "remediate" practice (Bensimon, 2007; Bensimon & Malcom, 2012; Bustillos et al., 2011; Dowd, Bishop, et al., 2012; Dowd, Bishop, & Bensimon, in press; Witham & Bensimon, 2012). It would not be viable or productive to design action research in a way that would routinely provoke disturbances among colleagues in professional settings. In contrast, the strategy of evoking disturbances between practitioners and their instruments of professional practice—the "social media" of practice (Kemmis & McTaggart, 2005)—is a highly viable and necessary one.

Practitioners who experience contradictions between their ideals and practices as professionals may become motivated toward *praxis*, "doing the good" through individual and collective action to reconstruct unjust social arrangements. Praxis has a "reflective moment, involving the critique of existing social patterns and the search for alternatives, and an active moment, involving mobilization and collective action" (Seo & Creed, p. 230). Recognizing praxis as those efforts to reconstruct institutional practices through collective agency and actions rooted in critical consciousness situates praxis as a necessary element in the work of nonoppression called for by the standards of justice as care. Institutional contradictions can be productively engaged as catalysts of change because "the likelihood of praxis increases as contradictions within and across social systems develop, deepen, and permeate actors' social experience" (Seo & Creed, 2002, p. 230).

The case analyses presented in this chapter are again set in California, at several community colleges and one state university. These settings were among a dozen where we conducted inquiry with Equity Scorecard evidence teams and workshop participants over the past few years. The cases are drawn from 10 doctoral dissertations produced through studies where the doctoral researchers were participant observers at Equity Scorecard evidence team meetings and workshops. In each study the doctoral researchers collected observational data at planning meetings, evidence team meetings, workshops, symposia, and other project activities over a period of 9 to 12 months. At several sites multiple studies were conducted over a period of 3 years, making them uniquely rich sources of data (Little, 2012). The students' interpretations of observational data were triangulated with data from interpretive or cognitive interviews, documents collected at evidence team meetings and workshops, and our own direct interpretations generated through participation as action researchers in the settings of study. In our findings we draw particularly on settings where multiple doctoral researchers conducted studies simultaneously or sequentially, thereby extending the depth and scope of the findings.

OVERVIEW OF THE CHAPTER

This chapter revolves around a case study in which college faculty conducted inquiry into their teaching practices using CUE's Equity-Minded Syllabus Review Protocol. The syllabus review protocol is a faculty-oriented version of a more general document analysis protocol that we have used in multiple settings over the past 5 years. The action research design of practitioner inquiry using the syllabus review protocol invites faculty to reflect on the content and format of their syllabi, consider whether they communicate in an equity-minded manner, and make revisions to bring about organizational changes that will support racial equity. Several dissertation studies we supervised at the University of Southern California focused on practitioner inquiry using the syllabus review protocol as the primary inquiry tool or as one of several tools used in a setting over time. We list here the dissertations cited in the chapter below, each followed by the pseudonym for the college where the study was conducted: R. Z. Brown, 2012 (Monarch State University); M. Enciso, 2009 (Birch College); S. V. Levonisova, 2012 (Monarch State University); C. Salazar-Romo, 2009 (Cal College); P. Smith, 2012 (Monarch State University); T. Subramaniam, 2012 (Dynamic Community College); and C. R. Woerner, 2013 (Dynamic Community College). These studies provided us with a comprehensive understanding of faculty experiences of inquiry using this tool. The core section, "The Activity System of the Syllabus Protocol," presents our insights from synthesis and reanalysis of their findings.

The core section is preceded by two sections that apply theoretical lenses to frame the uses of the commonplace institutional document known as the syllabus as a cultural tool with power to construct and deconstruct organizational routines implicated in the reproduction of racial inequities in higher education institutions. Our findings describe the ways faculty members changed their pedagogical orientation toward students, articulating a greater sense of empathy and care. Even as faculty endorsed an ethic of care, however, they tended to insist on color blindness and equal treatment for *all* students.

The final section analyzes the commitment to color-blind educational practices using concepts of authentic care, subtractive schooling, validation, expertise, and collective agency. We conclude by arguing that the standards of justice as care cannot be realized through color-blind practices.

REMEDIATING THE ORGANIZATIONAL ROUTINE OF A SYLLABUS

The method of the syllabus review protocol is to use qualitative indicators of equity-mindedness (Bensimon & Malcom, 2012), culturally relevant pedagogies and curricula (Ladson-Billings, 1995), and "validation" (Rendón Linares & Muñoz, 2011) as prompts to invite faculty members to look at their syllabi "with new eyes." When facilitating inquiry using Equity Scorecard tools, we use the term *equity-minded* to refer to the dispositions of practitioners who actively engage in perspective-taking that motivates them to affirm and empower underrepresented students of color. Equity-mindedness contrasts with deficit-mindedness, which is a mindset that assumes students from groups that have been assigned minority social status arrive in class with nothing but deficits: learning deficits, motivation deficits, cultural deficits, and so on (Gutierrez et al., 2009).

The purpose of the Equity-Minded Syllabus Review Protocol is to facilitate a self-assessment of the syllabus by faculty to consider whether it is instantiating equity-minded and culturally inclusive practices. The current iteration of the syllabus review protocol (of which there have been many versions) provides the following explanation of the concepts of equity-mindedness and cultural inclusiveness:

Equity-mindedness is characterized by being

- Conscious of race in an affirmative sense
- Aware that one's own knowledge, beliefs, and practices—even if they are intended to be race-neutral—can disadvantage students of color
- Responsible for eliminating inequities by changing practices
- Aware that racialized patterns may be embedded in institutional policies and practices that perpetuate inequitable educational outcomes

Cultural inclusivity adds to equity-mindedness the ideas that

- All students, regardless of their background, are capable of excelling academically
- Instructors are responsible for students' learning and for maintaining equitable relationships with all students
- The knowledge and experience that students bring into the classroom should be heard, valued, and engaged in meaningful ways
- Students' capacities to act as social change agents to address racial inequities should be fostered in college

The qualitative indicators that serve as prompts for inquiry are listed in a formatted document with instructions regarding the instructional design of the syllabus review inquiry activity. As shown in Table 3.1, a worksheet groups the indicators in three categories: 1. Diversity, Inclusiveness, and Multiculturalism; 2. Student Learning and Success; and 3. Empowerment. These three categories were developed over time to make the indicators of empowerment distinct from the others because faculty found it easier to discuss prompts related to diversity and active learning than prompts related to equity (Dowd, Sawatzky, Rall, & Bensimon, 2012; Levonisova, 2012).

The process for a participating faculty member involves asking herself or himself, in reference to the series of prompts, "Does the document communicate . . . ?" the attribute indicated in the prompt. As shown in Table 3.1, examples of prompts in the category of Diversity and Multiculturalism are "respect for students," "diversity is valued," and "color consciousness in an affirming way." The category of Student Learning and Success has prompts such as "confidence in the capacity of students to be successful learners and achieve their goals" and "an expectation that students and educators will coconstruct knowledge in educational settings." The category of Empowerment includes indicators such as "a commitment to social justice and elimination of racial discrimination" and "a goal of education in this setting is to empower students as agents of change to reduce racial and ethnic inequities." We have discovered firsthand that faculty members—if they have any familiarity with these concepts at all—tend to have greater exposure to the concepts of diversity and student validation than to concepts of empowerment and social justice.

The formatted worksheet provides space for evidence team members to record their thoughts in response to the prompts as they review the syllabus at hand (their own or others). Once faculty have had a chance to reflect on each prompt and jot down notes, the protocol then calls for discussion about the cultural practices of pedagogy and curriculum design reflected in the syllabus. A series of questions is included for group discussion following individual review and reflection. The purpose of this activity, from a cultural historical perspective utilizing activity theory (Ellis, 2011; Engeström, 2001, 2008; Lee, 2011; Roth & Lee, 2007), is to remediate the historically accumulated aspects of educational activity systems that are experienced as marginalizing by students of color.

THE ACTIVITY SYSTEM OF THE SYLLABUS PROTOCOL

Figure 3.1 uses an activity system triangle (Engeström, 2001, 2008) to illustrate the functioning of the syllabus as an artifact of practice and the syllabus review protocol as a remediating artifact of practice. We utilize activity theory in our analyses to emphasize that while syllabus workshops focus on the syllabus as a means to engage faculty in inquiry regarding a familiar or-

Table 3.1. Equity-Minded Syllabus Review Indicators

Dimension for Inquiry and Description	Indicators: Does the document communicate . . . ?
Diversity, Inclusiveness, and Multiculturalism Communicates the value of diversity.	• Respect for students. • Diversity is valued. • Inclusiveness is an institutional priority. • Cultural pluralism is valued. • Bilingualism (and multilingualism) is valued. • Color consciousness in an affirming way.
Student Learning and Success Positions educational settings as places to create and capitalize on knowledge about culturally responsive practices.	• Confidence in the capacity of students to be successful learners and achieve their goals. • Institutional responsibility to provide students with the information and resources needed to meet high expectations. • Student success is a collaborative effort among the student, peers, faculty, administrators, counselors, and students' families and communities. • Educational settings are designed to capitalize on diversity of cultural practices and learning. • Learning is situated in real-world problems and authentic opportunities for learners to engage in academic work. • Differences in students' prior educational and life experiences are affirmed and engaged in positive ways. • An expectation that students and educators will co-construct knowledge in educational settings. • Educational programs and activities are designed to promote critical thinking about racial inequities and how to dismantle them.

ganizational routine, we understand that, as a cultural artifact, the syllabus is a document that is both a product and producer of organizational culture. The lines linking the points of the activity system triangle on Figure 3.1 indicate a key tenet of activity theory: that changes occurring at one point of the triangle impact the other points. Changing a cultural artifact like the syllabus therefore has the potential of bringing about organizational change.

The instruments in this activity setting are the syllabi of the participants, CUE's syllabus review protocol, and the physical setting and materials of the syllabus workshop (e.g., a meeting or conference room, handouts

Table 3.1. Continued

	• A commitment to social justice and elimination of racial discrimination.
	• The institution fosters constructive discussion of discrimination, racism, and marginalization.
	• Dominant social and cultural assumptions regarding culture, intelligence, language, objectivity, and knowledge are questioned.
Empowerment Creates an environment that promotes social consciousness, collective responsibility, and agency to create a more just society.	• A goal of education in this setting is to empower students as agents of change to reduce racial and ethnic inequities.
	• One of the purposes of education is to promote social responsibility and agency.
	• Institutional policies and practices are designed to generate awareness of the experiences of marginalized racial and ethnic groups and the privileges of dominant groups.
	• Members of the educational community seek to be agents of change to reduce racial and ethnic inequities.
	• Stereotyped assumptions about "minority" group members are not accepted as part of everyday language and institutionalized discourse.

with supporting information, PowerPoint slides, and so on). As indicated in the annotations on the figure, the subjects in syllabus review workshops are faculty members who over time have been participants in a variety of CUE projects. Some have been engaged in a long-term Equity Scorecard process and others participated in a small number (two or three) of workshops in a short span of time such as a semester. Faculty participants are sometimes joined by administrators and student affairs professionals, who are part of the broader campus community whose practices influence and are influenced by the organizational routine centered on the creation or updating of a syllabus. Students are part of the community as well, and their behaviors influence the kind of information that appears on many syllabi, which typically communicate institutional policies and the class "rules" of the professor.

The twofold object of our action research design of bringing about, first, a syllabus redesign process utilizing principles of culturally responsive pedagogy (Ladson-Billings, 1995) and, second, the adoption of equity-minded practices, represents our action research strategy of syllabus review.

Figure 3.1. Equity-Minded Syllabus Review

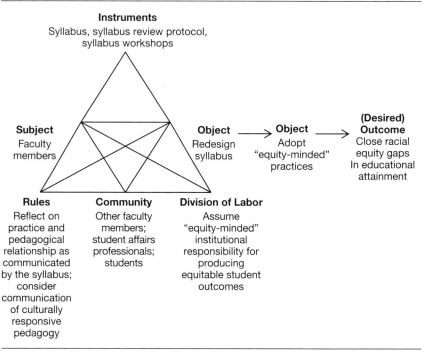

Source: Diagram features reproduced from Yrjö Engeström (2001), Expansive learning at work: Toward an activity theoretical reconceptualization. *Journal of Education and Work,* *14*(1), 133–156, reprinted by permission of the publisher (Taylor & Francis Ltd, www. tandfonline.com)

The desired outcome of these "task-level" objectives (Engeström, 2001, 2008) is organizational change at a scale that would close racial equity gaps in educational attainment. This differs from the typical object of creating a syllabus, namely, to communicate course content, expectations, assessment and grading procedures, and norms to students.

As Engeström (2008) points out, "This uppermost triangle, however, is but the tip of an iceberg. The less visible social mediators of activity—rules, community, and division of labor—are depicted at the bottom of the model" (p. 26). The social interaction among the faculty participants in the syllabi workshops invited the participants to reflect on the type of educational community that existed at their college (and that they wanted to exist); the rules and norms of the classroom and curriculum; and the division of labor between them (in their roles as professors) and their students. On Figure 3.1, we label that division of labor in an aspirational manner, reflecting the mission of our center and of the Equity Scorecard, that the faculty would assume equity-minded institutional responsibility for producing equitable student outcomes. In discussing the findings below, we annotate the activity system again to present the predominant characteristics of the activity of syllabus review, as we experienced it, and the changes that took place as a result of faculty participation in the syllabus workshops. As we show below, the rules, norms, community, and division of labor of the syllabus activity system were all amenable to remediation through the inquiry process.

The Syllabus as Artifact

Organizational culture can be influenced through the remediation of the syllabus because the syllabus is a cultural artifact with "historicity" (Engestrom, 2001, 2008). As a cultural artifact, the syllabus is a powerful instrument for the reproduction of academic roles, rules, and norms. Most professors can recall the day when, stepping into their first teaching role, someone else handed them the most recent version of the course syllabus, designed by the previous instructor or someone who had first taught the course long ago. This act, recurring as it does semester after semester, year after year, campus after campus, is an act of professional socialization and cultural reproduction.

The syllabus does much more than state the subject of study and the modes of assessment. It tells the new professor what it means to teach a particular course and even what it means to be a professor. The syllabus communicates the role of the different actors in the activity settings of the classroom, the course, and the curriculum. It sets out the rules of interaction between professor and students, for example, by stating office hours or permissible forms of communication (e.g., email, Skype, and so on). Norms may be stated ("turn off your cell phones!") or unstated (students will sit in desks in rows and the professor will stand at the front of the class). What "counts" as learning is typically indicated by the percentage of the grade carried by each assignment and by the modes of assessment: multiple choice, essay, research paper, presentation, or multimedia portfolio.

The syllabus acts on an instructor's thinking, actions, and planning about what it means to teach and be a professor. Thinking of a syllabus redesign process as an object acting on the identity and actions of a professor draws on a key tenet of activity theory contributed by Leont'ev, one of Vygotsky's students whose work engendered what is often referred to as "second-generation" activity theory (Lee, 2011): "Leont'ev's (1978, 1981) radical insight was to locate motives not in the subjects but in the *objects* of activity" (Engeström, 2008, p. 88). Objects shape "action-level decisions" as well as "future-oriented activity-level envisioning" (p. 205). Engeström explains:

> Mediating artifacts such as an alarm clock typically serve as signs that trigger a consequential action. They are mediators of action-level decisions. . . . But humans also need and use mediating artifacts to stabilize future-oriented images or visions of their collective activity systems. (p. 205)

As professors prepare to teach a course, the act of updating a syllabus leads to decisions about which books to place on order and which articles to upload into the learning management system. Preparing weekly course topics generates invitations to guest speakers, the reservation of learning labs, and perhaps (for those of us lucky enough to have one) the scheduling of weekly planning meetings with a teaching assistant. These are action-level decisions.

Future-oriented envisioning occurs in tandem with the consequential action-level decision making about what ideas to commit to text on a syllabus. Instructors envision the type of pedagogical relationship they will have with students in the class. These relationships (e.g., sage on the stage or mediator of active learning) are structured by the instructor's selection of course, content, activities, and assessment criteria, the latter being of high importance when it comes to counting credits and awarding credentials. Envisioning takes place as an instructor asks what she or he hopes students will learn and be able to do as a result of taking that course. Because every course is part of a larger curriculum, updating a syllabus inherently also involves future envisioning on a broader scale. For example, an instructor may recall that in prior years students began the course without sufficient exposure to prerequisite knowledge or skills earlier in the curriculum. This may lead to a mental note or immediate action to talk with other course instructors or to redesign the curriculum to omit a topic that is an ongoing trouble spot.

Organizational Routines. The doctoral studies discussed above, which examined the experiences of practitioners involved in inquiry using the Equity-Minded Syllabus Review Protocol, generated understanding of the meanings attached to the organizational routine (Spillane, 2012) of creating and using a syllabus. Observational studies of the use of an artifact of practice in multiple settings over time are necessary in order to understand, as Spillane (2012) urges, "how a new organizational routine transforms (or not) work practice" (p. 136). It is through these "multiple performances of an organizational routine, from the design stage through institutionalization (and failure to institutionalize) that we can better understand how practice is transformed and maintained over time in the ongoing interaction between formal structure and everyday practice" (p. 136). By synthesizing the findings of these doctoral studies, we gained insight into the ways the syllabus functions within organizational routines that can be productively disrupted through action research.

Looking at the syllabus as a mediating artifact elicits the application of several key points of activity theory. "Activities are not short-lived events or actions that have a temporally clear cut beginning and end. They are systems that *produce* events and actions and that evolve over lengthy periods of sociohistorical time" (Engeström, 2008, p. 26, italics in original). Even when a professor has authority over the design and content of a syllabus (which is not the case for courses taught as part of highly structured curricula), the document still reflects the "collective intentionality and distributed agency" (p. 201) of a larger system. The activity system of a college, a program, a discipline, and of a course "contains and generates a variety of different viewpoints or 'voices,' as well as layers of historically accumulated artifacts, rules, and patterns of division of labor" (p. 26). Within this collective system, individual agency still exists. The purposeful design of new artifacts can therefore serve as a "means of eliciting or triggering voluntary action" (p. 223).

Historicity of Artifacts. A statement that appears on our own course syllabi advising students that if they wish to receive accommodations for learning disabilities they should contact the office of disability services provides an example to illustrate this point of historicity. This statement (and similar ones on many other syllabi across the country) represents the accumulated history of legal decisions and institutional responses to the Americans with Disabilities Act (ADA) of 1990. The ADA statement, which is a standardized or "boilerplate" one, reflects the intentions of the U.S. Congress, the lawyers at our university who have gauged the risk of institutional liability, educators who provided leadership in universal design for learning, and disability rights activists who brought about passage of the ADA. The syllabus carries this history and is part of an activity system that includes academic and student affairs personnel who hold specialized training, titles, and functions to serve students with learning disabilities. It also creates a division of labor for us and other professors where we can defer to specialists in realizing the intention of the law. Recognizing that objects have the power to shape actions and an actor's identity provides a theoretical foundation for action researchers to utilize common instruments (artifacts) of professional practice, such as the commonplace syllabus, to peel back the layers of history.

Equity-Minded Syllabus Review

Across the multiple settings in which the syllabus review protocol was used as part of structured inquiry activities, we observed a number of common reactions among participating faculty. The first reaction concerned what faculty learned about the tone of their syllabi. Faculty realized much of the language was overly bureaucratic and harsh sounding—harsher than they intended. This led some, in an attempt to be more encouraging, to add information to the syllabus to let students know where they could find additional academic services on campus. In some cases, these steps preserved the division of labor between themselves, students, and student services personnel, but for others it involved questioning and reenvisioning the nature of the pedagogical relationship with students. Some faculty decided they wanted to communicate their willingness to help students by connecting them to available resources and by making themselves more available to students.

We noted, second, that this questioning and reenvisioning led to the addition of new, more welcoming language, including language celebrating diversity. The welcoming and "diversity" statements added by faculty to their syllabi reflected a desire to communicate "authentic caring" toward students (Noddings, 1992; Valenzuela, 1999). They took the first steps toward a relationship of authentic care by inviting students into relationship with them through more welcoming language. However, their capacity to engage in authentic care in its core essence of "sustained reciprocal relationships" (Valenzuela, 1999, p. 61) was constrained by their lack of knowledge of Latino and African American communities. These limitations were evidenced in faculty attempts to provide caring guidance to students that awkwardly took the form of paternalistic exhortations, for example, encouraging students to serve their communities and to take advantage of all a college education has to offer. The ethic of care expressed held a respectful and pitying perspective on students' communities in tension (Matias & Zembylas, 2014).

Discussions in syllabus review workshops served to bring to the surface faculty members' sense of the otherness of their students, articulated in statements like "they are not like we were." With a few exceptions, faculty appeared to lack the expertise to redesign their courses to incorporate the "funds of knowledge" (N. González, Moll, & Amanti, 2005) of students of color into the course activities and curriculum. Several faculty members reflected on their lack of knowledge and expertise to engage in critical pedagogy and were troubled by it.

Faculty changed their syllabi and began to envision new pedagogical relationships with students. This reenvisioning had the potential to be equity-enhancing and to contribute to a significant change in organizational culture. However, due to a variety of reasons including lack of knowledge, lack of leadership, and lack of agency to tackle systemic injustice, these change efforts were fairly limited in scope and did not appear to be substantial enough to initiate substantial change. With only a few exceptions, faculty who described how they changed their syllabus by adding welcoming statements or directing students to on-campus resources did not mention more substantive changes, such as revisions in the course content, assignments, learning assessments, or grading.

Remediating Pedagogical Relationships

In the cases presented in this section, the inquiry activities we designed using the Equity-Minded Syllabus Review Protocol led to "problem posing," where faculty looked at their syllabi with new eyes (McTaggart, 1997). A statement made by a community college professor, referred to in Salazar-Romo's (2009) study as Cindy, articulated this experience of seeing anew: "I basically looked at everything . . . how it was formatted . . . the text . . . the fonts . . . the tone" (p. 72). Another community college professor, at Dynamic Community College, referred to as Kathy by Subramaniam (2012), said, "Now that I look at my syllabus, it looks threatening. I need to change the whole thing" (p. 123). The sentiment that the syllabus looked threatening was echoed by other faculty members at Dynamic Community College, who discovered that their syllabi "sounded harsh" (p. 154), "legalistic" (p. 127), or "cold and intimidating" (p. 155). A participant at Cal College, Cindy, described the tone of syllabi for mathematics courses as "condescending and punitive." She observed, too, "there is only one mention of 'we' in the syllabus" (Salazar-Romo, 2009, p. 71).

Expressing Care. Realizing that their syllabi were harsh-sounding, a number of faculty decided they wanted the syllabus to offer an "embrace" to students; they "wanted it to be more inviting" (Subramaniam, 2012, p. 123). Communicating such an "embrace" involved changes such as shifting from strictly using the third-person voice on the syllabus to using "I," or to using "you" with a more "humane touch," as Subramanian expressed it (p. 154). One professor, Brian, rewrote his syllabus to revise the language from asserting "here is what you need to know" to "let me describe what the class is about." With the words "let me," the tone shifted from an instructional command to an invitation to relationship and helpful support.

A few participants in syllabus-focused inquiry opted to provide more background context about the course in order to help students understand how to study effectively. Faculty took steps to make the course schedule clearer so students would know what to focus on when they studied. They added more explanatory text to make the objective of learning activities more transparent. Others communicated to students their willingness to give students a break, for example, by letting them retest or earn extra credits. One instructor, called Brian in Subramaniam's (2012) study, communicated his side of the class "contract," as he expressed it, by stating on his syllabus: "I expect myself to be present and on time as well as prepared for all lecture and laboratory sessions and I also expect the same of you" (p. 154). This statement was intended to communicate the instructor's respect for his students and his commitment to them and the class. It explained the purpose of the class rules to students in a way that also imposed responsibility for respectful relationships on the professor, rather than imposing the rules in a one-sided, strictly bureaucratic manner, and expecting compliance.

Providing Resources. In an effort to sound more helpful, several workshop participants subsequently added information about the resources, advising, and counseling services available at the college. There was a "big list of places to go," as Joanna at Cal College explained it, and "a list of resources that [students] should know about," as indicated by Cindy (Salazar-Romo, 2009, p. 91).

That the act of providing "tips" to students on a syllabus was interrelated with a reenvisioning of the pedagogical relationship was clearly expressed by a professor referred to as Michael in Enciso's (2009) study. Michael described how he had begun to routinely create study guides to help students prepare for exams and how he encouraged students to form study groups. "I emphasize office hours," he said, adding that when you add some "tips" to your syllabus, students "realize you're there to help" (Enciso, 2009, p. 97). He continued:

> I think most of our students are pretty poorly informed about those things and so it's made me—when I have a student in at office hours say—I'm more likely to ask them more personal questions about their goals, their career goals, their major, and that will lead to financial aid and other things. It's made me realize their need for guidance. Again, it's so easy to just think your job is to teach them the subject and [attend] office hours [to] make sure they're clear on the subject, but I'm really trying to see it more as an opportunity to mentor them in a variety of ways. (p. 98)

Brian, who was also a participant in Woerner's study (2013), which followed a year after Subramaniam's (2012) at the same community college, described his efforts to forge a new type of pedagogical relationship with students. As he reflected on changes he had made to his syllabus, Brian expressed a sense of professionalism and care for students. In his mind, revising his "just the facts" syllabus was part of positioning himself in relationship with his students as a "life coach":

> When the Academic Senate did the workshop, personally I found it valuable. I'm thinking about things I haven't thought about for a long time. I love having

these conversations. . . . For many years, I had the "just the facts" syllabus. . . .
One page, one side. I got the important information to them. . . . So I decided
I'm going to shift. Instead of meeting my dean's needs, I'm going to meet my
students' needs. I see how that works. . . . I need to be more of a life coach. . . .
It can only help with what I do. The conversations I have with colleagues have
changed as well as with my students. (p. 84)

Although the action of listing resources on a syllabus is a simple step,
and one that might be taken in a very bureaucratic manner, in the context of
the syllabus review inquiry process it was evident that these changes reflected a change in the faculty members' role. Michael's reflections above depict
a professor who is actively experimenting and assessing his own efforts to
support students. Brian, referencing the "conversations" he is having with
his colleagues, clearly situates the changes to his syllabus in the CUE inquiry
process. His statement that he is "thinking about things I have not thought
about in a long time" captures the heart of the reflective practice of inquiry.
The notion of inquiry as a "cycle" is captured by Brian's reflection on his
past, present, and envisioned future practice as a teacher. The fact that he is
not engaging in these reflections alone suggests the potential for the collective agency of praxis to emerge.

Changing Attitudes. A statement made during a discussion of student
success rates by a professor referred to as Lucy in Enciso's (2009) study
echoes the relationship between the syllabus review and broader change:

The bottom line is it is the person in the classroom [who matters] and until the
attitude of the instructor changes nothing is going to happen . . . change has to
come and that's why I liked doing the syllabus workshop. It was a small thing
but it opened up people's minds and it even opened mine. The emphasis needs
to be on changing how we teach and it has to start in the classroom. (p. 89)

It is clear that Lucy associates the process of dialogue and of taking
small actions to change the syllabus as a process of changing habits of mind
and dispositions toward students, the shift in thinking and behavior we
refer to as moving from deficit- to equity-mindedness. Lucy's words stood
out in our minds because they support our theory of change, which relies
on changes in faculty members' beliefs and attitudes to bring about broader
organizational change. Viewed theoretically in terms of the potential of artifacts to remediate activity systems, the changes that these faculty members
made to their syllabi were not trivial. Of course, the revised syllabi continued to include rules, regulations, grading standards, and deadlines, but the
revisions were made to communicate expectations for compliance within a

caring instructor–student relationship. Faculty clarified the purpose of procedural information rather than simply stating it in an authoritarian manner. Joanna's description of why she added a list of resources to her syllabus indicated that she was taking responsibility for helping students gain access to the information they needed to be successful.

These revisions represent a change in the division of labor between faculty and students and the implicit rules governing the distribution of resources by revising the actual and legitimate uses of a faculty member's time. In an initial discussion among members of Joanna's inquiry group, several participants tended to emphasize, when discussing racial equity gaps, that students were not taking advantage of available resources. Through facilitated discussion using the concept of "equity-mindedness," individuals with this perspective became open to the possibility that the problem was not that students were too poorly motivated to take the trouble to access resources and help themselves, but rather that the college was doing an inadequate job of making those resources available to students. This realization led them to consider taking a personally active role in making students aware of those resources, in effect to catalyze resources that lay dormant in the absence of a relationship of "authentic care" (Valenzuela, 1999).

These faculty members sought to shift away from the use of impersonal language—the technical and standardized imperatives of an "aesthetic care" that is concerned only with "things and ideas" (Valenzuela, 1999, p. 22). They sought to shift away from a tone that primarily communicated the desire to "control" and elicit compliance from students, which is too often the overarching pedagogical relationship between teachers and "at-risk" students (Ladson-Billings, 2009, p. 30). Whether stating that "You just need to back off with the 'should' and just see what they need," or professing interest in playing a role as a "life coach," these faculty were experimenting with expressive communications that invited students into relationship with them as caring individuals who felt a sense of responsibility for their success in the classroom.

An ethic of care is marked by reciprocal, humane, and validating relations with students (Rendón Linares & Muñoz, 2011; Valenzuela, 1999). It should not be motivated by pity (Matias & Zembylas, 2014). If care is pitying of the cared-for it imposes what we call a "self-worth tax," undermining the participatory ideal. As we noted in Chapter 1, the validating role of institutional agents is especially important to counter the social harm students of color experience in racialized settings where they have been subject to deficit assumptions about their academic capabilities and interests (Dowd, Pak, & Bensimon, 2013; Museus & Neville, 2012; Rendón Linares & Muñoz, 2011; Stanton-Salazar, 2011; Teranishi & Briscoe, 2006). Students of color are often told in implicit and explicit ways that they do not belong in college. Consequently, students may well hesitate to seek help when college procedures, policies, or expectations are unclear to them. As Rendón-Linares and Muñoz (2011) point out,

> Nontraditional students will likely find it difficult to navigate the world of college by themselves. They will be unlikely to take advantage of tutoring centers, faculty office hours, or the library, because they will be working off campus, will feel uncomfortable asking questions, and/or will not want to be viewed as stupid or lazy. Consequently, it is critical that validating agents actively reach out to students to offer assistance, encouragement, and support, as opposed to expecting students to ask questions first. (p. 17)

The professors who participated in the syllabus review workshops were motivated by an ethic of care to reach out to students, to initiate validating communications, particularly in the form of information about how to navigate college or to take advantage of resources available for academic tutoring and guidance.

The Practice of Diversity

For a number of these professors, the expressive communications that they added to their syllabi took the form of statements acknowledging and welcoming the diversity of student backgrounds and communities. The diversity welcome statements were the outcome of faculty reflection on their syllabus as prompted by the indicators on the syllabus review protocol we provided. We had not taken the approach of providing a "best practice" model or boilerplate language with the recommendation that participants in our inquiry workshop adopt given language. The references that were added represented the faculty member's effort to be culturally inclusive of the students' lives outside the classroom. The diversity statements reflected the efforts of faculty who were acting through reflective practice with an ethic of care. However, most participants did not have the expertise to translate the concepts of critical race theory and culturally responsive pedagogy into practice, even if they might have been inclined to do so, and it was clear that several were not.

Welcoming Diversity in All Forms. For Joanna, a faculty member at Cal College (Salazar-Romo, 2009), the addition of the diversity statement to her syllabus represented an opportunity to reflect on and change her relationship with students to one that was more welcoming of diversity:

I've created a very specific diversity paragraph because I felt like I was just implying that appreciation of our diversity and eagerness to incorporate their [students'] life experiences. . . . And so I wrote a paragraph that I'm now going to put in all of my syllabi to say that look around us: we have different ages . . . and ethnicities, races, combinations of races, and life experiences, and if we collectively welcome that, we're going to have a rich welcoming experience. I certainly welcome you as an individual and you as part of our class with all these features. (p. 76)

At the state university that was the site of studies by Brown (2012), Levonisova (2012), and Smith (2012), other faculty took similar steps. One added a videotaped introduction of herself discussing her own racial and ethnic background and explaining her teaching philosophy to her course website. Another added images of students of color to his syllabus, which he also reformatted to make more appealing than a conventional syllabus by adding typographic features, clip art, and quotations.

The emphasis in all of these statements on welcoming students reveals an ethic of care for students' well-being and a commitment to their success in the professors' courses. These values and dispositions are important to validate the participation of students from minoritized racial and ethnic groups. In defining validation, Rendón-Linares and Muñoz (2011) emphasize that when faculty engage in validating behaviors, they "validate students' cultural experiences and voices in the classroom, provide opportunities for students to witness themselves as capable learners, and actively reach out to students to offer support and academic assistance" (p. 20). When syllabus workshop participants added welcoming diversity statements to their syllabi, their motivation was to validate nontraditional students.

However, as illustrated by Joanna's reflection, the diversity statement tended to take the form of "a homogenized 'we' in celebration of diversity" (Ladson-Billings, 2009, p. 29). Rather than engaging in the "deconstruction" and "reconstruction" of racial inequities in educational settings, such statements retained a race-neutral stance by celebrating the *individual* diversity of all students. The statement does not attempt an acknowledgment of racialized histories of discrimination and exclusion that would locate it within an equity paradigm informed by justice as transformation.

Color-Blind Equal Opportunity. Some faculty participants did not endorse a transformative agenda focused on race and ethnicity. The sentiment of "I treat all my students the same. I don't treat them differently" was often expressed (Subramaniam, 2012, p. 140). For example, Nancy, a faculty member whose experiences were described in Subramaniam's study, indicated during an interview with the researcher that she preferred a broader understanding of the term *equity* and did not like the term *racial equity*:

Nancy stated that she did not like the term racial equity; instead she liked using just the term equity since she felt that she treats all of her students based on their needs and not based on their race or ethnicity. She argued that a Vietnam veteran should be considered even if he is White since he is disadvantaged. She asserted, "So rather than discussing racial issues, we should be addressing equity issues without looking at ethnicity." (p. 140)

Interviews with practitioners in the area of student services at Monarch State University led to findings reported in R. Z. Brown's (2012) study that provide insight into the damaging consequences of such color-blind approaches for the practice of equity. Collaboration and meaningful communication among White faculty and student services personnel—an area of college and university operations with a higher proportion of Latino and African American staff members—was damaged by repeated endorsements of color-blind approaches. Responding to an interview question asking, "What factors add to your comfort or discomfort when talking about these issues?" one participant in Brown's study responded:

> It's ok to talk about difference as long as it's not at the expense of the majority. When I hear "we can't just do that for Black students" I feel locked in. . . . It's more of a "let's not do anything if it's not for everyone." [But yet] sometimes people have to have unique experiences. (p. 107)

The tense nature of these differences, which suggest that the view of equity based in justice as fairness was dominant in this setting, was revealed by one respondent who stated in an interview with Brown (2012) that talking about racial and ethnic issues seemed to be taboo at Monarch State. The respondent stated, "Colleagues across the board, even colleagues of color don't even talk about this."

A meeting held at Birch College revealed a similarly high level of tension. As facilitators of the Equity Scorecard process, CUE's project specialists and research assistants often take the work of the evidence teams and write a draft of the final report. In the draft, Birch was identified as a Hispanic Serving Institution, which took the team members by surprise. Michael, the faculty member introduced above who had become more interactive in his relationships with students, raised concerns. He reminded the team of the hostile reaction received when the group initially looked at their student success data disaggregated by race and ethnicity at the Flex-Day (professional development) workshop in late October. He worried that in response to the use of the term *Hispanic Serving*, faculty who read it would say, "I don't teach races, I teach students." Michael also tried to steer the group away from using the term *equity-mindedness*, which he feared would elicit negative reactions from his colleagues as well as the president. Michael suggested that if they wanted to elicit broader participation in their change efforts, they "might need to reword the same idea . . . ; [others] may react more positively if we write it in a different way" (Enciso, 2009, pp. 102–102).

Ideological Tensions. Michael's hesitation reveals the strong ideological tensions surrounding conversations about diversity and equity conversations at Birch College. His fears struck us as highly revealing of a culture of race muteness because, of all the faculty participants we involved in syllabus review in the California community colleges, Michael was the person to most clearly articulate a perspective of justice as transformation.

Michael acknowledged racial discrimination as a factor that influenced student experiences in college as well as their chances of success. In an interview with Enciso (2009), Michael raised issues of social justice. Referring to "institutions of slavery and racial prejudice and all that," he articulated the importance of examining student success data disaggregated by race and ethnicity. He observed that the institution could be contributing to equity gaps and social injustice whether it "was trying to or not" (p. 91), a perspective that reflects an awareness of structural racism (Chesler & Crowfoot, 1989).

Michael said he felt many of his peers took the stance that "becoming more color conscious is just going to exacerbate the problem." He reflected, seeing the limitations of a color-blind approach, "If we're totally colorblind at this point in time then we won't see gaps that we're perpetuating." He added, "eventually, sometime in the distant future, we should all be colorblind, but today I think that's to put your head in the sand" (Enciso, 2009, p. 92)

According to one respondent who was interviewed by R. Z. Brown (2012), talking about diversity was a challenge at Monarch State University because practitioners there "don't have the language" to do it. An inability or unwillingness to refer to specific racial or ethnic groups in conversation led to awkwardness and discomfort:

> "We have to create comfort and dialogue regarding diversity." Asked to explain further, he responded, "like calling Black students Black, feeling comfortable saying gay instead of LGBT (Lesbian, Gay, Transgender), referring to people as needed. Because we don't have the language, it's been the stumbling block to true change." (pp. 110–111)

Another statement from an interview participant in Brown's (2012) study indicates that masking was prevalent at Monarch State. The respondent stated, "there is more of an interest in people being comfortable than addressing the issues. The people who work on campus are more uncomfortable discussing racial and ethnic issues than the students. I think that students would be okay, if we were" (p. 108). The following excerpt from Brown's study also suggests that there was a "culture of silence" on the campus about racial issues, even in the face of discriminatory statements.

> During the [workshop], one of the male participants described an incident in which a faculty member used a derogatory term in reference to Japanese students: "During one of our staff meetings while discussing the internationalization of our campus, one of the faculty members stated, 'what are we trying to do? Jap out the campus?'" According to the participant, no one responded to the faculty member's comment. He stated that "a few people even added to the faculty member's comments with 'yeah! What are we trying to do?'" It sends a message that this behavior is ok. Later, the participants were asked how we can make sure that students do not have these experiences. The same male who provided the example suggested "making it okay to say that I have a problem with that statement." This seemed to make some of the participants uncomfortable. A female participant responded, "okay, you say that, then the room goes flat, what happens then?" The male participant suggested, "well, I guess I would imagine, perhaps, there would be some type of dialogue. I think it [is] less about the conversation had and more about making it okay to say to I have a problem with that. We have a culture of silence here at Monarch." Many people in the room nodded in agreement. (p. 107)

As at LFCC, the organizational routine of masking operates at Monarch State to silence discourse critically conscious race talk and actions that have transformative aims.

Commitment to Color Blindness

The faculty members in syllabus workshops often communicated a sense of their students' "otherness" as being most often located in their "bad behavior" in class or their lack of academic preparation. Perceiving their students as having a dire need took an emotional toll on the faculty. The syllabus workshops provided an opportunity for participants to discuss their sense of frustration with one another and to explore new approaches.

Speaking to her faculty peers, the faculty member referred to as Lucy in Enciso's study (2009) emphasized that the students at Birch College were not the way the faculty themselves had been when they were students: "These are not the students—these students are not like we were. They're really not." This difference is attributed to students' behavior when Lucy articulates that it is "difficult" for her to teach students enrolled in basic skills courses because "the students misbehave so much in class" (p. 83). Lucy does not express the view that "these students are not like we were" in terms of race or ethnicity. In fact, just the opposite, as she insists that the faculty at her college "don't see color":

> When they look at their class [the faculty] don't see color. And to give attention to more—more attention to one ethnic group [than] to another knowing that they struggle more . . . Is—is not what most teachers do. 'Cause that's—that's biased as well. (pp. 88–89)

Referring back to the conversations about acknowledging the college's Hispanic Serving identity, Lucy continued in a manner that illustrates she adopts a color-blind ideology as part of an instinctual approach to move beyond the "othering" of students that she is experiencing as a contradiction in her organizational setting:

> It's not going to make any difference [referring to adopting a race consciousness]. . . . Okay? I mean I—I've had students of all ethnicities. Do really well, do really poorly. And so you just—you just look at the student. You don't—I don't look at the—what their ethnic race is, ethnic background is. I look at how well prepared they are for the course. And then work on those issues. (Enciso, 2009, p. 83)

Another community college professor, Leslie, also expressed her sense of frustration. "I was getting more and more frustrated as the semester . . . progressed," she recalled in an interview with Salazar-Romo (2009, p. 69). Through the syllabus review process, Leslie developed what Salazar-Romo referred to as an "empathic disposition" toward her students, which was articulated when she said, "You just need to back off with the 'should' and just see what they need" (Salazar-Romo, 2009, p. 80). Like Lucy, Leslie related the challenge of developing the reciprocal relationships of authentic care with the challenge of managing students' "bad behavior":

> They may not get to where they have to be by the end of the semester but if you can connect, then you can at least help them do what they can do if they're willing to if you can help them grow as far as they're willing to grow. . . . Even the ones with bad behavior, I try to just mellow out to see if we can improve that, that they'll not be so defensive and to trust me. (p. 80)

Joanna is committed to helping her students and hopes they will come to trust her, but she is also opposed to adopting a critical race perspective. Salazar-Romo observed:

The recognition of classroom diversity was for Joanna a significant addition to a syllabus in terms of analyzing a tool through the lens of culturally responsive teaching; however, she adamantly denied race and strived to see her classroom as color-neutral: "I think about these statistics [disaggregated by race and ethnicity] and I wonder how the outcomes of success for various ethnicities ought to influence me. I continue to want to work to see individuals in my group, but it is a group and it's a diverse group, but I really want to treat people equally, yet with sensitivity to what I perceive as their background. But I may not know their background. And certainly I'm not going to plant their background on them by the color of their skin—I'm not gonna do it!" (p. 71)

Lucy and Leslie are both experiencing a disturbance in their organizational routine, evoked by the syllabus review protocol, with its prompts for equity-minded and culturally responsive practices. They would not only like to help their students, but themselves as well. They would like to escape from their frustration and "do something about it," as Leslie expressed it. As noted above, Lucy feels that the syllabus review inquiry process has "opened" her mind and Joanna added a diversity welcoming statement to her syllabus. Yet they are uncomfortable when called on to exercise "race consciousness in a positive way," as we do when presenting the concept of an "equity-minded syllabus review."

Their reactions suggest that they view acting in a color-conscious way as uncaring and unjust. They are concerned that if they see race and ethnicity as social constructs shaping the lived experiences and multiple identities of their students, they will take something away from the students of color as individuals and from *all* their students, which by the norms of color blindness amounts to taking something away from White students.

Yet Lucy and Leslie clearly also believe that all of their students, and more generally all the students at the college, have a high level of academic need that deserves to be met. In fact, Lucy is angry with those of her colleagues who she expects would react to the syllabus protocol by saying: "I teach content; it's not my job to teach what office hours [are]; have them take an intro to college class" (Enciso, 2009, p. 100). She feels that "change has to come in the classroom . . . even now students have resources and students don't use services that are here. If the professor doesn't change, success rates will fall." Lucy's comments suggest that she feels that something else is needed above and beyond a just distribution of resources based on the principle of vertical equity, providing more resources to those students with greater educational needs. Justice as care provides a meaningful alternative for Lucy and Leslie to articulate the need for changes at their colleges. They are not espousing justice as transformation in a critical sense. To give attention to racial and ethnic characteristics, or to racialized experiences of discrimination and exclusion, is faulty because to do so places the needs of one group over another. This violates their sense of justice as fairness, which means ideology is at play. Deeply held ideological values have emotional intensity; yet the views engendered by ideological values are seen as normal, and therefore go unexamined.

Mal Educado?

Without engaging the historical and contemporary forms of racism, the community college faculty members were left struggling within a disenfranchised sector to make a difference in individual students' lives. Their sense of frustration and lack of efficacy was evident. Their impulse to renew their relationship with students within the realm of their classroom interactions reflected their agency within the one educational bastion within their control. However, they were not expert or skilled in their application of these impulses toward authentic relationships, or *educación*, as Valenzuela (1999) terms it, drawing on her study of Mexican American students in Texas schools. A young person who is the beneficiary of *educación* is *bien educada* or *bien educado;* she or he has "competence in the social world, wherein one respects the dignity and individuality of others" (p. 23). Those who are *mal educado* have been subject to an impersonal form of schooling, which leaves them alienated from teachers, schools, and the dominant society. The faculty members, while expressing care, were hard-pressed to respect the individuality of their students of color while at the same time acknowledging that race, skin color, immigrant status, and language all mattered in U.S. society and educational settings, including their own classrooms.

Acting to address the desire to help their "diverse" students, several professors included aphorisms that sought to impart educational values. The diversity statements and the aphorisms emerged in tandem, suggesting that the undertaking of writing a welcome statement for "diverse" students was informed by a belief, subconscious or otherwise, that such values were in deficit among students of color. For example, one instructor added (under a section still somewhat harshly labeled "cheating") a statement that read "Live your life with integrity—why would you want to cheat yourself out of your education?" (Subramaniam, 2012, p. 154).

In a second example, a community college English as a Second Language instructor shared with a group of faculty who were being invited to participate in syllabus-focused inquiry how she had revised her own syllabus (Woerner, 2013). As others had, this instructor added a welcoming statement that celebrated diversity in its broadest sense. She read aloud:

Welcome to our class! I am excited to have you in this class. All students have an opportunity to succeed in this class and at the college. We appreciate the richness of your ideas, your cultural background, and your life experiences. Education is a gift to yourself. Take advantage of the opportunity to improve your English language skills and your life in our community. (p. 85)

With the advice to "Take advantage of this opportunity to improve . . . your life in our community," this statement features guidance similar to the guidance provided by the professor who advised students to live their lives "with integrity."

As Rendón observes, although "many nontraditional students come to college needing a sense of direction," they do not want to receive that guidance "in a patronizing way" (cited in Rendón-Linares & Muñoz, 2011, p. 16). The concept of authentic care and validation, therefore, is an asset-based model that calls on faculty to develop reciprocal relationships with students, through which they seek to understand and draw on the "reservoir of assets" (Rendón-Linares & Muñoz, 2011, p. 16) that students possess for learning and knowledge creation in and out of academic settings. When faculty enter into validating pedagogical relationships with underrepresented students of color, "the dominant view that poor students only have deficits is shattered and decentered" (p. 25). Gaining insight through such reciprocity will be difficult for faculty who see their role as imparting moral education in a one-directional manner.

Acknowledged Lack of Expertise

The evidence from the dissertation studies of faculty inquiry using CUE's Equity-Minded Syllabus Review Protocol shows that most participants were "ill equipped," as one participant expressed it, as institutional agents who would engage in what Stanton-Salazar (2011) refers to as *empowerment*. The motivation of an ethic of care articulated by participants did not translate into an endorsement of justice as transformation. In part this was due to the use of color-blind ideologies to judge what type of wording would be most appropriate for text appearing on a syllabus.

Several of the participants stated that they wanted to make changes to their syllabus, but as they attempted to incorporate culturally responsive pedagogy into their classroom teaching to address equity issues, they were uncertain how to go about it.

Figure 3.2 uses the activity system triangle to illustrate the critical disturbances that faculty members became aware of quite acutely by self-assessing their practices using the syllabus review protocol. Their belief in color blindness hampers the object of equity-minded syllabus review of entering into validating relationships of authentic care with students. The rules and norms of their practice do not support the task facing higher education of crafting a new division of labor with students to realize critical agency and empowerment.

Brian said that he wanted to make changes but he did not know how to include culturally inclusive pedagogy into his practices:

> I am still ill equipped to do a lot of this even though it is my intentions to do better at it. Most faculty have the best interest in helping their students but on the most part we don't know what to do. Tell me what I can do and I will do it. I am doing all I can. We all agree that we need to do it but most of us don't know how so then what. Yeh! We need to help them. So, how? I don't know how to teach writing nor reading so that is where we get frustrated. We have moved along and tried this and that but we feel that we are groping around in the dark as we hope we will find something. (Subramaniam, 2012, p. 138)

Brian continued, "I am still not sure of the difference between ethnicity, race and culture, so I am uncomfortable to try to figure a way to approach the issue. . . . How do I talk with students about inequity? Do we need to say, 'You come with inequitable backgrounds'? Do we use squishy language?" (pp. 141–142).

Efforts we took to provide a tool for understanding the causes of racial inequities based on the concept of microaggressions (Sue, Capodilupo, et al., 2007; Sue, Nadal, et al., 2008) led a female faculty member at Monarch State University to express similar frustration. The professor, whose field was not education, social science, or cultural studies, indicated she would not attempt to draw on what research says about the nature and experience of microaggressions because she did not have sufficient in-depth knowledge or "background" on the topic. Revealing a strong sense of risk, she asked, "How do I know that I am not perpetuating other kinds of stereotypes?"(R. Z. Brown, 2012, p. 109). Results reported by Smith (2012), whose study also took place at Monarch State University and included faculty members in science and engineering fields, suggest that this sense of frustration and lack of expertise was not uncommon. Seven of eight faculty members included in Smith's study valued the inquiry process of syllabus review, but the same proportion expressed that they were not trained to engage with diversity or equity issues. As one respondent stated it: "I found I could not do this—this diversity stuff" (p. 98).

Although the faculty could engage with students from a sense of justice as fairness and justice as care, engaging in the transformative work called for by justice as transformation was typically not within the realm of ambi-

Figure 3.2. Remediating Pedagogical Relationships

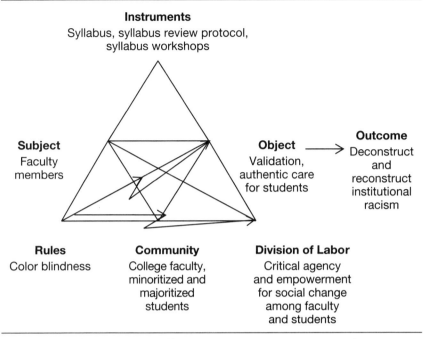

Instruments
Syllabus, syllabus review protocol,
syllabus workshops

Subject
Faculty
members

Object
Validation,
authentic care
for students

Outcome
Deconstruct
and
reconstruct
institutional
racism

Rules
Color blindness

Community
College faculty,
minoritized and
majoritized
students

Division of Labor
Critical agency
and empowerment
for social change
among faculty
and students

Source: Diagram features reproduced from Yrjö Engeström (2001), Expansive learning at work: Toward an activity theoretical reconceptualization. *Journal of Education and Work,* 14(1), 133–156, reprinted by permission of the publisher (Taylor & Francis Ltd, www. tandfonline.com)

tion or capability for faculty we interacted with. As Rendón-Linares and Muñoz (2011) emphasize in describing the tenets of validation theory and practice, ideally validation "engenders transformative consequences for students as well as for validating agents" (p. 25). The act of validation and the development of reciprocal relationships with students of color are intended to be empowering for faculty and students and to produce collective agency for the social change needed to create a just society. Validation is not fundamentally rooted in a desire to "help disadvantaged students," although it is necessary to recognize the social context of privilege, racial discrimination, and inclusion/exclusion. Stanton-Salazar (2011) similarly defines empowerment agents in terms of their agency for social change and distinguishes empowerment agents from institutional agents based on their willingness to empower themselves and their students to change social structures.

Although faculty members in our workshops were not moved toward collective agency as empowerment agents, many developed agency to direct their own personal resources as well as college resources toward students. Beyond that, we observed the potential for faculty actions based in an ethic of care to lead to greater knowledge about the need for justice as transformation. This was articulated very clearly by Salazar-Romo (2009), who captures the complexity of the emerging relationships of authentic care well in the following passage. She describes Leslie's experience in the classroom as she became more comfortable sharing her own personal experiences as a student and learning about students' experiences:

> Discussions with her students . . . informed Leslie of how students have been previously treated in their academic life. During a classroom discussion on an essay that discussed a student coming to terms with being called stupid by his teacher, Leslie was shocked that an overwhelming majority of her students were not surprised. After asking her students whether or not a teacher would really call a student "stupid," she recounted her students' comments:
> . . . "Oh my gosh, of course," and . . . "I've had people tell me that." I was so appalled, and it really opened my eyes to the fact I have no idea sometimes what they're walking in with. . . . Doing these types of activities opens my eyes to what they need. They need somebody who truly believes that they can do something. I think for a long time they've been told, "you're not going to amount to anything." . . . I think what could potentially happen is that I'm planting a seed somewhere that along the way they'll kind of start to get it . . . at least there's a little more positivity. (p. 79)

Salazar-Romo (2009) concludes that "Leslie was not entirely aware of the complex experiences of her students" (p. 79), and this exercise influenced her to use a text in class that she would not have previously thought to use. Overall, Leslie strengthened her commitment to developing caring relationships with students. Leslie was willing and able to engage in some aspects of validating behaviors, even if she did not endorse the critical agenda of transformative social change. As indicated above, she did not interpret her students' negative experiences of being called "stupid" in racialized terms, despite having many Hispanic students in her ESL classroom.

The story recounted by Salazar-Romo (2009) is highly evocative of a similar account by Valenzuela (1999), who describes the tense relationship between a teacher she refers to as Mrs. Hutchins and a student named Susana. Mrs. Hutchins had asked Valenzuela, who was doing participant observation research in Mrs. Hutchins classroom, if she could discern why Susana was so disengaged and disaffected in class. After speaking with Susana, Valenzuela discovered that Susana had an experience with a science teacher who had humiliated her and made her feel stupid by asking her not to raise her hand so much in class. "'All the students laughed at me,' Susana explained. 'I was trying to learn and he was a new teacher . . . hard to understand. I felt so stupid. . . . But now it's like What's the use?'" This resigned question was followed by Susana's avowal to merely get through the day at school and mind her own business "without no problems" (p. 72).

Upon hearing this explanation from Valenzuela, Mrs. Hutchins is exasperated and expresses a "rather self-absorbed, emotional response" (Valenzuela, 1999, p. 73). Mrs. Hutchins complains about having to "deal with" Susana's problems, because she is not "paid to be a social worker." In this way, Mrs. Hutchins locates the injustices of Susana's negative schooling experiences on the family, the community, or society outside the walls of the school, despite the fact that Susana's disaffectedness is completely a product of her prior educational experiences.

It is important to us, therefore, that when Leslie learns her students have been called stupid, she does not see this as beyond her responsibility. On the contrary, and unlike Mrs. Hutchins, she seeks to develop the capacity to understand her students' experiences, albeit in a color-blind manner. As Valenzuela points out, even short of a critical social consciousness, this leaves the door open to the development of alternatives: "In most cases, there is likely some room to maneuver—that is, if the situation is approached literally 'with care'" (p. 73). This ethic of care is expressed in Leslie's statement, "You just need to back off with the 'should' and just see what they need" (Salazar-Romo, 2009, p. 80). In this, Leslie and the other faculty who articulated impulses toward authentic care are moving away from deficit perspectives that focus on the perceived behavioral problems of students of color and neglect institutional responsibility for creating a positive environment for students' learning.

Collective Agency for Professional Development

Many faculty who participated in our syllabus inquiry workshops acknowledged a lack of knowledge of racial equity issues and of culturally responsive practices. Through the syllabus workshops they had opportunities to express their frustration and sense of inefficacy. Perhaps more important, these reflective moments led to action in many cases. Faculty added welcoming and diversity statements to their syllabi; they adopted a sense of responsibility to inform students about available resources and to personally assist them in locating those resources; and they developed more caring attitudes toward their students. They also designed professional development activities to educate themselves about new ideas and practices and to share materials that they had developed. At Monarch State University, an administrator and a faculty member teamed up to design and obtain a small amount of institutional funding for a series of faculty seminars, in which faculty met and discussed readings about culturally responsive pedagogies (Smith, 2012). In three of the community colleges that were settings for our action research, faculty members who were involved in the first syllabus workshop held at their campus later became involved in introducing others to the syllabus protocol. They hosted workshops independently of our involvement, taking roles of faculty leaders in professional development.

At Birch College (Enciso, 2009) a three-part series of syllabus workshops was held and faculty, with support from the institutional researcher, developed activities and materials. The materials included a video of students in Lucy's class doing a Stand Up exercise, in which students stand up when a statement is read that characterizes their home or family situation, such as having one parent who has a bachelor's degree, having two parents who expect them to complete a degree, or having access to a working computer. When the video was shown to Lucy's peers in the syllabus workshop hosted by our inquiry participants, responses were audible at different points: "Wow, many students stood up"; or, in relation to the question about parental degree attainment, "Wow, nobody in the class stood up." Enciso concluded from these observations that faculty members' "preconceived beliefs about the students were challenged and sometimes disproved as a result of the exercise" (p. 106). One participant expressed a sense of being "floored" by the exercise because "our students are much more similar than we thought . . . I always hear basic skills students are coming from disadvantaged backgrounds" (p. 107).

Lack of Leadership

These powerful learning experiences led the faculty at Birch College to propose to the president of the college that ongoing funding be provided to support faculty inquiry groups that would be organized as teaching communities. However, at this point the inquiry group, and the organizational change process intended by our action research design, "hit a wall" due to lack of support from the college president and other executive leaders. Thus Enciso (2009) related this development:

> The leaders on campus did not support inquiry as an accountability strategy to promote equity. Therefore, although the participants were able to learn at an individual level, they "hit a wall" when they tried to share the learning beyond the group. The manner in which the senior administrators perceived equity and issues of equity on campus impacted what team members utilized as a result of the project. Although the team was able to develop an environment that encour-

aged dialogue about equity, administrative leaders did not respond positively to the team using equity-minded language. Leadership at the institution, especially at the higher levels, prevented further learning about equity amongst individuals working at an institution. (p. 120)

A similar lack of leadership support was articulated by faculty at Dynamic Community College (Subramaniam, 2012) and at Monarch State University (Cornell, 2012; Smith, 2012). Although faculty had taken individual and group actions to introduce greater use of culturally relevant pedagogies, they felt stymied by a lack of symbolic or material endorsement from university leaders. Leaders play an important role in embedding cultural norms and values. Through their actions, language, and what they pay attention to, they communicate priorities, values, and expectations (Schein, 1985b). When campus leaders show ambivalence or outright opposition to the idea of equity as a matter of institutional accountability to Black, Latino, American Indian, and other marginalized racial/ethnic groups, as they did at Birch College and Monarch State University, the benefits of action research driven by faculty inquiry are limited to the individual and group levels. The potential for broader organizational change is constrained. We return to a focus on the role and importance of leadership in Chapter 4, where we discuss the role administrators and faculty leaders played in the implementation of the Equity Scorecard in Wisconsin as part of a system-wide initiative supported by college, university, and system leaders.

THE EMOTIONAL GEOGRAPHY OF AUTHENTIC CARE

We see through these dissertation studies that the faculty who participated in the syllabus workshops engaged in both the reflective and the active moments of praxis (Seo & Creed, 2002). Faculty became willing to renew their praxis, reflective practice in combination with action, and reframe their relationship with students and their institutions as change agents. Their strongest sense of agency stemmed from the ability to change their own teaching practices. However, for the most part, faculty did not have the requisite cultural competencies to engage in empowering pedagogies with a strong sense of self-efficacy. That faculty became motivated to acquire this knowledge through collective action was encouraging to us.

The disturbances experienced by faculty in the syllabus workshops and expressed as frustration as well as an impulse to provide care and help to students of color reveal an "emotional geography" (Zembylas, 2011) of racial equity work on college campuses. These emotional responses led faculty to take action, though they were not always well equipped to do so. They were not prepared to engage racism as a root cause of the "otherness" of students of color. Egalitarian views constrained mobilization of race-conscious practices. Where Valenzuela (1999) saw "subtractive schooling at work," we observed a fear, fueled by color blindness and perhaps a measure of pity, of engaging in race-conscious practices. Faculty worried that race consciousness would amount to zero-sum schooling, where attention to race and ethnicity would take away from other relationships with White, Asian, and immigrant students and students with other types of diversities. They did not see this as privileging Whiteness as the norm; they viewed it as embracing diversity.

Despite a lack of expertise or leadership support for culturally responsive pedagogies, faculty made changes individually in their syllabi and developed collective agency to improve their knowledge and expertise. They sought to be caring, based on what they understood to be their role in helping disadvantaged students. The role of providing resources to help someone compete for an education on a "level playing field" is well established in conceptualizations of equity rooted in the dominant ideology of educational policy. Justice as fairness calls for equal opportunity (not empowerment for social change) and for color blindness (not engagement with racial discrimination and the legacies of racism institutionalized in educational practices). This partial progress affirms for us that cycles of inquiry design based on principles of expansive learning are valuable and deserve broader adoption in institutional and state accountability policies.

CHAPTER 4

Enacting Justice as Fairness

> We were throwing money at a problem without understanding [it], and
> the results were disappointing.
>
> —UW Equity Scorecard team member

This chapter opens with a quotation from a University of Wisconsin (UW) Scorecard participant who highlighted how typical it is to "throw money at" problems without understanding them, leading to disappointing results. Structural changes tend to be introduced by the reproduction of "best practices" that have been developed at another institution. The quotation reflects a growing awareness on the part of the speaker that it is difficult to bring programs back from a professional conference and make them work without tailoring them to local contexts and needs. In addition, any large-scale change effort requires ownership and buy-in on the part of local actors (Kezar, 2011; Marsh, 2012). Organizations need to engage in a structured and sustained learning process in order to gain understanding of the ways institutional practices are contributing to racial inequities in student experiences and outcomes.

When institutional agents engage in "divergent" organizational change, they challenge dominant institutional logics, which are the "taken-for-granted social prescriptions that guide behavior of actors in fields" (Battilana, 2006, p. 656). Institutional logics represent "a field's shared understandings of what goals to pursue and how to pursue them" (p. 656). When the faculty members featured in Chapter 3 changed their syllabi to communicate a welcoming classroom environment to students of color, they were challenging institutional logics of control, which attempt to counter the behaviors and perceived lack of motivation of disengaged students through bureaucratic procedures (Ladson-Billings, 2009).

For organizational learning and social change to have occurred on a broader scale in the settings we featured in Chapter 3, the faculty involved would have required institutional structures that supported their ongoing professional development as well as the support of institutional leaders—

important resources that were not forthcoming. The scope of the change efforts was limited, for the most part, to changes in the tenor of the syllabus and in faculty approaches in their interpersonal communication with students.

This chapter draws lessons from CUE's work in the state of Wisconsin to illustrate how reflective practice at the individual and group level supports collective action to design more equitable educational programs and structures. We show how Equity Scorecard tools function through an expansive learning (Engeström, 2001, 2008) process to remediate practices that are reproducing racial inequities. The Scorecard tools, acting as task-oriented objects, motivate reflection and action, which in turn influence norms in the community of practice. The chapter illustrates how Equity Scorecard participants came to understand, through the Scorecard's inquiry process, what it means to be color-conscious "in a positive way." It shows how they were motivated by their new understanding of equity issues to take action. The reflections of Equity Scorecard team members presented in this chapter highlight the importance of involving practitioners in purposeful, task-oriented discussions of disaggregated data, in other words the "joint productive activities" of activity theory discussed in Chapter 3.

The individuals and groups featured in this chapter were members of Equity Scorecard teams at University of Wisconsin campuses. The Equity Scorecard was adopted as a tool for organizational learning as part of a systemwide accountability initiative begun in 2005 to improve diversity and student success. Since that time, we have collaborated with many practitioners and system leaders in Wisconsin to develop equity-based assessment and accountability practices.

OVERVIEW OF THE CHAPTER

The remainder of this chapter is presented in four sections. The first section presents the setting for the chapter, the University of Wisconsin system. The second section illustrates the changes in beliefs about equity that came about as evidence team members collaborated to make sense of inequities represented in their institutional data. UW Equity Scorecard participants reflected on what they learned through close examinations and discussions of their campus data during evidence team meetings and in settings outside the team meetings. Seeing gaps in participation and outcomes among racial and ethnic groups, the inquiry process led participants to start "thinking about what the institution can do differently," as one participant explained it. These participants were moved to stronger conceptions of equity and a willingness to act on them. Not every Equity Scorecard participant adopts a strong equity perspective. We present dissenting voices in this section to illustrate the range of understandings Equity Scorecard participants bring to the inquiry process.

As shown in the second section below, those who have a strong commitment to racial equity take on institutional responsibility for addressing inequities. Practitioners who hold these beliefs do not necessarily or quickly have a remedy available to improve the situation. The inquiry process enables Equity Scorecard participants to generate a range of strategies to address particular problems of institutional practice. These problems were revealed through the Equity Scorecard data analyses and other analyses that were conducted as the campuses institutionalized disaggregated data use in their assessment practices. The strategies the team implemented involved local experimentation, such as curriculum restructuring, as well as the adoption of programs and policies viewed as "best practices" by the field, such as peer mentoring, intrusive advising, supplemental instruction, summer bridge programs, and academic learning communities.

In the third section, we include a detailed description of changes in the admissions policies for students in the UW–Eau Claire Honors Program. This case illustrates the types of changes that administrators and faculty enact when they hold a deep commitment to the principles of justice as fairness. As we discuss, the case exemplifies the change enacted based on strong conceptions of equity that exist within the family of philosophical traditions that advance tenets of justice as fairness. The fourth, and concluding, section reflects on the capacity of practitioners acting as "institutional agents" to carry out justice as fairness by adopting stronger standards of equity (Stanton-Salazar, 1997, 2011).

THE EQUITY SCORECARD IN WISCONSIN

The opportunities for expansive learning were more numerous in the Equity Scorecard settings in Wisconsin than in the California settings described in Chapter 3 because the process had leadership support at the system and institutional levels. Wisconsin has a long history of stated commitment to ensuring excellence through diversity. The Equity Scorecard was adopted as part of the state's institutional assessment efforts after it became apparent that a major diversity initiative, called Plan 2008, was not achieving the desired goals even as diversity issues were taking on more prominence in the state. Although Wisconsin is predominantly White, it is experiencing a significant increase in its minority population. At the time of our study in Wisconsin, racial and ethnic minority groups constituted over 10% of the total population (U.S. Census Bureau, 2000) and the Hispanic population had doubled in the span of a decade (U.W. Extension & Applied Population Laboratory, 2001). In the same time frame, the African American population had increased by nearly 25% and the American Indian population increased by 20%. In contrast, the White population (the largest racial group) grew by only 4.8%. These demographic trends created greater impetus for UW system leaders to examine their efforts at increasing racial equity in the university system.

Plan 2008 had required the 19 campuses in the UW system to create their own 10-year plans to diversify their student populations and to identify accountability measures to monitor their success in achieving diversity goals. By 2005, it appeared that although Plan 2008 had produced many diversity-oriented programs, the system had few if any indicators to evaluate progress in access and success for historically underrepresented groups. The Board of Regents began to consider the adoption of standardized indicators of progress that would be applied across all the campuses. The system leaders were skeptical about the value of standardized metrics of progress. With the regents' approval, they adopted the Equity Scorecard as an accountability approach that was responsive to the regents' needs for indicators of progress while at the same time sensitive to individual campus contexts and need for autonomy.

We focus on reflective practice by participants in the Equity Scorecard initiative at UW–LaCrosse, UW–Milwaukee, UW–Oshkosh, UW–Parkside, UW–Whitewater—all 4-year, comprehensive universities—and the UW Colleges, the 13 associate's degree–granting campuses of the UW system, which participated as a group led by the Colleges' central academic office. These institutions were part of the first wave of the Scorecard in Wisconsin, which took place from 2006 to 2008 with coordination from the UW system office. By 2012, all 19 of the comprehensive universities in Wisconsin had also completed the Equity Scorecard (in whole or in part).

In Spring 2009, 19 participants were interviewed about their experience doing the Equity Scorecard. These respondents included two faculty members, five institutional researchers, three student service directors, two equity officers, and seven upper-level administrators (in roles such as provost, associate dean, vice chancellor, and chancellor). What we learned from these interviews complements the insights presented in Chapter 3, which were derived from interviews and observations with faculty members only.

At least two people who had participated on the Equity Scorecard evidence teams at each of the five UW universities and the UW Colleges provided their thoughts. Semi-structured interviews were organized with questions designed to elicit respondents' personal beliefs about equity, how their involvement with the Scorecard may have influenced their professional practices, and broader impacts of the Scorecard on institutional practices, structures, policies, or culture. The interview findings were also triangulated through our direct interpretations of our experiences in the Wisconsin context.

DEEPENING COMMITMENTS TO EQUITY THROUGH INQUIRY

In our application of inquiry, we focus on generating insights about institutional practices that contribute to racial disparities in college participation and outcomes. Our tools are designed to assist practitioners in seeing racial patterns of inequality in educational outcomes and how their own practices may be contributing to inequities. The Equity Scorecard's iterative process of data review, from the Vital Signs to fine-grained measures, is intended to offer numerous opportunities for race-conscious data discussions. It is common for members of the evidence team to disagree on the meaning and causes of these gaps and for some members to disagree with one another and with us about the definitions of equity that we provide in our materials or that participants articulate.

Equity Scorecard participants are typically drawn to or agree to participate in the Equity Scorecard because they care, at least to some extent, about equity issues. The majority of participants are not steeped in formal theories of justice, but they often intuitively relate the concept of equity to the liberal egalitarian ideal of equal opportunity. When we point out that the terms *equity* and *equal opportunity* are not synonymous, the variation in participants' responses reflects the range of beliefs present in the room about the obligations of a just society to provide equal opportunity. These differences in perspective surface in the dialogue about inequalities in educational participation among racial and ethnic groups observed in the data presented in this chapter. They help us understand what is involved in a change process that calls on practitioners to apply stronger standards of equity in their day-to-day work.

Practitioners' culturally acquired knowledge often operates in practice "below consciousness" (Polkinghorne, 2004), often revealed in their "sense-making" conversations concerning the causes of inequalities revealed by disaggregated data on educational outcomes (e.g., persistence after the first semester). Articulating understanding about racialized experiences in higher education is a step toward adopting equity frames for viewing problems of student outcomes, because it involves taking note of racial/ethnic differences.

Seeing Patterns of Inequities

The Equity Scorecard aims to enable practitioners to exercise race consciousness in a positive manner. This involves learning to see racialized patterns in the ways that institutions select, involve, and communicate with students of different racial and ethnic groups in educational programs, services, and classrooms. Developing the capacity to observe and notice problems, including problems of racial inequities, is a necessary first step in any inquiry process.

For example, evidence team members at one UW university who were part of the faculty in the Math and Science Departments started a conversation in those departments about the effects of gatekeeper courses on students of color. After reviewing retention Vital Signs, the departments started offering tutorials and secured grants to, in the words of one faculty member who was interviewed, "understand what we can do . . . to ensure students are not flunking and retaking, flunking and retaking." In this section, we illustrate the way Equity Scorecard participants change how they talked about racial equity issues by using Scorecard tools and begin to formulate ideas for change.

Revealing a change in sense-making about equity issues, one UW Equity Scorecard participant explained the value of looking at data in the following way:

> Looking at data disaggregated by race and ethnicity was really useful for us. I found it personally interesting to realize where some ethnic groups' scores were different. In some cases, the [outcomes of] students of color were better than their White peers and it suggested that we have people and programs that were successful. Also we could see patterns in which students of color were falling behind. Identifying those areas was good.

For this participant, the data tools had revealed "patterns" that had previously gone unnoticed. The amorphous problem of inequities came into sharper relief. The comment articulates the speaker's sense of optimism, in part evoked by seeing some areas where students of color were doing well, that the institution was not powerless in the face of racial disparities.

This experience was expressed by another respondent who emphasized the value of looking at disaggregated data for gateway courses and majors. "Diving into institutional research in a different way," the team members had "talked about data in lots of new ways." The attention given in CUE's action research design of the data tools enabled two people who brought different assumptions about data—a science faculty member with "an engineering bent" and a participant who had previously "resisted" data—to be "in the conversation." As the science professor articulated:

Prior conversations about diversity and campus climate left me cold. But once it became quantitative—looking at numbers—then I had a way into the conversation. And a way to get passionate about the conversation—get revved up about it.

This professor's initial disposition toward using data contrasts with the participant who saw herself as a newcomer to data use. Yet both spoke positively about the Scorecard experience and, perhaps more important, both respondents understood that the data themselves were not the "end-point." As the newcomer to data expressed it:

I really learned that you can use data to provoke a discussion, and not use it as an end-point. It was totally transformative for me . . . what's really important is the discussion. Data provokes mining for more data, which in turn provokes more discussion, which leads to more inquiry.

Gaining Race Consciousness

These participants saw that the data were a way to produce shared understandings through group discussions, the "social interactions" of the inquiry process. The ongoing nature of data analysis through inquiry is built into the design of the Scorecard data tools. After getting a sense of the data presented by the Vital Signs, team members proceed to ask "fine-grained questions." They then obtain or collect "fine-grained data," which may be quantitative or qualitative.

An example of fine-grained data is data on incomplete applications. Several Scorecard teams, upon learning that admissions rates for African Americans were twice as low (or more) than the rates for Whites, asked why that was the case. Rather than assuming that African American students were not academically qualified, which is a deficit assumption that often quickly surfaced, these teams used the inquiry process to dig deeper into their institutional data to see if institutional practices were creating a barrier to equity in admissions. They discovered that those students who did not fully complete their applications—meaning that transcript data, an application fee, or SAT scores were missing—were disproportionately African American. This finding led to closer monitoring of applications and more outreach efforts to assist students in completing their applications.

The desired result of this iterative process of data discussion and interpretation is for team members to gain "race consciousness in a positive way" (Bensimon & Malcom, 2012). The participant quoted below explained how race consciousness can motivate inquiry on a routine basis:

I am always race-conscious now. We had a discussion regarding the guaranteed transfer program—the first thing I did was look at how it would affect students and broke it out by race. I'm also very conscious of outcomes. I never stop at access anymore.

This type of growing awareness, of consciousness about racial issues and how they can be observed in patterns of data and patterns of student outcomes, illustrates the central role that beliefs play in enabling change. This participant's sense of agency to make a difference is predicated on race consciousness and the ability to construct knowledge about the nature of inequities through ongoing inquiry. The statement "I never stop at access anymore" also reflects the value of the four-perspective design of the Equity Scorecard. The Scorecard report includes indicators of institutional effectiveness that represent the functioning of the system as a whole. After using baseline data to identify inequities, participants are asked to recommend improvement targets, strategies for improvement, and equity goals for longer-term monitoring.

Through this process, participants are making decisions together about what type of knowledge to generate through the inquiry process. This design is based on the principle at the heart of activity theory and sociocultural theories that learning is socially constructed (Tharp, 1997; Tharp & Gallimore, 1988). Participants reflected on the benefits of using data to interact in new ways with their colleagues, saying the Scorecard data provided "another avenue to work with people" and a way to "suggest we do things differently." The emphasis on communication was reflected by one interview respondent who said, "The Equity Scorecard helped us go through all the data and present it so it's compelling and helpful to the conversation."

In addition to providing a means to start conversations about racial disparities in student experiences, the language we use in introducing the Scorecard process, such as "equity-mindedness" and "equity gaps," provided cognitive tools for active reflection and knowledge construction. The comments below reflect the value one participant placed on "learning about cognitive frames":

I began to understand where people come from regarding diversity or equity. It deepened my desire at meetings to draw people out to determine where they were coming from, the frame in which they were operating. It was tremendously valuable to me to reach out to those people and pull them into the process.

Another participant spoke about how the inquiry process focusing on group differences had helped clarify the meaning of equity:

Participating in Equity Scorecard clarified my thoughts on equity. Once you looked closely at the data and disaggregated it by race/ethnicity, and understand there are differences between and amongst groups—it solidified that in my mind.

The concept of equity-mindedness is a cognitive tool for reframing assumptions about the causes of racial disparities. Often educational practitioners hold unexamined assumptions that gaps in participation and success among racial and ethnic groups are completely attributable to student deficits, such as lack of preparation, motivation, resilience, or attention to required procedures. Without saying these factors do not matter at all, we ask Equity Scorecard participants to be open to the possibility that their own practices are contributing to racial disparities, and then to use inquiry to investigate that possibility. One participant reflected the influence of this cognitive reframing process, indicating that "There has been increased discussion and awareness in policy's differential impact." These discussions helped to create an understanding of how inequities can be "manifest" in normal routines of practice:

The ways inequity manifests are more visible to me. Before the project, equal access and equal opportunity had always been beliefs I've held strongly. Equity Scorecard allowed me and the team to dig into unseen effects of policies that are overlooked. You get busy and don't think of the pervasive effects of policy, how it can have differential impact on different groups of students.

Growing Awareness of Disparate Impacts

An inequity addressed by one evidence team illustrates how seemingly neutral policies can have disparate impact on students of color. The team found that the determination of whether a student was included on the dean's list was based on a grade point average calculated on a minimum credit load each semester. Evidence team members realized that this policy penalized part-time students, who were also disproportionately students of color. The team then introduced a recommendation for a change in policy to the academic senate, which would allow part- and full-time students equal opportunity to be included on the dean's list.

The following participants articulated the shift in point of view toward institutional responsibility for student outcomes that can be achieved through equity-minded inquiry. Their words highlight the ways that an equity-minded data review informs the knowledge practitioners bring into dialogue about racial inequities:

This study gave us very detailed evidence that we could point to . . . so that we give equal opportunity to students of color. So not only do students come in, but we can help them stay. It is not just getting into the institution, it is helping them graduate.

At this stage of inquiry, where the focus is on problem-framing and knowledge construction, participants do not yet necessarily have the answers to "fix" inequities. However, through inquiry they have acquired and are mutually constructing artifacts, whether in the form of language, data, or organizational structures, to generate knowledge to assess the impact of their practices on students of color. This "naming of the problem," as we emphasized in Chapter 1, is a crucial building block to change. As one participant expressed this:

A huge take-away for me has been the role of institutional responsibility as it relates to equity. I always thought that institutions are responsible, but did not have the language to talk about it. We can all agree that we have underprepared students. But they are in our walls now, so what can we do for them?

That the Equity Scorecard process supported a shift away from prior efforts that focused on student deficits, rather than institutional responsibility, was also articulated by a team member at another UW campus:

(We're) not just looking at what students are or are not doing, and focusing on student deficits, but thinking about what the institution can do differently. This is different from other work that has been done.

Finally, in featuring this series of quotations from UW interview respondents, we note the local nature of problem framing and idea generation in the Scorecard, as explained by a participant who focused on patterns of student progress through the curriculum:

[Findings from the Equity Scorecard] made us more conscious of the curriculum. We look at success rate the curriculum has with students, not the other way around. We look at patterns of success and failure in the curriculum more—we are more sensitive to race.

A willingness to direct resources toward students of color or develop new practices and policies depends on the belief that equal opportunity and equitable outcomes are institutional responsibilities. As one speaker stated it, endorsing an equity perspective promotes the view that practitioners are responsible for students within their walls, rather than blaming them for lack of preparation or other real or perceived deficits. Returning again to the quotation that begins this chapter—"We were throwing money at a problem without understanding [it]"—we are reminded how important these insights are to problem solving to reduce racial inequities. Those who name the problem in terms of institutional responsibility are positioned to solve the problems of educational practice.

Changing Educational Structures Through Inquiry

When practitioners take action to improve social conditions they are engaging in *praxis*, which can be understood in a general sense as "doing the good" through reflective practice and collective action to reconstruct unjust social arrangements. Praxis is at the heart of professional accountability to teach and administer programs equitably. It involves both reflection and action (Seo & Creed, 2002). Institutional agents take actions when they are motivated by a sense of injustice. This section shows how reflection and action are integrally related. As action researchers, we need to understand what types of inquiry processes support reflection and action in a sustained way to not only critique but to mobilize against the practices (e.g., teaching and in-class student assessment), systems (e.g., admissions and standardized aptitude testing), and structures (e.g., differentiated curricula) that produce unequal educational experiences and outcomes among racial and ethnic groups.

Data can influence reflection and action if they are used in situ (Spillane, 2012), in other words, in ways connected with the daily work of teaching and administration. The data that motivate faculty and other student-oriented practitioners to make changes in their practices differ from the data favored by policymakers. The typical data collected through public accountability systems is too far removed from what matters to practitioners in their day-to-day work world. In the previous section, we provided examples of structural changes made by Equity Scorecard participants in their own programs and institutional practices.

Through our work as action researchers we see four strategic leverage points for change to improve racial equity: (1) recruitment, assessment testing, admissions, and student placement; (2) curriculum and pedagogy; (3) professional development and networking; and (4) recruitment and hiring of faculty and administrators. While in some ways the steps taken by the UW practitioners in the examples presented in this section may seem small to those who have not engaged in this type of work, they are not. The Equity Scorecard participants in the UW system were taking action at the strategic leverage points available to institutional change agents. In addition, they were doing so within an inquiry process that held the potential for the expansive learning process to continue, meaning that the participants would have the opportunity to deepen their knowledge about racial equity issues and their capacity to act as institutional agents. The institutionalization of data use to generate knowledge about particular policies and practices that were having disparate impacts on students of color were therefore among the most important outcomes we observed. Those who were interviewed were able to directly link the development of new policies and practices to the review of specific data.

Recruitment and Admissions. Three examples of change revolving around ongoing data use and inquiry that we gathered through the interviews with UW evidence team members are centered on recruitment and admissions practices. One campus began to generate demographic reports of high school students in their service area and to recruit at schools with a higher number of students of color. In a second example, another campus realized that African American applicants were more likely than others to begin but not complete the application process. The admissions office began to contact students with incomplete applications to offer them assistance in submitting required documentation.

In the third case, findings from the Equity Scorecard helped a participating university begin "conversations regarding holistic admission practices and cut-off dates for applications; it helped us think through abandoning cut scores for scholarships and looking at scholarships in a more holistic fashion." In addition, the application deadline for admission was reexamined. The application had previously closed just before the first day of class. The evidence team found that 1st-year African American students "came to campus very late without orientation or getting the courses they needed, and also needing developmental education work and feeling shortchanged because no one told them they would need that." The deadline for freshman admissions was therefore moved to earlier in the summer to allow students time to prepare for the fall semester. With this shift, students could then use the summer months to take English and Math placement exams, participate in summer bridge programs, and attend orientation programs. The university also shifted to portfolio admissions for its nursing and architecture programs, and observed an increase in applications and admissions of students of color in both programs.

Curriculum and Pedagogy. Several examples of data use that informed curricular restructuring or changes in pedagogy were provided by interview participants. After receiving a $200,000 grant to improve retention efforts, one university issued a call for proposals from faculty to improve students'

1st-year experience. The call required proposals to draw on data summarized in the university's Equity Scorecard to focus on a problem evident in the data. An evidence team member explained that this requirement "shifted faculty to look at the data. If you give faculty data, they want to see students succeed, and look beyond grades. They can ask themselves, how can I teach or do things differently? Without data, that would not have gotten their attention." The proposals reflected a willingness to make changes in the curriculum. Several proposed, as one interview respondent described it, "restructuring entry-level courses and involving junior/senior faculty across disciplines."

Moreover, by digging deeper into their Scorecard data, one university discovered that although they had high retention of students of color in the 1st year, they were losing them afterwards. An evidence team member explained: "we tend to frontload a lot of resources in the 1st and 2nd years . . . and after that year hope they get it by then, but we were finding they were not." Subsequently, the campus extended its mentoring program to 2nd-, 3rd- and 4th-year students, with programming focused on employment and graduate education opportunities for juniors and seniors. In a related example at a different university, Equity Scorecard participants found that students of color received grades of D/F/W at higher rates than their White peers in most courses. To address this finding, the academic support center "stepped up their mentoring program" and one college added supplementary instruction periods to gatekeeper courses. The college also created a program in which students took a summer week-long course to see what college is like.

Professional Development. Through the Equity Scorecard at one UW university, the evidence team learned that students of color were not having the same success in STEM courses as White students. As a result, the team initiated efforts to improve the classroom experience for students of color. Like the faculty at Monarch State University featured in Chapter 3, faculty from the team reached out to colleagues and started a Teaching to Diversity book group. This professional development activity represented a change in practices directly aimed at increasing the faculty's own knowledge of culturally responsive pedagogies. The book group was set up to actively read and apply what was learned through the readings.

The equity-focused inquiry process of the Scorecard prompted the team to avoid structuring the program as a remedial program. This was articulated when one participant described the program as "not remedial, but an honors-type program." The literature the team had read suggested the value of creating opportunities for students to study together, and the "honors-type program" was a way to build a study cohort without stigmatizing students of color. This example illustrates how the Scorecard team focused on their own capabilities to educate the students who were enrolling at their university, rather than blaming students for their lack of preparation or wishing for different students.

At another university, Equity Scorecard participants learned that African American students were disproportionately enrolled in developmental mathematics. They saw that, in general, the university was losing a lot of students of color from developmental education. The evidence team conducted a focus group with African American males and other students of color to better understand the challenges they were experiencing with developmental education.

What they learned led to a hiring process that prioritized faculty searches for candidates with demonstrated interest and capacity in teaching developmental and lower-level math courses. This search led to greater faculty diversity when, among three hires, an African American female and a Latina were added to the predominantly White faculty. Responsibility for developmental education was not placed entirely on the new hires. The curriculum was restructured by adding a fourth hour of instructional contact time to several courses and introducing academic learning communities. These changes created time within the curriculum for faculty collaboration, as faculty worked together to coordinate instructional delivery of three courses offered within the learning community. These problem-solving steps show the faculty recognized they lacked sufficient knowledge and expertise to effectively serve students of color in developmental courses. As a result, they extended the inquiry process we had introduced by conducting the focus groups with students and also made structural changes at a point in the curriculum where the university was losing students. Therefore, these changes held potential to improve equity in outcomes.

FROM WEAK TO STRONG CONCEPTIONS OF EQUITY

The Equity Scorecard asks participants to act on their ideals, as expressed by the word "equity," through their educational practice. The Scorecard offers evidence team members tools to pursue equity through practitioner inquiry. How team members use those tools—and to what effect—depends largely on their individual and collective belief systems.

Equity Scorecard teams usually include people with a variety of beliefs about what equal opportunity, equality, and equity mean. The range of views echoes ideas present within the family of philosophies that articulate the values of justice as fairness. Some traditions, such as libertarianism, advance weaker standards of social intervention than others, such as compensatory approaches. Some emphasize the need to provide formal structures of schooling and equal access to them, without making a commitment to equalizing outcomes (Howe, 1997). Still other traditions, such as liberal egalitarians, advance a stronger conception of equity.

Strong conceptions of equity place a greater demand on society to equalize outcomes, viewing "any group differences in educational attainment that are systematically linked to [social] goods such as employment, income, and health [as] *prima facie* unjust" (Howe, 1997, p. 66). In our work, as in these strong forms of liberal egalitarianism, we argue that the sorting of minoritized groups into lower-quality educational systems and of dominant groups into higher-quality systems is a sign of racial inequity. It is these systemic and racialized inequalities that bear investigation, intervention, and remedy.

Yet, clearly, all inequalities do not represent inequities. Different individuals obtain different (unequal) outcomes due to natural variation in interests, talents, and motivation in the population as a whole. We argue that when unequal outcomes are observable not only among individuals but among racial and ethnic groups as well, then they are suspect.

Those who are comfortable with formal provision of equal access do not view any inequalities as a sign of inequity. They argue that students (and families) with different values, talents, educational interests, and cultural practices naturally will have unequal outcomes. Those with strong conceptions of equity acknowledge that some individuals with weak academic interests will opt out of educational systems after compulsory schooling. However, when a systematic pattern exists among racial and ethnic groups in which those groups that have experienced racial discrimination opt out of education earlier or opt out of more robust, well-resourced, or advanced forms of education with greater frequency, then the pattern of inequality demonstrates educational inequity. For a society to pursue egalitarian ideals, such inequities must be addressed through educational policy and by practitioners acting on their ideals concerning the features of a just society.

Weak Conceptions of Equity

The idea that inequalities in outcomes represent inequities is rejected by many Scorecard participants who hold more formalist, or weaker, conceptions of what equity and equal opportunity entail. Two respondents among the first wave of UW Scorecard participants who were interviewed by CUE researchers articulated their belief that equity should be measured in terms of equal opportunity, not in terms of outcomes. One participant used the concept of a "normal curve," or a normal distribution, of human abilities and talents to understand differences in student success.

Asked to explain the meaning of *equity*, the participant replied:

Equity of opportunity for all people, regardless of race/ethnicity, creed, religion, gender, sexual orientation. Not necessarily equity in outcomes. There are people on a normal curve. Some people will do better than others.

The speaker's comment represents a weaker conception of equity, giving little credence to the impact of the history and contemporary forms of racial discrimination on today's students. Another participant rooted disparities in outcomes firmly on individual student performance, viewing this as a more "neutral" view of the gaps represented in the Scorecard data:

Frankly, I don't think the title "Equity Scorecard" is the best. To me, the project is about looking at performance gaps. . . . The subtle connotation . . . when we saw a performance gap and labeled them inequitable or unfair, [was that] someone was acting in a way that was causing the unfairness. Performance gap is a more neutral way to talk about the Equity Scorecard approach.

These participants disagreed with the idea of defining *equity* in terms of equality of outcomes. Further, the inquiry process had not led them to adopt new beliefs about the meaning of equity or about the obligations of a just society to produce conditions for equitable outcomes. As one stated, "Participating in the Equity Scorecard did not change my perception of equity."

While many Equity Scorecard participants are moved by the inquiry process to view racial inequities in a new light and to change their practices, whether individually or through collective action, this is not true of all participants. For participants who embrace stronger conceptions of equity, the Scorecard process supports praxis, which is the mobilization of collective action through reflective practice.

This chapter illustrates the types of changes Equity Scorecard participants who are motivated by liberal egalitarian ideals make in their educational practices to act as change agents in support of equity goals. We do not view the examples of change presented in this chapter as deeply transformative (a challenge we take up in the next chapter). What the examples do show is how participation in the Equity Scorecard led participants to examine the relationship between their ideals, specifically their conceptions about equality of opportunity in education, and their practices. Reflective practice engendered through the inquiry process led participants, in many cases though certainly not all, to adopt stronger conceptions of what constitutes equality of opportunity and a stronger commitment to acting as change agents to pursue those ideals.

Strong Conceptions of Equity

In this section, we present text from a speech given at a national professional conference by an Equity Scorecard team member from Wisconsin. We have chosen to present this excerpt for two reasons. First, it represents a case of enactment of the principles of justice as fairness based on a strong conception of equity, where gaps in program participation among racial and ethnic groups were viewed as inequities. Second, it illustrates the relationship between the reflective phase of inquiry, based on race-conscious data use, and the active phase, in which programs and structures, such as admissions policies, are changed to promote equity.

In his speech, reproduced below from the speaker's prepared remarks (which he shared with us), the team member describes the iterative process of data review, action, and ongoing inquiry. Through reviewing the Vital Signs of the Excellence perspective of the Scorecard and obtaining fine-grained measures of participation in the university's honors program, the evidence team learned that the program had practically no students of color. In the speech, the team member explains how the Equity Scorecard team had asked two questions during the inquiry process: (1) "How many students are in the Honors Program and what is their racial/ethnic background?"; (2) "Is the representation of students by race and ethnicity proportional to their representation in the overall student body?"

The data to answer these questions showed that students of color were underrepresented. Instead of guessing why that might be, they systematically inquired into the situation by asking: "How does a student join the Honors Program?" The team member described the answers to these questions and what he and other program leaders had done about the situation.

It is fair to say that our Equity Scorecard, specifically the Interim Report on Excellence from June, 2009, motivated me, and my colleague, and the four faculty and two Honors student members of the University Honors Council, to [quoting from the Scorecard report] "respond to known inequities with purposeful actions." The Equity Scorecard team's analysis of multicultural participation in our University Honors Program showed beyond mistake that the Equity Scorecard report's conclusion was correct: that "students of color," when compared to their percentage representation at our campus as a whole, "[were] seriously underrepresented in the Honors program." Out of 392 students then officially enrolled in the program, only 7 students (1.7%) were known to be students of color: 4 Asian or Asian American and 3 Hispanic/Latina(o) students.

Just as significantly, the Equity Scorecard report was able to give us a concrete and manageable prescription for change. It specified exactly how many students in each underrepresented group Honors would need to be recruited into the program to achieve equitable representation and to provide such groups with equitable access to the manifold benefits of an Honors education:

African American: Increase by at least 2 students
American Indian: Increase by at least 2 students
Asian: Increase by at least 8 students
Hispanic: Increase by at least 2 students

The Equity Scorecard report also surmised that "the current admissions criteria for the Honors Program unfairly disadvantage students of color," and urged us to re-examine our rationale for our particular ACT and class rank admissions requirements. At the time, students were admitted to our program only if they had 28 or higher ACT composites (1280 SAT) and were in the top 5% of their high school classes. After earning a 3.67 GPA on 15 academic credits, students could also be admitted, but only if they had achieved an ACT score of at least 26.

In the ensuing self-study of our Honors admissions history and practice, we learned many interesting things, but two stand out. The program literature at that time boasted that our Honors program "uses the most rigorous admissions criteria of the UW system institutions, with the exception of UW–Madison." And a member of the original Honors advisory board confided to us that the ACT and class rank criteria were set at 28 and top 5% not for any academic or intellectual reason, but simply to keep the numbers of admitted Honors students manageable for the program.

Clearly it was time for a new approach.

In response to the Equity Scorecard, and based on what we learned in our self-study, we designed a holistic admissions pilot project to answer this question: in restricting admissions to students with 28 ACT and top 5%, are we missing students with great Honors potential? Not surprisingly, the answer turned out to be "yes."

(During our pilot projects, we also continued our traditional admissions procedures.)

We asked the Admissions Office to make us a list of all accepted applicants for Fall 2010 who matched these characteristics: 26 and up ACT, class rank top 10%, or (and that "or" is very important) 3.75 GPA. This gave us a printout of nearly 2,100 names. We then made our first cut by applying some simple selection criteria. We took all students with geographical diversity (i.e., not WI or MN), all students with racial and/or ethnic diversity, all valedictorians, and all students with at least one outstanding academic characteristic (GPA, ACT or SAT, class rank)—and there were a couple other categories. This resulted in a sublist of some 350 students.

We then developed an Honors pilot rubric and used it to read and rate all 350 of these students' university applications. Our rubric categories, in alphabetical order, were academic accomplishments and potential; employment /extra-curricular/service activities; potential to diversify the Honors Program; rigor of senior-year course work; special talents, abilities, experiences, achievements.

At the end of the process, we chose 57 great students to invite to join the University Honors Program, all of whom our traditional admissions procedures would have missed: 5 African Americans, 2 American Indians, 1 Egyptian American, 6 Hmong, 6 Other Asians, 8 Hispanic, 4 Native Hawaiian/Pacific Islander, 25 White.

At least 19 of these students were first generation [college students]; 5 were discernibly low income; and 22 recorded having overcome serious obstacles in their lives. ACT scores ranged from 21 to 34; median score was 28. In the end, 19 of these students decided to attend UW–Eau Claire, and 18 joined the University Honors Program: 4 Hmong, 2 Other Asians, 3 African Americans, 5 Whites, 4 Hispanics.

In the pilot's second year, 2010, we again culled records of some 2,100 admitted students, and we chose more than 500 names. We invited colleagues and staff members from across campus to join us in reading and rating applications, and 8 people responded. At the end of the process, we invited 83 students to join the Honors Program, 49 White students and 34 students of color: 4 African Americans, 3 American Indians, 10 Hispanics, 17 Hmong and other Asians.

Twenty-four of these students enrolled at [our university], and 20 joined the Honors Program: 0 African Americans (none enrolled), 1 American Indian/Alaskan native, 3 Hmong and Other Asians, 2 Hispanics, 14 Whites.

This case illustrates a strong conception of equity. It asserts a view of the validity of assessment tests and admissions standards based on the view that "Testing practices must be evaluated in terms of the broad social consequences that result from their use" (Howe, 1997, p. 92). The growth in the numbers of students from minority groups illustrates the improvement in racial equity brought about through the Equity Scorecard team's reflective practice using the Vital Signs data and finer-grained measures that they obtained during the inquiry process.

The inclusion of Hmong and American Indian students among the list of racial and ethnic groups listed highlights that the inquiry process was local. The data were local and enabled a "particularized" inquiry process, right down to stating the number of additional students who needed to be recruited to create equitable enrollment in the honors program. The program leaders were able to see racial inequities in their own data, and in their own admissions practices, and to act on them. They questioned the assumptions and history of the "artifacts" of admissions to the honors program, asking, "Why is this the way we do it?" What might have seemed a normal assumption—admit top scorers—took on the dimension of a contradiction between practice and the ideal of justice as fairness.

PRACTITIONERS AS CHANGE AGENTS

An indicator of the validity of action research is whether the knowledge generated through the inquiry process is acted on by practitioners in their own educational settings (Kemmis & McTaggart, 2000). The examples of changes in educational practices presented above show the value of using action research as an accountability strategy. Practitioners can learn to observe inequities, document them, and take action on their own campuses to address them. Action research processes involve practitioners in looking at campus data in new ways, assuming new roles and relationships in their work, and examining unstated assumptions of what is "normal" in a new light.

The insights and actions described by UW Equity Scorecard participants in this chapter have the potential to be transformative. When "knowledge is consciously reflected on, struggled with, and shifts the individual's sense of self or social position," it involves a practitioner in a "consequential transition." Such transitions lead practitioners to want to act on their newly acquired identity and social position to spread what they have learned, that is, to engage in "knowledge propagation" (Tuomi-Gröhn, Engeström, & Young, 2003, p. 6).

Institutional agents are individuals who have status, power, authority, and control of resources in a hierarchical system (Stanton-Salazar, 1997, 2001, 2010). Institutional agents contrast with a student's "protective agents": parents, extended family members, and peers who "have the best interest of the student in mind and care the most about their futures" (Teranishi & Briscoe, 2006, p. 598). Practitioners act as institutional agents when they use their status, authority, or resources to enable a person who has been ascribed low social status to gain access to their high-status setting or related networks of opportunity (Stanton-Salazar, 2011).

All high-status individuals in educational settings have the potential to assist low-status youth in navigating structural and interpersonal barriers to educational success. Those who use their experience, knowledge, networks, and commitments to do so are said to be "manifesting" their potential to serve as institutional agents (Stanton-Salazar, 2011, p. 1067). Not all individuals with high status take on the role of institutional agents. Some individuals use their networks and resources to assist other high-status individuals; in this case, they are not viewed as institutional agents, since they are not acting to improve equity.

Through certain behaviors, roles, and commitments, institutional agents may also act as "empowerment agents" (Stanton-Salazar, 2011). Like other institutional agents, empowerment agents provide low-status students with emotional support and access to resources through their networks. Whereas institutional agents might be motivated by a liberal, progressive point of view to assist the disadvantaged, empowerment agents are motivated by what Freire termed a "critical consciousness (*conscientizacao*)" (Stanton-Salazar, 2011, p. 1089). Empowerment agents are not motivated by the desire to teach students how to get by within an existing system. They strive to teach students how to "change the world" and act on their behalf to create opportunities and structures where their collective agency can develop (Stanton-Salazar, 2011, p. 1093).

Where some institutional agents may use their time, resources, and networks to promote the individual status attainment of particular low-status students, empowerment agents take steps to address institutional racism. They act to fill "structural holes" that disadvantage low-status youth by using their networks to create a bridge to resources in other settings (Stanton-Salazar, 2011, p. 1095). Empowerment agents are motivated by a *critical*, transformative sense of their role in promoting social justice. The case discussed above of the honors program leaders who changed their program admissions criteria and redefined the meaning and purpose of "merit" illustrates the types of actions practitioners take in their everyday practices when they are motivated by a critical consciousness.

In order for practitioners who were moved to act as institutional agents through the Scorecard process to engage more extensively in the "deconstruction" and "reconstruction" (Ladson-Billings, 2009, p. 19) of justice as transformation, they would need to be able to transfer what they had learned as part of the Scorecard evidence team in other professional settings. Where transformative change enters the realm of politics and power, practitioners need to assume the social position and strategies of empowerment agents—those institutional agents who act with a critical consciousness to dismantle unjust educational structures.

Praxis depends on practitioner agency fueled by critical consciousness, which is developed through reflective practice. As Seo and Creed (2002) emphasize:

The likelihood of praxis increases as contradictions within and across social systems develop, deepen, and permeate actors' social experience. Although actors can become reflective at any time, the likelihood of a shift in collective consciousness that can transform actors from passive participants in the reproduction of existing social patterns into mobilized change agents increases when actors continually and collectively experience tensions arising from contradictions in a given sociohistorical context. (p. 230)

The Equity Scorecard changes participants' social position, enabling agency for those who are willing to invest their own resources and to develop networks in the organizational field of accountability in higher education, but it does not necessarily empower them. That aspect of a change agent's work depends, at least in part, on institutional and system-level leadership.

What accountability policies and practices will support such transformation? Our experiences with Equity Scorecard teams in California, Wisconsin, and other states highlights four key ingredients for the mobilization of institutional agents in higher education: (1) system leadership; (2) ongoing inquiry involving data disaggregated by race and ethnicity; (3) professional development to acquire the cultural competencies for equity work; and (4) professional networking in an organizational field committed to equity.

The cases presented above of practitioners in the UW system acting to make changes to their own programs and practices are instructive. Higher education in the United States is facing many accountability pressures that are intended to produce the kinds of changes that were instituted by the UW Equity Scorecard teams. The UW cases above show what accountability looks like when practitioners deepen their commitment to professional accountability and take action. Practitioners see where their practices are lacking; they collectively improve their understanding of the improvements that need to be made; and they change programs and curricula to make them more effective and equitable.

Public accountability policies, such as performance-based funding and performance dashboards like President Obama's College Scorecard, aim to change the prevailing institutional "logics" (Little, 2012; Spillane, 2012) of educational practice, which are viewed by many outside higher education as too entrenched and self-serving. Policymakers may well have authority to make structural changes in educational programs and degree requirements. They certainly have authority to articulate new ideals for institutional functioning. However, new structures, mandates, and marketlike accountability structures will not motivate institutional actors to make changes if they are too distant from the world of educational practice. Policies may simply be ignored if they target organizational routines at the periphery of the educational core. Or they may unleash resistance if they are instituted as an exercise of power that challenges the institutional logics of professionalism that motivate professionals in their day-to-day work.

To bring about change in educational practices that promote equity, accountability policies must pair the creation of data systems with inquiry structures that allow practitioners to articulate their beliefs about equal opportunity and reflect on institutional responsibility for equal outcomes.

CHAPTER 5

Enacting Justice as Transformation

To form relevant and effective ideals, we must first be acquainted with
and take notice of actual conditions.

—John Dewey, "The Underlying Philosophy of Education"
(1933/1989, p. 97)

The objective of the Equity Scorecard is to move participants involved in
practitioner inquiry from a passive position about the role of colleges and
universities in producing inequities to a socially conscious position where
they assume responsibility to undertake institutional changes to address racial inequities. Prior chapters have illustrated the action research processes
and outcomes of the Equity Scorecard at the individual and institutional
levels. We showed how faculty and administrators engaged with racial equity issues, adopted new beliefs, and made changes to their educational
practices. However, to have sweeping effects that will approach the level of
transformative change in higher education, change must occur at the individual, institutional, *and* systemic levels.

In this chapter we discuss two state-level accountability initiatives that
had the potential to bring about changes at the systemic level. Both attempted to address educational problems that are instances of institutional racism: transfer access to bachelor's degrees through technical colleges, in one
case, and basic skills education at the postsecondary level, in the other. The
racial dimensions of the two problems of educational practice in focus in
this chapter are very clear when viewed from a critical race perspective. The
Wisconsin Transfer Equity Study, which developed from the Equity Scorecard work described in the previous chapter, and the Basic Skills Initiative
of California's community colleges each took aim at systemic educational
problems that have their roots in histories of racial discrimination and are
carried forward by contemporary practices. Both provide opportunities to
examine the characteristics of institutional racism, which occurs, "absent
prejudiced actors," through an inertia that comes with privilege and an ac-

ceptance of "deeply entrenched material inequalities" (Haney-López, 2010, p. 824).

Both the Wisconsin Transfer Equity Study and the Basic Skills Initiative had extensively developed structures and tools for practitioner inquiry, which were intended to ensure that the inquiry process would be meaningful. In each case, our progress and the progress of system leaders in restructuring the policies and practices that were perpetuating institutional racism were "partial and halting" at best (Chase, Dowd, Pazich, & Bensimon, 2014). Thus these two cases are illustrative of the potential and limitations of inquiry as a driver of organizational and systemic change. They show that institutional racism is difficult to address on a system level absent a coordinated political process that will generate impetus for change from within and from outside colleges and universities. In each of these cases, inaction on the part of higher education system leaders perpetuated racial inequities that might have been addressed had there been greater political will.

The two cases in this chapter had transformative potential, but did not yield transformative changes at the system level. Justice as transformation calls on institutional change agents to inform the enactment of their ideals with knowledge of institutional and structural racism. As John Dewey (1933/1989) observed over 80 years ago, "To form relevant and effective ideals, we must first be acquainted with and take notice of actual conditions" (p. 97). The purpose of developing critical race consciousness is to engage in "deconstruction, reconstruction, and construction: deconstruction of oppressive structures and discourses, reconstruction of human agency, and construction of equitable and socially just relations of power" (Ladson-Billings, 2009, p. 19).

The systems and structures that require deconstruction and reconstruction are those that offer only "bare opportunities" to equal education, which Howe (1997) defines as opportunities that "hardly seem to count for anything," and that "hardly seem worth wanting" (p. 18). Where weaker standards of equity are content to provide bare opportunities to achieve equal educational outcomes, stronger standards demand "real opportunities" (p. 18). Students, families, and communities have real opportunities when they have sufficient information, capacity, and resources to make choices about how they will interact with the educational system. At the level of higher education, real opportunities can only exist when students receive adequate preparation in compulsory schooling. Real opportunities also require a "favorable context of choice" (p. 19) in which nondominant group members do not experience challenges to their sense of self-worth.

Opportunities to participate in "second chance" curricula for which one is not well prepared are bare opportunities, as are educational experiences that threaten one's sense of self-worth (Howe, 1997, p. 19). Postsecondary vocational education and basic skills education, the two forms of education that provide the case examples in this chapter, often take the form of bare opportunities.

OVERVIEW OF THE CHAPTER

This chapter is organized in three sections following this introduction. The first long section discusses the Wisconsin Transfer Equity Study and the next long section examines the California community colleges' Basic Skills Initiative (BSI). They present empirical analyses that we conducted, with the assistance of CUE researchers and doctoral students, during the time these initiatives were unfolding. Megan Chase and Loni Bordoloi Pazich were instrumental in collecting and analyzing data during the Wisconsin Transfer Equity Study (see also Chase et al., 2014). Laura Lord collaborated with us as a CUE staff member to generate the empirical results of our analysis of the BSI's "action plans." In the Wisconsin case, our methodology was participatory critical action research (Kemmis & McTaggart, 2000), and in the California case, it was document analysis (Althede, Coyle, DeVriese, & Schneider, 2008; Prior, 2008). In discussing the Wisconsin study, we draw on data and artifacts we collected or produced as we facilitated the inquiry process involving Wisconsin system leaders. In the case of California's BSI, where we were not integrally involved in the inquiry design or implementation, consistent with document analysis methods we interpreted public BSI documents as "actors in a web of activity" (Prior, 2008, p. 117).

Our purpose in conducting these analyses was to interject race-conscious discourse and data tools into the inquiry process at the heart of both initiatives. The transfer equity study was designed by us, and therefore racial equity was the explicit point of departure. It is less clear to us to what extent the architects of the Basic Skills Initiative (BSI) intended to make racial equity a central driving focus of the BSI. As we show below, the initiative had potential to enact transformative changes because of its substantial focus and investments in basic skills instruction, which disproportionately enrolls students of color. In a variety of supporting roles to the BSI over the course of several years, such as advisory group members, invited panelists or presenters at task force or working group meetings, workshop facilitators, and data coaches, we observed an ebb and flow of attention to racial equity issues in BSI activities and documents.

Taking stock of our results, which highlight the limitations of practitioner inquiry to bring about more equitable educational policies, we conclude with a brief section emphasizing the importance of adopting a critical consciousness during policy design and implementation. Seemingly apolitical, color-blind approaches to educational reform will not produce the deeper understandings of institutional racism that will be required to pursue justice as transformation.

THE WISCONSIN TRANSFER EQUITY STUDY

We conducted the Wisconsin Transfer Equity Study with leaders of the University of Wisconsin (UW) and Wisconsin Technical College System (WTCS) from 2008 to 2010. The Transfer Equity Study followed several years of Equity Scorecard work at the UW campuses. As described in Chapter 4, the UW system (UWS) office had provided coordination and leadership for the implementation of the Equity Scorecard in the 13 associate's degree–granting UW Colleges and the 19 bachelor's degree–granting UW universities in three "waves" of participating institutions from 2005 to 2012.

As a result of organizing available enrollment and transfer data and viewing it in the Vital Signs of the Equity Scorecard, there was a growing awareness and concern among educational leaders in Wisconsin about the lack of transfer pathways for African Americans and Latinos in the Wisconsin system. During the same period, other initiatives in Wisconsin were also calling attention to the need to expand and improve transfer pathways. For example, in 2004 the Committee on Baccalaureate Expansion (COBE), a joint WTCS and UW committee, had identified the technical colleges as an important source of working adults and students of color who could and should be tapped to increase the number of baccalaureate degree holders in the state of Wisconsin (Pruitt & Smith, 2005).

The Action Research and Inquiry Process

To address issues of transfer access and equity highlighted by the Equity Scorecard, from fall 2008 to fall 2010 we convened a team of system-level administrators from the UWS and WTCS to review, discuss, and reflect on ways to change Wisconsin's transfer policies and practices to enable more students of color to transfer. In bringing together a system-level evidence team whose members held leadership positions such as provost, vice president, institutional researcher, dean, and transfer services director, we were expanding the action research focus from local practices and institutional actors to the system level. While the UW leaders knew us and CUE's practitioner inquiry model from the previous Equity Scorecard work, the WTCS leaders were new participants.

We designed a number of inquiry tools for the Wisconsin Transfer Equity Study system-level team to engage in an action research "cycle of inquiry" (Cochran-Smith & Lytle, 2009; Kemmis & McTaggart, 2005; Reason,

1994). The objective was to involve the system-level evidence team members in seeing, reflecting on, and discussing the state's transfer data in new ways. As action researchers, we designed tools and activity settings for the social construction of knowledge, such as a transfer policy and practices survey and a multistate policy scan; protocols for reflective dialogue; data tools for problem identification in race-conscious ways; problem-solving ideas generated through comparison with practices in other states; and project design features that could be incorporated over time as organizational learning features by our Wisconsin partners.

The UW and WTCS system leaders were convened as a system-level evidence team. They engaged in the practitioner inquiry process in a number of ways tailored to the fact that their schedules were even more constrained than campus-level practitioners. We devoted more of our own staff resources to data collection and analysis, in order to present more "boiled-down" findings for discussion and reflection among the system evidence team members. Although the system evidence team did not collect data and draft reports of their inquiry findings the way campus inquiry teams do, we retained the fundamental self-assessment and knowledge-producing characteristics of practitioner inquiry by involving the team members in review and dialogue about existing data, data collection instruments, and results at each step of the study. Evidence team members participated in planning and goal-setting meetings; reviewed and discussed numerical and qualitative data; reviewed and modified data collection protocols we created to collect new data; reviewed policies and policy documents; developed recommendations; and communicated with colleagues and the UW Board about the project, its findings, and its recommendations. This interactive process of data use enabled us to draw out the insider perspectives that are central to action research methodologies, produce trustworthy interpretations, and involve our UW and WTCS partners in the knowledge construction process.

Planning Process. Our first step in getting the project under way was to hold a 2-day planning meeting at CUE's offices in Los Angeles with UW leaders. The agenda included practical concerns such as scheduling, staffing, and clear specification of project goals. We also devoted a block of time to a "hopes and fears" exercise, in which we discussed what we each hoped would come of the study and the potential pitfalls that might undermine its success. These "fears" ranged from the practical (e.g., lack of time) to the political (e.g., crafting clear PR messages). We did not want the project to unfold as a series of steps divorced from the praxis of equity work. We also understood that asking educational leaders to engage in transformative change posed political risks; the early reflective dialogue was intended to raise attention to these risks among all the participants.

The planning meeting was followed by a day-long evidence team meeting in Wisconsin, where the UW leaders were for the first time joined by WTCS leaders. The meeting started with time for discussion to acknowledge that the success of the study would depend on the willingness of the group to interact in new ways that were outside the norms of the existing organizational routines. The UW and WTCS are independent systems, with their own missions, funding sources, and organizational cultures. We made sure to begin with an opening segment that involved dialogue in order to maximize our prospects of building a trusting relationship with the new participants.

Subsequent to the initial planning process, it became evident that the project would benefit from a complementary inquiry process at the campus level. In spring 2010, evidence teams of faculty and staff at two of the UW universities, one of the UW Colleges associate's degree–granting colleges, and two of the WTCS technical colleges were convened. The role of these campus representatives was to provide a campus-level perspective on transfer issues and to identify choke points or barriers in the transfer pathway within or between institutions. The campus evidence teams also conducted inquiry into student progress through developmental education and more advanced courses on their campuses to understand student experiences navigating transfer pathways. One of the campus teams used CUE's Equity-Minded Syllabus Review Protocol (discussed in Chapter 3) to review syllabi for developmental education classes.

System Structure. At the first planning meeting in Wisconsin we also reviewed the existing academic structures and policies that governed opportunities for students in the UW 2-year colleges and in the technical colleges to transfer to bachelor's degree–granting institutions. Wisconsin is unusual relative to other states in that it has two separate systems of associate's degree–granting colleges, each with its own governance structures and funding streams. The WTCS is a much larger system than the 2-year UW Colleges. There are only a few more WTCS colleges (16 compared with 13 UW Colleges), but reflecting the location of many WTCS campuses in urban areas, the WTCS enrollment is roughly 30 times larger. At the time of our study, there were about 400,000 students enrolled in the WTCS compared with less than 12,500 in the UW Colleges in 2006–2007 (WTC System Administration, 2014; UW Office of Policy Analysis and Research, 2014).

The mission of the WTCS does not include transfer. The system was founded in 1911 (Wisconsin Technical College System, 2010), and its focus remains squarely on the mission established at the time of its founding: vocational and technical education. The technical colleges in Wisconsin have statutory authority to grant applied associate degrees and certificates earned through programs with a technical and occupational focus. The curricula for these applied programs include general education courses and technical courses.

Typically, only the credits earned in the general education courses, but not in the technical courses, are eligible for transfer toward a bachelor's degree awarded by the University of Wisconsin. Therefore, students who transfer with an applied associate's degree must make up extra credits once they are enrolled at a UW university. Graduates of the WTCS who hold applied associate's degrees may transfer to private universities in or out of state through any one of the numerous institution-to-institution or program-to-program articulation agreements that were in place. Many of these agreements allowed students to transfer credits earned in both general education and technical courses.

In an effort to broaden transfer access from the technical college system to the UW system that had been brokered prior to the Transfer Equity Study, 5 of the 16 technical colleges (Madison Area, Milwaukee Area, Nicolet Area, Chippewa Valley, and Western) were permitted to offer a transfer-oriented liberal arts curriculum awarding an associate of art or science degree. Only about 5% of WTCS students were enrolled in these new programs, compared with almost 30% in the applied associate's degree programs (Wisconsin Technical College System, 2014), which were still clearly the core of the WTCS degree programs. A further 10% of students were enrolled in technical diploma programs. Other students were taking basic skills courses or involved in community service programs that did not count for credits toward degrees or diplomas.

African American, Latino, and Southeast Asian students were more likely to be enrolled in basic skills courses, making it more difficult for them to accumulate the number of college-level credits necessary to transfer. In fall 2007 the proportion of new 1st-year White students at the UW 2-year colleges needing English or math remediation was 40%. The corresponding percentages were 60% of African American students, 47% of Hispanic/Latino students, and 54% of American Indian students (UW Office of Policy Analysis and Research, 2008a).

In addition to detailing these academic structures and transfer requirements, at the initial planning meeting with the system leaders we reviewed existing structures to provide students with information about how to earn the credits necessary to transfer. At the time of our study, these included a formal position within the UW system known as the "transfer advocate"; an online Transfer Information System (TIS); and documentation about the numerous articulation agreements, each with its own particular requirements.

Lack of Transfer Accountability Data. Given that the inquiry process of the Transfer Equity Study would rely on data about transfer, our early discussion with the system evidence team raised issues of transfer data availability and quality. The UW Equity Scorecards, which had included transfer Vital Signs, provided a knowledge base going into the study. However, it became clear through preliminary discussion and document review that transfer accountability data were lacking.

For example, the UW system had an annual accountability report summarizing system performance on a number of accountability metrics. At the start of the Transfer Equity Study, transfer was only marginally included in the accountability report. A hyperlink in a "More to Know" section of the main report directed readers to a bureaucratic, informational memorandum with transfer regulations, but otherwise did not systematically report on the number of students transferring or transfer rates. WTCS annually conducted a survey of employment outcomes among its graduates, but the survey did not include any items that would gather data to indicate that a student had transferred to a bachelor's degree–granting institution. Disaggregated data or indicators that would reveal the status of transfer access for students of color were scattered among various informational memoranda and data reports published by UWS and WTCS. No one report focused on transfer access as an equity or diversity issue or on transfer as a structure that could be actively strengthened to increase diversity on bachelor's degree–granting campuses.

New Data Collections and Displays. The lack of accountability data or reports on transfer led us to develop new data displays from information available in a variety of reports and to collect new data. Drawing on campus-by-campus information about the numbers of students who transferred to each of the UW universities, we created a series of maps to gauge the robustness and geographic location of transfer pathways. These "transfer maps" were Wisconsin state maps showing the location of the college and university campuses superimposed with lines and numerals graphing the number of students utilizing each pathway for vertical transfer. Two sets of maps documented the number of White students and the number of students of color moving from one of the technical colleges or a UW associate's degree–granting college to a UW university. These maps could be read similar to reading an airline route map with the number of miles or approximate travel time between cities in an airline's service network.

We conducted or facilitated several other types of data collection, including a survey of administrators with responsibility for transfer services, a document analysis or "scan" of accountability policy documents (in Wisconsin and in six other states), student cohort progression analyses, and syllabus review. In conducting the survey, we were particularly interested to learn more about the responsibilities of the transfer advocate, a position that would seem to hold important implications for the equitable implementation of transfer policy. The system evidence team was uncertain to what extent the transfer advocate functioned to improve transfer access for students of color.

Action Research Findings

Mapping Inequitable Transfer Pathways. Based on their formal positions and job responsibilities, the UW and WTCS system leaders were the most knowledgeable group of people we could have convened to examine transfer access in Wisconsin. Nevertheless, the data gathering and analysis we did together through the Wisconsin Transfer Equity Study proved fruitful for "sensemaking" about transfer access and equity issues, as we introduced new "logics" of data use (Little, 2012; Spillane, 2012), offering new perspectives on what might count as accountability data.

The transfer maps displayed the "spatial inequalities" (Metcalf, 2009) of transfer access to university degrees in the Wisconsin public higher education system. It was already known that the dual associate's degree–granting system was a largely segregated system. The transfer maps made it easy to see that this segregation carried over to transfer access. This is not surprising, but because transfer is often viewed as one of the most equity-enhancing features of the higher education system—providing students with a second chance to enroll at a university and earn a bachelor's degree—it was sobering to see the extent of the "separate and unequal" systems. The "geography of access" (Metcalfe, 2009) was racialized; the placement of college campuses with different missions and degree-granting capacities severely limited transfer access for students of color. Equally, the maps highlighted that White students were privileged in transfer access by the existence and geographic dispersion of the UW Colleges.

Most of the 2-year UW Colleges are small, rural institutions serving a predominantly White student body. The ratio of students of color (including African Americans, Hispanics, and Native Americans) pursuing associate's degree, diploma, or basic skills coursework at the technical colleges in comparison to students of color at the UW Colleges is about 50 to 1 (University of Wisconsin Office of Policy Analysis and Research, 2012; Wisconsin Technical College System, 2012). African Americans and Hispanic students are overrepresented in the technical colleges when compared to the 2-year UW Colleges (UWC) and the UW 4-year institutions, whereas White students are overrepresented in the UWC and UW 4-year institutions. For example, African Americans represent 12.4% (26,045) of the student body at the WTCS, but only 1.6% (216) of the total UWC population and 3.4% (5,294) of the total UW 4-year institution population (UW Office of Policy Analysis and Research, 2012; Wisconsin Technical College System, 2012).

Students of color predominantly enroll in the technical colleges in the southeast corner of Wisconsin: the Milwaukee Area Technical College, Madison Area Technical College, and Gateway Technical College. As noted above, students of color are 12% of the WTCS student body; in contrast, students of color are 25% of the Milwaukee Area Technical College student body (data based on average enrollment from 1999–2007; WTC System Administration, 2008). These enrollment patterns follow from the residential patterns in the state; the majority of African Americans and Latinos live in the southeastern urban area.

Transfer from the Technical Colleges. The transfer maps highlighted that the relatively small number of students, nearly all White, enrolled in the 2-year UW Colleges had more numerous transfer pathways available to them than the Black and Latino students enrolled in the technical colleges. The two transfer maps in Figures 5.1 and 5.2 show the numbers of African Americans, Hispanics, American Indians, and Southeast Asian students who transferred (Figure 5.1) and the number of White students who transferred (Figure 5.2) from the Milwaukee Area Technical College (MATC) to any UW university. We have featured the transfer map for MATC here because MATC had the largest number of transfer students who were students of color. (The complete set of transfer maps is available on the Center for Urban Education website at http://cue.usc.edu/projects/wi/transfer_maps. html.) The lines on the maps represent "transfer pathways," with different lines indicating the number of students in the increments noted on the legend.

Figure 5.1 shows that there were five receiving universities that provided transfer pathways for MATC students of color in 2008. UW–Milwaukee received most of these transfers: 45 African Americans, 11 Hispanic/Latino students, 1 American Indian, 3 Southeast Asians, and 5 students categorized as other Asian. The other four institutions acting as receiving institutions for technical college students of color were UW–Parkside, UW–Whitewater, UW–Oshkosh, and UW–Stout, but none of them received more than 6 students of color. With the exception of the 11 Hispanic students who transferred to UW–Milwaukee, no UW campus received more than 1 Hispanic transfer student.

Taking a longer-term view shows that the data in the map, from fall 2008, were not unusual. In the period from 1999 to 2007, the average number of African American students who transferred annually from MATC was 41, compared to an average number of 213 White students transferring

Figure 5.1. Transfer Pathways of Students of Color

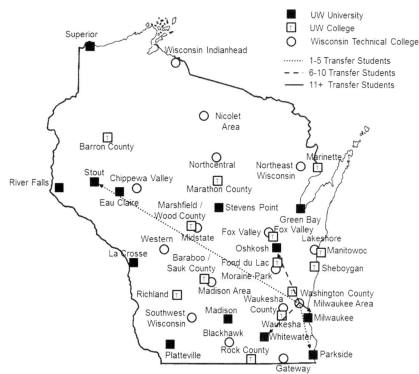

Source: University of Wisconsin, Office of Policy Analysis and Research (2008b)
Notes: Transfer students to Milwaukee 45 African American, 11 Hispanic/Latino, 5 Other
Asian, 3 Southeast Asian, 1 American Indian; Oshkosh 4 African American, 1 American
Indian, 1 Southeast Asian; Parkside 1 African American, 1 Hispanic/Latino; Stout 1 African
American, 1 Hispanic/Latino; Whitewater 2 African American, 2 American Indian, 1
Hispanic/Latino, 1 Other Asian

annually (based on number of transfers between 1998 and 2007; UW Office of Policy Analysis and Research, 2008b). To put these small numbers
of transfer students of color in perspective, it is important to realize that at
that time MATC enrolled about 13,000 African American students, a number greater than all of the students enrolled at the UW campuses combined.
Clearly, the higher education system was not well structured to serve the
bachelor's degree aspirations of students of color in the Milwaukee area.

A comparison of Figures 5.1 and 5.2 shows that transfer pathways were
far more numerous for White students at MATC. In addition to the transfer
pathways utilized by students of color, at least one White student transferred

Figure 5.2. Transfer Pathways of White Students

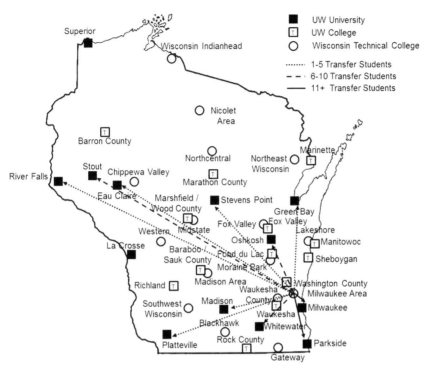

Source: University of Wisconsin, Office of Policy Analysis and Research (2008b)
Notes: White transfer students to Eau Claire 2; Green Bay 3; Madison 1; Milwaukee 120; Oshkosh 7; Parkside 13; Platteville 1; River Falls 1; Stevens Point 3; Stout 10; Whitewater 8

from MATC to UW–Madison, UW–Eau Claire, UW–River Falls, UW–Platteville, UW–Stevens Point, and UW–Green Bay. In each transfer pathway that existed for White students and students of color, fewer students of color transferred than their White peers. For example, 13 White students transferred from MATC to UW–Parkside, but only one African American student and one Hispanic student transferred to the same institution.

Transfer from the UW Colleges. Consistent with overall enrollment, we expected the number of transfer students of color from the 2-year UW Colleges to be small, and this proved to be the case. From 1998 to 2007, the sum total of the number of African American students who transferred from each of the UW Colleges to the UW universities fell in the range of 0 to 23. (The sum of the annual number of transfers was calculated over 10 years because for many years at many colleges the value was 0.) Reflecting the predominantly White population in rural and suburban areas of the state, 8 out of 13 UW Colleges transferred a total of 5 or fewer African American students over the course of the 9-year time period (UW Office of Policy Analysis and Research, 2008b). The number of Hispanic, American Indian, and Southeast Asian transfer students was similarly low, averaging 25, 10, and 21 students respectively for all 13 of the UW Colleges. This compared with an average of 1,589 White students transferring in the same period.

In sum, 92% of the transfers from the UW Colleges to the UW universities were White. Three percent of UWC transfer students were American Indian, 2% were classified as Hispanic/Latino, and 1% or less were African American or of Asian descent. Clearly, the UW Colleges were not positioned to compensate for the lack of transfer access from technical colleges to provide equitable transfer pathways for students of color in Wisconsin's public higher education system.

Relative to urban Black and Latino students, rural White students had much more viable pathways to bachelor's degrees through transfer from the UW 2-year colleges. The UW Colleges serve as the designated transfer pathway to bachelor's degrees at the state's public universities, but an even smaller number of students of color were transferring from the UW Colleges than from the technical colleges. Transfer pathways from the technical colleges to 4-year institutions in the UW system were extremely narrow, and in some cases nonexistent.

Policy Road Blocks. In addition to the fact that rural students had much greater access to transfer pathways than urban students, the policy scan that we conducted highlighted a number of barriers to technical college transfer that disadvantaged technical college students. The UW system had a set of Transfer Principles of Accommodations that established policies for students at 2-year colleges in Wisconsin to enroll at the 4-year universities. The principles made it easier for students from within the state to transfer to the UW universities. Prior to the adoption of the principles of accommodation, continuing university students were given priority in course enrollment over transfer students. After the change of principles, transfers from the UW Colleges were treated as "on a par" with continuing students (Chase et al., 2014).

At the beginning of our study this recognition was withheld from transfers from the technical colleges, who were not included in the Transfer Principles of Accommodations. Similarly, under the principles of accommodations, transfers from the 2-year UW Colleges are not charged an application transfer fee, but this fee waiver was not available to technical college students. Though the fee is fairly minimal ($44 in 2009), the amount might still be enough to dissuade a student from applying if it were not a simple matter for them to write a check; additionally, waiving of the fee can be seen as an unfair incentive.

Through the inquiry process of the Transfer Equity Study, with its focus on racial equity, one transfer policy change was enacted in 2010. The accommodation available to transfers from the UW Colleges that treated them on a par in access to course enrollment with continuing students was extended to WTCS transfers (Chase et al., 2014). However, the transfer application fee waiver was not similarly extended, despite the fact that a fee waiver exemption for WTCS students was discussed, endorsed, and recommended by the system evidence team to the UW Board. The fee waiver was ultimately opposed by the UW College system leaders and defeated.

This policy defeat was extremely disappointing to us because the system leader who opposed the change had repeatedly articulated and in many ways enacted a strong commitment to racial equity. The inquiry process, although conducted in a coordinated manner and involving all the relevant system leaders, was only strong enough to bring about "partial and halting" changes (Chase et al., 2014), including changes in monitoring transfer access that may provide leverage for policy changes in the future.

Two new accountability indicators were adopted. The first reports the number and percentage of students who transferred to UW universities from sending colleges (including the UW Colleges and WTCS colleges) by institutional type. The second disaggregates the composition of transfer students by race and ethnicity. Previously, the accountability report had only included indicators of students' success after transfer, providing no information about the larger pool of students at UWC and WTCS institutions who may have been eligible for transfer and no information on racial equity in access. Such disaggregated data are essential for keeping the conversation going about racial equity issues. Unfortunately, despite the fact that the transfer maps had illustrated the racial inequities in transfer pathways, the new indicators did not enable tracking of transfer by race and ethnicity from each of the sending institutions.

The differences in treatment of students from the UW Colleges and the WTCS highlighted the fact that the systems were quite separate, that the separateness of the systems disadvantaged potential transfers from the technical colleges, and that current policies were structured to privilege UWC transfer students over WTCS transfer students. There were clearly historical and political dimensions to this policy—for example, embedded separateness—as leaders of the WTCS, the UW Colleges, and the UW universities all had vested interests in keeping the status quo.

The UW Colleges were defined by their transfer mission and their status within the UW system. Unlike the technical college, the associate's degree–granting UW Colleges were not separate institutions; they were part of the UW system and were expressly charged with providing the first 2 years of baccalaureate education to students who were in rural areas not in close proximity of a 4-year campus or were not ready, able, or interested in enrolling directly in the UW universities. WTCS leaders were committed to their original mission of vocational and occupational education, for which they were funded and governed independently of the UW through local communities and boards. From the start of the project it became clear that increasing transfers was not an aspirational goal of the WTCS leaders; in fact, creating enhanced transfer pathways was viewed by WTCS leaders as antagonistic to their mission. With the historical differences in status between technical colleges and universities still palpable, WTCS leaders hold greater status and authority in the domain of technical education. Being the lower tier of a transfer system does not convey much glory. And, finally, as in other states, the associate's degree–granting institutions shielded the UW universities from enrolling any additional students who would require developmental education before completing degree-credit coursework. No strong incentives, aside from racial equity considerations, existed to dislodge these interests.

Ultimately, the system leaders, acting on behalf of their colleges and universities, were stymied when it came to making larger structural changes. Despite their positive track record and the impressive momentum of equity work in the UW system, the system-level evidence team, like the faculty members in Chapter 3, "hit a wall" when they moved to take the next step, to implement policy changes based on what they had learned through the inquiry process. To some extent, the inaction reflected political changes in the state, which shifted during this period from Democratic to Republican control of state governance. However, in large part, the inaction stemmed from conflicting interests among the participating leaders, who sought to protect the interests of their institutions.

Institutional Racism

Such conflict in the form of "turf wars" is not unusual. Administrative leaders represent and are charged to ensure the fiduciary sustainability of their institutions. The outcome of policy stasis was particularly problematic in this case because the inequities in transfer access to bachelor's degrees fell so heavily on African American and Latino students in Milwaukee and other population centers of the state's urbanized southeastern corridor. The "partial and halting" nature of transfer policy changes in Wisconsin to address racialized inequities in transfer (Chase et al., 2014) illustrate the challenge of coordinating change in an environment of political tension, demographic

change, and greater political pressures on colleges and universities to produce more certificate and degree holders, and to do so more efficiently, operating under a "do more with less" expectation.

For us, the transfer maps provided a simple and clear depiction that
Wisconsin had two associate's degree–granting systems, yet neither provided a real opportunity within its public postsecondary system for students
of color to earn a degree through transfer. The WTCS students had only a
bare opportunity to transfer to pursue a bachelor's degree, and many were
mired in basic skills courses that hampered their opportunities even to earn
vocational certificates. While students and families are at liberty to choose
vocational education—and it is important to note that many programs yield
high returns for individuals as well as positive social benefits—the racialized
pattern of access to different types of educational opportunities in the Wisconsin public system represented racial inequities. As Howe (1997) argued
in regard to the tracking of poor students into vocational education at the
secondary level, "the mere fact that an individual affirms a choice does not
mean the freedom and opportunities worth wanting exist" (p. 22).

The lack of transfer opportunity for students of color could be traced,
in part, to the fact that the UW Colleges are primarily located outside the
southeastern urban corridor of the state, where the majority of African
Americans and Latinos live. Once we focused on the racialized nature of the
geographic placement of the colleges, the racial disparities in transfer access
could not be viewed in an ahistorical manner. The placement of the colleges
was not ahistorical; the creation of the dual system was situated in histories of housing discrimination, enforced segregation, and racial discrimination in education, where the placement of colleges of different institutional
types was a primary policy tool for creating separate and unequal systems
(Metcalf, 2009; Minor, 2008; Olivas, 2005b). The legacy of racist views
assigning African American, Latino, and Native American students to "the
manual arts," "voc-ed," and "tech prep" lived on within the postsecondary
system.

The racial segregation of transfer access in Wisconsin in two "separate
and unequal systems" struck us forcefully as an example of institutional racism. Structural and institutional models of racism stress that racism occurs
due to the "deeply entrenched material inequalities and the inertial tenden-
cies of privilege and disadvantage even absent prejudiced actors" (Haney-
López, 2010, p. 824). No single individual needed to act on explicitly racist
views for the racial marginalization and exclusion that were part and parcel
of the system to be perpetuated. Educational systems institutionalize "systemic inclusion" and "systemic exclusion" unless someone acts to change
existing systems (Howe, 1997, p. 71).

THE PROBLEM OF BASIC SKILLS EDUCATION

For decades it has been clear that workable strategies to improve institutional effectiveness in producing student success in basic skills courses are critically needed, both in California and across the United States (Bahr, 2010; Bettinger & Long, 2007; Grubb et al., 2011; Jenkins & Boswell, 2002; Kirst, 2007; Merisotis & Phipps, 2000). With 72 districts and 112 colleges and an annual enrollment of more than 2.5 million students, approximately one of every five community college students in the United States are enrolled in California Community Colleges (CCC). Some estimates indicate that as high as 90% of incoming CCC students are not prepared to succeed in degree-credit courses and require basic skills coursework to earn a college degree (Hill, 2008). This compares with the 40% of all students nationally in both 2- and 4-year institutions who enroll in at least one remedial course (Adelman, 2005). At the time we conducted our study of the Basic Skills Initiative, remedial education placement rates were very high. Approximately three-quarters of California community college students who took assessment tests in 2006–2007 were assessed as requiring basic skills coursework (Fulks & Alancraig, 2008). Estimates indicated that somewhere between 1.8 million and 2.2 million California community college students were "basic skills" students. A much smaller number, in the range of 400,000 to 800,000, were *not* basic skills students.

The problem of basic skills in California is also fundamentally a "Latino problem," not only because it is a problem facing Latino students—who in comparison to other racial/ethnic groups disproportionately attend community colleges and are disproportionately placed in basic skills and English as a Second Language (ESL) classes (Board of Governors of the California Community Colleges, 2008)—but also because the existence of such a large number of undereducated young adults in one state is emblematic of a collapsing commitment to public education. Data current at the time of our study indicated that Latino students represented 41% of the credit-bearing basic skills and ESL enrollment and 43% of the noncredit courses in those areas. In comparison, White students were 23% of the credit and 19% of the noncredit basic skills and ESL enrollments.

Basic skills classrooms have been characterized as having a "revolving door" because students enroll and leave so quickly and continuously (Grubb & Gabriner, 2013). The statewide average rate of course completion is approximately 60%. However, the curriculum sequence is lengthy (consisting of three or more courses), which makes the prospects of moving into the degree-credit curriculum quite slim. In some colleges with a particularly high need for basic skills instruction, 80% to 90% of entering students begin in non-degree-credit courses and fewer than 1 in 10 ever successfully complete an associate's degree or transfer-level course (Hill, 2008).

Such a large proportion of Latino students are placed in basic skills courses on entering the California community colleges and so few are successful in navigating the lengthy basic skills curriculum to the first college degree–credit courses that the issue of basic skills education in California postsecondary education is emerging as an issue of fundamental civil rights. The high need for basic skills instruction at the college level is a failure of the educational system as a whole. The loss of potential college graduates represents a tremendous loss of human potential in a state where Latinos will make up 50% of the state's working-age population by the year 2030 (Moore & Shulock, 2005). Without significant improvements in basic skills education, degree completion among Latinos will inevitably continue to lag behind that of their White and Asian counterparts.

The Development of the Basic Skills Initiative

The California Community Colleges' Basic Skills Initiative was a multi-million-dollar effort to improve the quality of basic skills education (also known as remedial and developmental education) in the state's community colleges. As a major statewide accountability initiative, the BSI, which began in 2006 (Hill, 2008), was unusual in that it emphasized practitioner inquiry as the cornerstone for bringing about improvements in institutional performance. It was instituted after a strategic planning process identified "student success and readiness" in basic skills as a systemwide priority. The momentum for the initiative peaked in 2011, as indicated by a declining budget allocation and growing attention to new policy initiatives since then.

The BSI is a valuable case study for examining strategies for accountability in higher education because it represents a high point in system-level reliance on practitioner inquiry as a driver of broad-scale change. The BSI placed faith in practitioners to address problems of educational practice, in this case the intractable problem of educating adults who enter community colleges without the foundational knowledge and skills to complete college degree coursework. With 110 colleges receiving $148 million in funding between 2006 and 2013, the BSI represents a major investment by a state system of higher education in practitioner inquiry.

The Basic Skills Initiative was funded by the California State Legislature and developed by a large number of different participants. These included the California Community College Academic Senate; the RP Group, a steering group of institutional researchers from the nonprofit Research and Planning Group for California Community Colleges; the California Community Colleges' Success Network (3CSN), a professional development network of community college faculty and administrators that was created with BSI funding; and program developers and researchers who received funding from the William and Flora Hewlett Foundation. (For a summary of the early development of the BSI, see Academic Senate for California Community Colleges, 2007.) An advisory group was convened to inform the development of the initiative by the California Community College Chancellor's Office (CCCCO). Estela Bensimon served on this advisory group on a subcommittee referred to as the Student Readiness and Success Action Group.

Benchmarking Effective Practices. The BSI's inquiry design was notable in its comprehensiveness as well as its ambitious scope. After a 1-year pilot project, all of the 112 colleges in the system (at that time) were required, in order to receive their BSI funding, to document a prescribed inquiry process focused on the effectiveness of basic skills programs and practices on their campus. Numerous structures and tools were created to guide the inquiry process. Many colleges created BSI committees to respond to the accountability mandate, and the state provided funds for Basic Skills Coordinators to lead the work of the initiative on the college campuses.

A primary resource was a three-part report titled *Basic Skills as a Foundation for Student Success in California Community Colleges* (hereafter called the *Basic Skills* report; RP Group, 2007), which was commissioned by the statewide Academic Senate and written by a team of institutional researchers, community college faculty members, and administrators affiliated with the RP Group's Center for Student Success. Part I of the report presented a literature review of effective practices in basic skills education ("Review of Literature & Effective Practices"). The review highlighted models and strategies for improving basic skills instruction and support services. Part II, "Assessment Tool for Effective Practices in Basic Skills," provided an inquiry protocol for the colleges to conduct a self-assessment of their developmental education programs. The self-assessment process culminated in the completion of an action planning matrix to improve developmental education programs, pedagogy, and administration. Part III, "A Tool to Estimate Costs and Downstream Revenue," provided a cost-benefit analysis tool for comparative review of developmental education program models.

The literature review, self-assessment tool, and action planning matrices created by the RP Group for the *Basic Skills* report served as a blueprint for the templates the CCCCO required the colleges to complete in order to receive their BSI funds. The CCCCO required the colleges to submit an action plan for improving basic skills education at their college, and this action plan was to be developed through the college's use of the self-assessment tool.

As explained in the documents, the purpose of the self-assessment tool was to encourage practitioner reflection and inquiry based on "evidence." The introduction to the self-assessment tool explains that its purpose is to help teams of college practitioners "to reflect" on their current practices and consider how their "current practices" compare with the effective practices documented in the review of the literature (RP Group, 2007, p. 98). In this respect, with its emphasis on comparison of local practices with effective practices identified in the research literature, the underlying change strategy of the BSI was similar to other national initiatives, such as the What Works Clearinghouse (What Works Clearinghouse, 2006). The logic model is one of diagnostic and peer benchmarking, where practices proven to be effective in one setting are held up for replication in other settings (Barak & Kniker, 2002; Bender & Schuh, 2002; Dowd & Tong, 2007). Effective practices were defined in the *Basic Skills* literature review as "organizational, administrative, instructional, or support activities engaged in by highly successful programs, as validated by research and literature sources relating to developmental education" (RP Group, 2007, p. 13). The campus practitioners who were to participate in the self-assessment process were "strongly" recommended to invest time and effort to become familiar with the indicators of effective practices before attempting to complete the self-assessment and to "frequently consult" the literature review during the self-assessment process (RP Group, 2007, p. 99).

Yet, in a pairing of benchmarking and inquiry principles, that knowledge was to be generated through a team approach to organizational change in a process relying on reflection and planning. The BSI documents instructed the colleges to create cross-functional practitioner teams charged with leading a collaborative review of their own campus practices. After studying the literature review and completing the self-assessment matrix, the college teams were expected to "reflect in more detail" on the effective practices that they had identified for use or in use at their own college. This reflection phase was guided by prompts and questions, which signaled the importance of identifying barriers to effective practice and fixing them. Guiding questions posed in the *Basic Skills* report include, for example, "What barriers/limitations exist to implementing or enhancing this practice?" "What would be required to remove or substantially decrease the barrier?" During action planning, the colleges were instructed to indicate the "specific problem(s) the action is expected to remedy," and ask, "What will it fix and how will it work? What sorts of results are expected? What evidence can be used to verify results?" (2007, p. 100).

Color-Blind Inquiry Tools. The self-assessment tool of the *Basic Skills* report was the main instrument for organizing the inquiry process in the colleges. The report included a series of diagnostic indicators of effective practices based on the literature review, which included a listing of 26 overarching best practices. These were broken down into 107 strategies of effective educational practice and arrayed in the self-assessment matrix. The literature review and the self-assessment tool were both organized into four areas (A–D): A. Organizational and Administrative Practices, B. Program Components, C. Staff Development, and D. Instructional Practices. Each area had multiple subcomponents; for example, Section A, Organizational and Administrative Practices, included seven effective practices (labeled A.1–A.7). These were further delineated by specific actions that could be taken to put those practices into effect.

Despite the large number of Latino students in basic skills classrooms and the disproportionate impact of the problem of basic skills education on Latino students, however, the literature review and inquiry tools of the BSI did not give special consideration to educating Latino students. While repeatedly referencing "ESL students" and "ESL programs," the *Basic Skills* report did not include a single effective practice for educating Latino adult students or bilingual learners. Only one indicator of effective practice on the self-assessment tool addressed bilingual education, doing so quite vaguely. Indicator D.2.3 referenced ESL and read, "Developmental courses/ programs implement effective curriculum and practices in ESL" (RP Group, 2007, p. 129).

A key word count in PDF versions of the *Basic Skills* documents confirmed our impression that the literature review and templates were essentially color-blind. The word *Hispanic* was used only once as a parenthetical example of the "traditionally underrepresented groups" that benefit from small-group instruction in developmental math classes (RP Group, 2007, p. 45). The words *Latina, Chicano, Chicana*, and *undocumented students* did not appear. The words *Mexican* and *Latino* each appeared only one or two times in reference to the Mexican American Legal Defense and Education Fund (MALDEF) and to model programs. Including references to the Latino-serving programs Puente and MESA, each of which were noted once, the total number of references to Hispanic/Latino students or communities was only six.

HSIs Without Hispanics. Noting the color blindness of the inquiry protocols, we were interested to know whether the campus action plans were also color-blind. Informed by an earlier study by Contreras, Malcom, and Bensimon (2008), where the findings showed that Hispanic Serving Institutions (HSIs) tend to hide (or "closet") their Hispanic identity, we were particularly interested to look at whether HSIs in the California community colleges were paying explicit attention to the "Hispanic" nature of their student body.

We conducted a document analysis of a subsample of the BSI action plans that had been filed with the CCCCO as part of BSI compliance reporting. We selected 25 colleges, located primarily in Southern California and the San Francisco Bay area, that had participated in seminars and workshops convened through CUE's California Benchmarking Project (Dowd, 2008). We chose these colleges because we had met with and had had the opportunity to share our ideas about inquiry and equity with practitioners from these colleges who had attended Benchmarking Project workshops and symposia. This familiarity with the campuses gave us a larger context for interpretation than would be provided by the documents alone. Among the 25 institutions in this subsample, 22 were HSIs, which means 25% or more of their enrolled full-time students were Hispanic. Together these HSIs had a head count in 2005–2006 of over 286,000 Latino students. This number accounted for almost 35% of the nearly 821,000 Latinos attending the California community colleges that year.

An analysis of a subsample of HSIs was also most likely to lead us to institutions that were utilizing the BSI inquiry process as an opportunity to improve institutional effectiveness in educating Latino students in basic skills classrooms. If California community colleges with an HSI designation were using the BSI as an opportunity to delve into the conditions of basic skills education for Latinos, this sample was likely to capture at least a few of them.

We searched on the words *Hispanic, Latina, Latino, Mexican, Chicano, Chicana*, and terms such as *minority, culturally diverse*, and *underrepresented* students that may have served as proxies for references to ethnicity. The results of this search demonstrated that the words *Hispanic, Latina, Spanish, Chicano, Chicana*, and *undocumented* were not mentioned in a single action plan of the 25 colleges. The term *Latino* was used only once. *"Race," "racial," "racial/ethnic," "ethnic,"* and *"ethnicity"* were not used in any of the plans, nor were the terms *minority, underrepresented,* or *underserved.*

References to programs that serve Latino students, such as Puente, MESA, and the Adelante scholarship program, were referenced only four times in total. *Students of color* were referred to by two colleges, each using the expression once. The words *equity* and *equitable* appeared in the plans of four colleges a total of eight times. The most common terms used by the colleges to refer to the racial and ethnic composition of their students were variants of the words *diverse* and *culture. Culture* was used to reference the concept of a culture of inquiry as well as "culturally responsive teaching."

In light of the designation of the majority of the colleges as HSIs, the absence of terms associated with Hispanic, Latino, and Chicano students and communities by these colleges was striking. Despite the appearance of the terms *diversity* and *culture*, with only a few exceptions, none of the documents particularize the concept of culture to observe and reflect on the Hispanic ethnicity of the student body or surrounding communities. Even those colleges that incorporated the concepts of culture and diversity into their action plans were largely silent on the racial/ethnic characteristics of their students and communities. These 25 colleges, the majority of which were

HSIs, had produced action plans to improve their basic skills educational programs without ever explicitly referencing Hispanics or Latinos. To us, this indicated that the BSI was proceeding in a color-blind manner. Guided by the documents of the *Basic Skills* report, they did not seek to observe, through the self-assessment process, the sociocultural context of the college community or the racial/ethnic experiences of the student body.

Implications of Color Blindness

The expression "ESL students" appears to have served as a stand-in for references to Latinos in the *Basic Skills* report and the college action plans. The veiled reference to Latinos in the references to ESL students did not allow for deeper engagement with the issues of bilingual learning and educational inequities imposed on Latino students. Does this matter? Why is it necessary for practitioners and their colleges to pay attention to the racial and ethnic backgrounds of their students? There are many reasons why it would have been much better for the action plans at HSIs to reference their Latino students with specificity.

A greater focus on bilingual learners in the BSI would have made a great deal of sense because learning is rooted in language. Although not every Latino student in community colleges is an English language learner or bilingual, the poor quality of bilingual education has a disparate impact on Latinos, because Spanish speakers make up approximately 85% of bilingual learners in California primary and secondary schools (Gándara & Contreras, 2009, p. 94). The state's electoral Proposition 227 (passed in 1998) effectively outlawed bilingual education in schools. Proposition 227 diminished efforts to develop pedagogies, curricula, and teacher education programs to teach bilingual learners effectively. The disproportionate enrollment of Latinos in basic skills classrooms in community colleges is directly related to the lack of capacity in California's public education system to educate Latino youngsters effectively. With the quality of bilingual education reduced by Proposition 227's insistence on a narrow range of educational techniques intended to move bilingual students quickly into English-only classrooms, many of those students who passed basic language proficiency tests are ill equipped for academic reading and writing at the college level (Gándara & Contreras, 2009).

Learning involves trying on new identities in ways compatible with existing identities (Nasir & Hand, 2006). This is true not only for youngsters and teens but for young adults and older adults as well. Acting as though college practitioners do not need to engage Latino identities pushes this important aspect of learning into the background of the educational enterprise, leaving students to negotiate their identity development on their own, independent of validation from persons in authority at the college. The academic social identity of students of color is likely to be influenced by both the choices they have available to them and the "constraints of [their] history of participation" (Nasir & Hand, 2006). Students from minoritized groups are constrained in taking on college student identities by the history of marginalization that prevented their parents and ancestors from attending schools and colleges.

To support Latino students' developing academic identities, faculty and administrators need facility in communicating with students about their lives and aspirations. We showed in Chapter 3 that well-intentioned faculty members acting from an ethic of care were, by their own appraisal, ill-equipped to engage students' racial and ethnic identifications. Their lack of expertise led them, at times, to express their intention to develop more caring pedagogical relationships in patronizing ways. An ethic of care uninformed by critical consciousness can impose social harm by taking expression as pity (Matias & Zembylas, 2014). For their professional development and growing pedagogical expertise, faculty must be able to guide authentic inquiry among their students and produce "generative knowledge" (Ball, 2009) through their interactions with them. This involves interacting with students' racial and ethnic heritage in expert ways.

Color blindness eliminates this important aspect of professional development. "Color-blind" inquiry is problematic because it constructs practitioner expertise in a manner that suggests expertise can be generalized as effective practices disconnected from students' communities, cultures, or lived experiences. On the contrary, expertise is developed through inquiry when practitioners "particularize" their practices for local settings and communities.

Respect cannot be communicated through control or condescension, and pedagogical relationships cannot be developed through generic teaching skills. Ladson-Billings (2009) makes a point concerning the education of African American students that is equally relevant to Latino students in basic skills classrooms:

> Current instructional strategies presume that African American students are deficient. As a consequence, classroom teachers are engaged in a never-ending quest for "the right strategy or technique" to deal with (read: *control*) "at risk" students. Cast in a language of failure, instructional approaches for African American students typically involve some aspect of remediation.
>
> This race neutral perspective purports to see deficiency as an individual phenomenon. Thus instruction is conceived as a generic set of teaching skills that should work for all students. When these strategies or skills fail to achieve desired results, the students, not the techniques, are found to be lacking. (pp. 29–30, emphasis added)

Similarly, Valenzuela (1999), focusing on the relationships of teachers with Mexican American students, argues that schools are engaged in "subtractive schooling" that attempts to bring minoritized students into line with the Anglo culture that dominates the curriculum and social practices of schools. "Rather than building on students' cultural, linguistic, and community-based knowledge," Valenzuela argues, schools "subtract these resources." The resulting "psychic and emotional withdrawal from schooling are symptomatic of students' rejection of subtractive schooling and a curriculum they perceive as uninteresting, irrelevant, and test-driven" (p. 62).

Ladson-Billings and Valenzuela were writing about compulsory school settings. The negative implications of cultural distance and subtractive educational practices have also been highlighted in the postsecondary literature (Harper & Hurtado, 2011; Hurtado et al., 2012; Museus & Quaye, 2009). The constructs of validation (Rendón, 1994; Rendón Linares & Muñoz, 2011), sense of belonging (Hurtado & Carter, 1997), intercultural effort (Dowd, Sawatzky, et al., 2011; Tanaka, 2002), institutional agents (Bensimon, 2007; Bensimon & Dowd, 2012; Bensimon, Dowd, Chase, et al., 2012; Museus & Neville, 2012; Stanton-Salazar, 2011; Teranishi & Briscoe, 2006), and empowerment agents (Dowd, Pak, & Bensimon, 2013; Stanton-Salazar, 2011) have emerged as analytical tools to understand and remediate the dynamics of subtractive schooling in colleges and universities.

The participatory ideal requires the principle of nonoppression to protect minoritized groups from further "cultural imperialism," which is "the imposition of the cultural meanings of the dominant group on all groups" (Howe, 1997, p. 70). Schools and colleges impose opportunity costs and social harm on students of color when they fail to represent their communities in the curriculum and ignore the histories of marginalization that produced and reproduce racial inequities (Dowd, Sawatzky, et al., 2011; Howe, 1997; Kleinman & Copp, 2009). Such neglect constitutes a form of "environmental racism" and creates toxic learning environments (Carter-Andrews & Tuitt, 2013). Educational settings that undermine students' sense of self-worth are "bare" opportunities (Howe, 1997, p. 28). To provide "real" opportunities, colleges must engage with the historical roots of minoritized students' ascribed identity and the students' own emerging academic identities.

Practitioners should adopt practices of affirmation and validation to create educational settings based on the participatory ideal. Faculty and administrators who use culturally responsive pedagogy and practices not only affirm diversity and student belonging, they engage students of color as critical thinkers whose learning can and should engage them as community change agents. Praxis is not ahistorical and placeless. Praxis involves a "critical understanding" of the existing social conditions and mobilization to "reconstruct the existing social arrangements and themselves" (Seo & Creed, 2002). The colleges' lack of engagement with the racial and ethnic dimensions of the problem of basic skills education in community colleges was a wasted opportunity for critically informed praxis.

The Limitations of Technicism in Educational Policy

Viesca (2013), studying technicism, racism, and "linguicism" (discrimination based on language) in Massachusetts state bilingual education policy, emphasized (drawing on Bonilla-Silva's phrase), "We live in a time of *racism without racists*," in which individuals with "colorblind perspectives view racial hierarchies as an irrelevant artifact from the past" (p. 2). She continued:

> They perpetuate a belief that racism is only manifested in individual acts of prejudice rather than as a widespread phenomenon that is historically grounded in cultural and institutional practices. Further, [those with] colorblind perspectives suggest that the best way to achieve equality is to act as if race does not exist at all. (p. 2)

Those who adopt *technicism* as an orientation to educational reform believe that teaching "can and should be reduced to 'best practices' that support the acquisition of ideologically-free discrete pieces of knowledge valued by those in dominant positions in society" (Viesca, 2013, p. 10). The color blindness of the inquiry tools and action plans of the BSI indicate that the authors of these public documents felt that it was better, in such documents, to "act as if race does not exist at all" (p. 2) and to implement educational reforms in a seemingly apolitical manner focused on the dissemination of best practices. In light of the opportunity to capture legislative support for significant investments in basic skills education, however, it appears that the omission of references to race and ethnicity was itself a political calculation. At the time of the BSI, voters in California had already expressed their displeasure with race-based educational policies by passing ballot initiatives banning affirmative action (Proposition 209) and severely curtailing the provision of bilingual education and dual-language immersion programs (Proposition 227).

In her analysis of Massachusetts' state policy restricting the access of primary and secondary school students to bilingual education and dual-language immersion programs, Viesca (2013) emphasizes the ideological underpinnings of the English-language instruction ballot initiatives in

Massachusetts, California, and Washington, which were all animated by racist, anti-immigrant sentiments. Viesca demonstrates how linguicism, or language-based discrimination, and "technicism" go hand in hand.

Those who adopt the ideology of technicism take the perspective that "teaching and learning are not political endeavors" (Viesca, 2013, p. 10). Yet the advocates for the voter ballot measures drew selectively and in a biased manner on research findings to draw out ideological fears among the electorate. The subtext of claims that bilingual education programs did not teach English was that Mexicans and other Spanish speakers were not adopting English as their language. By remaining Spanish-speaking, they were threatening the national identity (see also Gándara & Contreras, 2009).

Did the silence on race represent the inertia of institutional racism or a pragmatic political strategy to capture resources for the BSI? The political rhetoric surrounding basic skills education tends to emphasize waste and inefficiency rather than the national identity. From this view, students who did not learn in primary and secondary school should be reschooled as quickly as possible in short-term, occupationally oriented programs from which they can enter productive occupations. Whether due to this ideological underpinning or merely to poor teacher preparation to teach basic skills, basic skills classrooms tend to be dominated by "drill and kill" exercises rather than social constructivist pedagogies. Despite pockets of innovation with contextualized curricula and constructivist pedagogies, teachers tend toward the use of skills worksheets that segment content knowledge into small pieces designed for rote memorization (Grubb & Gabriner, 2013).

The emphasis on identifying and disseminating validated effective practices to improve the quality of developmental education was established in one of the foundational documents of the BSI. As explained in the Executive Summary of the California Community Colleges System Strategic Plan, issued in 2006, "Goal B, Student Success and Readiness," seeks to "Ensure that basic skills development is a major focus and an adequately funded activity of the Community Colleges" (p. 5). The rationale and strategies to achieve this goal were further elaborated:

> To successfully participate in college-level courses, many Community College students need pre-collegiate math and/or English skill development. The goal is to identify model basic skills and English as a Second Language programs and their key features and, given availability of funds, to facilitate replication across the Colleges. In addition, best practices in classrooms and labs and descriptions of effective learning environments will be collected and disseminated widely to inform and assist both credit and noncredit programs. However, noncredit basic skills courses are funded at approximately 60% of the rate provided to credit basic skills courses, which is a disincentive for colleges to offer those courses. The Colleges need to gather practices with high-effectiveness rates, such as innovative

program structures, peer support, and counseling, and acquire funding to implement these approaches to reach all students needing basic skills education. (p. 5)

This framing of the purpose of the BSI, to "gather practices with high-effectiveness rates," indicates that the BSI was speaking to the policy concern of waste and inefficiency in remedial education (Mazzeo, 2002).

The paired emphasis in the strategic plan Goal B statement on the adoption of scientifically validated effective practices and the need for higher levels of funding for basic skills courses suggests that they were written to send a message to legislators that the community colleges would have the expertise to educate basic skills students effectively, but required sufficient funding to do so. This lobbying position, if carried out effectively, could have attracted badly needed funding to the community colleges, which would have had an equity-enhancing effect if they were well spent and distributed equitably.

Further, the BSI's emphasis on self-assessment of educational practices that are internal and within the control of institutional members reflects a commitment to inquiry as an organizational learning and change process. It reflects an equity orientation in its core assumption of institutional responsibility for student outcomes. The fundamental orientation of the BSI toward the problem of basic skills education was based on the assumption of institutional deficits in effectiveness, not on student or community deficits. In addition, the BSI did not adopt the ideological stance of technicism in isolation from an emphasis on practitioner knowledge and responsibility. The BSI was designed to make basic skills an "institutional priority" by refocusing the "responsibilities of the colleges, their faculty and their staff" (RP Group, 2007, p.9).

With its emphasis on using practices validated in the research literature as benchmarks for practitioner inquiry, the BSI clearly drew heavily on the rhetoric of best practices and articulated the ideology of technicism. However, given the historically racialized context and ideological dimensions of access to education in California, whether bilingual education or an elite education at one of the nation's most selective universities, the technicism of the BSI could not exist independent of the dominant stance in educational research today that "scientific" solutions are ideologically neutral solutions. They are not (Dowd & Tong, 2007; Ladson-Billings, 2009; Lather, 2004; Noddings, 1999; Pusser, 2011; Rodriguez, 2013).

The rhetoric of the BSI was ahistoric, because the problem of basic skills education in community colleges is directly related to the quality, or lack of quality, of education in primary and secondary schools. The BSI's color blindness renders Latino students, their concerns, and particular community needs invisible. Latinos and Spanish speakers are treated as part of a generic group of ESL students, when in fact the history of educational policy in the state was quite clearly marked by anti-Latino sentiment

in the passage of the voter ballot restricting educational opportunity fo
bilingual students.

The initiative attempted to strike a difficult balance between techni
cism and professionalism. Whether the embrace of technicism and colo
blindness of the BSI framers was an epistemological or politically pragmati
matter is uncertain. However, by attempting to combine the ideology o
technicism with the professionalism of inquiry, the BSI sacrificed attentior
to the social and political contexts of basic skills education.

ADOPTING A CRITICAL PERSPECTIVE

The results of our analysis conducted for the Wisconsin Transfer Eq
uity Study, which focused on the numbers of students of different racia
and ethnic groups who were transferring between associate's and bachelor'
degree–granting institutions in Wisconsin, highlighted the racial segregatior
and inequities structured into the state's higher education system. The re
sults of our BSI document analysis showed that although the BSI, by placin;
the quality of basic skills education squarely in focus, was tackling one o
the most troubling manifestations of institutional racism, it attempted to d(
so in a color-blind way, ultimately hampering its transformative potential.

A critical perspective is necessary during policy design and implementa
tion to call attention to institutionalized discrimination that occurs througl
routine educational practices and policies. Although occurring with no prej
udice or intent to harm, institutionalized discrimination nevertheless ha;
negative and differential impacts on minoritized populations and, often
beneficial implications for members of the dominant group. It occurs with
out the conscious intent of any one actor.

The principle of nonoppression guards against the cultural imperialisn
that is the source of dominance in schooling, in educational policy, and ir
educational research. In support of the goal of nonoppression, the partici
patory ideal states that educational institutions must take responsibility tc
instill self-worth in all students. The goal of instilling self-worth is under
mined when minoritized groups are rendered invisible by color-blind prac
tices and one-size-fits-all references to diversity. Like justice as care, justice
as transformation advances standards of equity that counter institutiona
discrimination by requiring respect for students and communities. Goin;
beyond that and entering into the political arena, justice as transformatior
calls for policies and practices that seek to identify and deconstruct struc
tural racism. Justice as transformation requires structural changes in the
systems, like unequal transfer pathways and monolingual basic skills educa
tion, which reproduce inequities.

CHAPTER 6

Designing Equitable Institutions

Two hundred fifty years of slavery. Ninety years of Jim Crow. Sixty years of separate but equal. Thirty-five years of racist housing policy. Until we reckon with our compounding moral debts, America will never be whole.

—Ta-Nehisi Coates, "The Case for Reparations" (2014)

As we noted in the Preface, in 2013 and 2014 as we were writing this book the United States observed several 50th anniversaries commemorating events and legislation of the civil rights era, including Martin Luther King's *I Have a Dream* speech in 1963 and passage of the Civil Rights Act in 1964. On each occasion, social and political commentators assessed the nation's progress in race relations, with many observers concluding that progress has been decidedly mixed. Their words echoed that of James Baldwin, whose words on another anniversary (the tenth anniversary of the 1954 Supreme Court's *Brown v. Board of Education* decision) provided us with "sustenance and perspective" (Ayers, 2006, p. 81) as we began writing this book.

New York Times columnist Charles Blow (2013), who succeeds Baldwin as an eloquent and insightful observer of race relations in the United States, weighed progress on the 50th anniversary of Dr. King's March on Washington with a "gnawing in [his] gut, an uneasy sense of society and its racial reality." Blow was, he wrote, "absolutely convinced that enormous steps have been made in race relations," most notably that laws that "codified discrimination have been stricken from the books." Yet he worried that "the more sinister issues of implicit biases and of structural and systematic racial inequality" endure. In other words, like us, Blow could see signs of progress, yet feared that premature celebration would deflect needed attention from the ways that institutions like schools and universities have racial biases embedded in their everyday routines.

Also like us, Blow (2013) worried about the muddled nature of the conversation Americans are having in regard to matters of race and equity, questioning:

I wonder if we, as a society of increasing diversity but also drastic inequality, even agree on what constitutes equality. When we hear that word, do we think of equal opportunity, or equal treatment under the law, or equal outcomes, or some combination of those factors?

Research on racial attitudes about social inequality shows that, in fact, we do not agree on what equality means or what constitutes just social policy to bring about equal outcomes in contemporary society. What we hear when we hear the word *equality* differs considerably by race and ethnicity (Bobo & Charles, 2009). Further, what we hear and say in navigating race talk is less pressing than what we do as a society with our resources to address endemic race-based inequality. Ta-Nehisi Coates (2014), writing in *The Atlantic*, argued that America, rather than observing the half-century mark of civil rights legislation, should take stronger action through financial reparations to compensate for a different set of numbers: "Two hundred fifty years of slavery. Ninety years of Jim Crow. Sixty years of separate but equal. Thirty-five years of racist housing policy. Until we reckon with our compounding moral debts," Coates argued, "America will never be whole."

Presenting a synthesis of research on race relations and the views Americans of different racial and ethnic backgrounds hold of one another, Bobo and Charles (2009) concluded that "prejudice and racism" remain a defining part of "the American social, cultural, and political landscape" (p. 244). Blacks, Whites, Latinos, and Asians hold different views, on average, of the severity of social injustice resulting from prejudice and racism, as well as the public policy mechanisms that should be used to compensate for race-based injustice. This means that American higher education has a sizeable challenge in addressing issues of racial equity. Yet, if indeed higher education is to function as a "public sphere" for debate and instantiation of democratic values, as some argue it must (Pusser, 2011), then colleges and universities must take up the challenge. Our experience with action research convinces us that colleges and universities can and must engage in critical self-assessment through action research and other methods to play a leadership role in improving racial equity in the U.S. educational system.

What is higher education's role in this social struggle, and how can social policies designed to promote racial equity have a chance of achieving their goals? In the preceding chapters we shared what we have learned as action researchers involving college and university practitioners in addressing racial equity in American higher education. As in the broader social, cultural, and political landscape of American society, our progress and the progress of the field of higher education in addressing racial inequality has been mixed. Diversity is valued by many in higher education. An array of special programs has been put into place to promote college access. Yet, although concerted efforts have been made to articulate the value of diversity, the "playing field" for the vast majority of students of color is not yet level. In fact, it appears to be getting worse. Even as access to college improves, broadening participation among Black and Latino students, the quality of that access is stratified by race and ethnicity (Posselt et al., 2012). Postsecondary settings are becoming more segregated rather than less (Carnevale & Strohl, 2013; Goldrick-Rab & Kinsley, 2013). The racial and ethnic group disparities in the college experience and educational outcomes of college students have not been reduced substantially, despite decades of effort.

Throughout this book, we have emphasized the importance of integrating the principles of justice as care and justice as transformation with principles of justice as fairness in educational policy and practice. Educational equity, conceived using the predominant application of principles of justice as fairness, calls for resources to be distributed equally among equals and unequally among those with disparate needs. As a repair for social injustice, greater resources are directed through educational policy toward those who have greater needs.

Deciding where such repair is needed, how to bring it about, and with what level of resources is, of course, contentious. Principles derived from justice as care and justice as transformation provide a guide to understanding how to pursue a racial equity agenda. Justice as care, recognizing that students have an equal right to experience a sense of self-worth in their educational experiences, insists on educational policies that do not impose a "self-worth tax" on the intended beneficiaries. Justice as transformation calls for the restructuring of racially segregated educational systems that currently reproduce race as a socially stratifying and hierarchical construct.

OVERVIEW OF THE CHAPTER

In this chapter we recommend steps that colleges and universities should take to make a commitment to racial equity and redesign themselves as equitable institutions. The redesign principles we present draw on the theories of justice as fairness, justice as care, and justice as transformation. There are three cornerstone principles that must inform a racial equity agenda:

1. Drawing on "strong conceptions" of equity, racial inequities in student outcomes represent a failure not of students but of society and educational institutions, whose practices are embedded in our histories and contemporary legacies of racial discrimination.

2. All students have the right to freedom from oppression in higher education; a "self-worth tax" may not be imposed on students, their families, or communities through educational policies.
3. The accountability field has a moral obligation to provide incentives to institutions of higher education to deconstruct and reconstruct the educational systems that are reproducing racial inequities.

The strategies for designing equitable institutions presented in this chapter involve practitioners in actively addressing the race question through their own practices. The equity design strategies presented in the first section below revolve around the use of artworks and humanistic expression to allow histories of racial discrimination to be discussed "with wisdom" during institutional self-assessment. These recommendations are informed by our analyses in Chapter 2 and Chapter 3 of color-blind responses to structural racism. The strategies presented in the second section emphasize equity-focused data use and goal-setting. These recommendations draw on the positive examples of individual and institutional change toward equity, presented in Chapters 3 and Chapter 4, which have taken place through action research using the Equity Scorecard. This section highlights the key data and inquiry practices practitioners and institutional leaders should use to embed equity principles into organizational routines.

The concluding section, recognizing the limitations presented in Chapter 5 of action research and inquiry to address structural racism, calls on educational leaders and policymakers to promote a public sphere in which racial equity is articulated as a core commitment. This recommendation engages the political dimensions of action research and of higher education accountability. Accountability policies and practices in higher education take shape within a broader organizational field. This field of practice includes state and federal officials, foundation officers, nonprofit think tanks, technical assistance providers, data intermediaries, postsecondary associations, and institutional leaders. These organizations must also play a role to change the national conversation from a focus on diversity to a focus on equity.

ENGAGING HISTORIES OF DISCRIMINATION

History is often celebrated in higher education: The year of a college's founding is proudly highlighted; important civic or college leaders are memorialized in the names of buildings, endowed chairs, or on statues; and alumni, administrators, and faculty celebrate local legends and sports heroes. History and sense of place are integrally intertwined. For example, land-grant institutions were founded to serve their states, and community colleges were created to serve local communities. However, the relationship between racial discrimination and the history of place is often not well remembered or understood.

This is despite the fact that when colleges and universities were located near (or distant) from particular populations, "place was crucially at issue: White public spaces into which Blacks were not allowed" (Olivas, 2005b, p. 170). To segregate Blacks and Whites, states created Black colleges; created incentives, such as scholarships, for Blacks to pursue higher education in other states; or created "roped-off areas or anterooms" (Olivas, 2005, p. 170). Mexican Americans were kept even further at bay, with their educational needs largely overlooked: "Education was so poor and inadequate for Mexican Americans in the 20th century that neither the state, nor private philanthropies, nor church groups established colleges for this population" (Olivas, 2005b, p. 180).

Court battles to dismantle de jure segregation in higher education have a long history:

> The issue of place has . . . been contested in [numerous] sitings, such as whether colleges can locate in certain "service" areas, whether college policies can be localized or tied to locales, whether regions and regional populations have legal claims to proportional college resources, or whether the setting of higher education can trigger racial claims. Indeed, each of these scenarios has been tested in court, each with its own incontestable racial calculus. (Olivas, 2005b, p. 170)

It is clear that "placing colleges near populations is a central feature of universal access"; for that reason, desegregation litigation is ongoing (Olivas, 2005b, p. 170; see also Metcalfe, 2009; A. Wells, 2014). Legal decisions do not bring immediate relief. The decades of court supervision and judicial review of Mississippi's postsecondary desegregation effort provide a clear example of the long delays that can ensue even after a moral and legal case for change has been made. Further, even when educational settings are desegregated at the institutional level, racially segregated tracks emerge.

Even brief consideration of the relationship between race and place demonstrates that no higher education institution exists independent of racially discriminatory policies and practices. Structural racism is embedded in the history of higher education, and the "problems and potentials" of organizations "can only be understood against their own history" (Engeström, 2001, p. 136). Celebrating differences of diversity under an "umbrella of inclusiveness" or claiming color blindness is problematic because it obscures the history of racial discrimination that lives on in contemporary educational institutions.

The cases of practitioner inquiry and change presented throughout this book illustrate that the perceptions practitioners hold of what is "fair" influences their willingness to engage in equity work. Varying beliefs about fairness, merit, and equity, rooted ideologically and often unconsciously in theories of justice, arise in tension whenever we undertake racial equity work in colleges and universities. Whereas principles of justice as fairness are often invoked to argue the virtues of "color-blind" practices, the principles of justice as care and justice as transformation insist on racial consciousness rooted in critical, historical perspectives. Educational settings are "racialized." The experiences of students in educational settings and their opportunities to be successful in them differ by race. We cannot begin to address racial inequities without acknowledging that.

Chapter 2 analyzed a critical incident in our action research where discussion of the "racism cartoon" (Figure 2.6) evoked awareness of a "critical disturbance" (Engeström, 2008) in the activity system of an Equity Scorecard evidence team. Critical disturbances that surface contesting beliefs are necessary and valuable to address root problems in any organization. As we noted at the beginning of Chapter 1, we set out to do this "with wisdom," to engender a sense of individual and collective responsibility to racial equity. Chapters 3 and 4 illustrated how practitioners developed a deeper commitment to equity issues and adopted stronger conceptions of equity through participation in critical self-assessment protocols that are part of the Equity Scorecard toolkit. To address the histories and contemporary manifestations of racial discrimination in higher education with wisdom, we recommend that equity initiatives

1. Use art and other forms of humanistic expression, such as essays, literature, and poems, to provide a shared reference and focal point for authentic communication about the experiences participants in equity initiatives have had with historical and contemporary forms of racial discrimination.
2. Actively distinguish the concepts of diversity, inclusiveness, and racial equity, using strong conceptions of equity that commit to equality of participation and outcomes among racial and ethnic groups.
3. Acknowledge the emotional dimensions of engaging in racial equity work.
4. Develop measures of progress in building individual and institutional capacity to realize racial equity goals.

Inviting the Conversation

Figure 6.1 displays an artwork we have used in quite a few presentations to metaphorically invoke the relationship between race and place in higher

Figure 6.1. Sundown Town

"Sundown Town," by Joel Ross. Used with permission.

education. Titled *Sundown Town*, the image is a photograph of a sculpture
made out of large wooden boards. The boards, placed vertically in a farm
field, spell out the words "Every Day at Six." A barn is also pictured. Closer
inspection reveals that the boards used in the sculpture have been cut from
the side of the barn, which now has a stenciled appearance. The caption to
the work explains that the expression "every day at six" refers to what are
known as "sundown towns," those towns that for decades relied on Black
laborers to work the fields, but then blew a daily whistle at sundown to tell
those laborers it was time to get out of town.

As the caption for this artwork explains, the intriguing relationship of
the boards, the barn, and the field is intended to invite a second, closer look
at the image and a historical reflection on the seemingly bucolic image:

> The phrase "every day at six" comes from the history of Villa Grove, a town in
> east central Illinois. For decades, there was a whistle mounted on the town's wa-
> ter tower and every day at 6:00 p.m., it sounded. Villa Grove was one of many
> Illinois towns where Blacks were not allowed to own or rent property, and this
> daily signal warned Black laborers that it was time to head home. There are a
> surprising number of towns in Illinois that utilized similar alarms, some even
> until the late 1990s. These places were commonly called *sundown towns*. It is
> important to me that there is a specific narrative or history being referenced in
> the work, one that is imbedded in this landscape and its vernacular architec-
> ture—a history that is often nearly invisible. (Joel Ross, 2007, *Sundown Town*)

Our first encounter with this work took place, appropriately enough, in Illinois. It was displayed outside a meeting room where researchers from the Office of Community College Research and Leadership (OCCRL) at the University of Illinois–Urbana-Champaign had held a convening of practitioners engaged in equity-focused action research using OCCRL's Pathways to Results (PTR) inquiry model (Bragg & Durham, 2012). During the meeting, a practitioner from a predominantly White rural college that had no Black students enrolled in a number of high-value health science programs commented that if any Black students were to apply to the programs, they would be welcomed, but none had. This seemed to pose an open-and-shut case in regard to issues of equity in access to the health sciences at the college. However, as the PTR facilitators debriefed in the foyer after the meeting, conversation about the "Every Day at Six" image hanging on the nearby wall brought out the history of racial discrimination that had produced the current-day absence of African Americans in Illinois's rural areas. This instructional dialogue was carried forward through our use of the image in other settings where college and university practitioners were convened to talk about and make plans to address equity issues.

The conversations this artwork has invoked in the multiple and varied settings where we have used it have been emotional, yet productive and instructional at the same time. They have made clear that memories of racial segregation lie right beneath the surface of our "normal" professional discourse, even when the express purpose of a project or initiative is to address racial equity issues. By inviting the conversation about the "architecture" of racial discrimination in our schools and colleges, we have experienced insightful reflection from our White colleagues who remember, or whose parents remember, living in "sundown towns" as well as from our African American colleagues who remember the ways that they or their families were driven from them. The conversations have brought us to other metaphors and images that have served as bridges to the not so distant yet often forgotten past.

When we display the "Every Day at Six" image as an entrée to dialogue about racial discrimination, we point out that higher education's discourse about "helping" students of color who are "disadvantaged" and "at risk" is not sufficient to disrupt historical amnesia about racial discrimination. We use the image of the barn, boards, and field to communicate that the "vernacular architecture" of higher education must be deconstructed and reconstructed to get at the root causes of racial inequities. To motivate commitment to strong conceptions of equity and a willingness to change the higher education systems that create structural racism, it is necessary to remember these histories of race and place. (For a comprehensive historical database, recent media coverage, and instructional materials including a map of sundown towns, see http://sundown.afro.illinois.edu/sundown-towns.php, which was created by James W. Loewen, professor emeritus of sociology at the University of Vermont and the author of *Sundown Towns: A Hidden Dimension of American Racism*.)

The case of technical education in Wisconsin, discussed in Chapter 5, with its bifurcated systems of associate's degree–granting colleges in the University of Wisconsin system and the Wisconsin Technical College System, provides an example of a system where the history of race and place create modern-day inequities. At one time in our nation's history, African Americans, Latinos, and other students of color were channeled by legal discrimination into vocational colleges (Gasman, 2002). These channels are no longer formal, discriminatory structures upheld by law. Yet they continue to exist, and the patterns of enrollment have not changed very much. By now, this history is hidden to many. That students of color are clustered in technical schools seems natural, a result of cultural differences in motivation or academic proclivities.

We can use data such as the Scorecard's Vital Signs to show inequities between the population of an area and a college population and ask Scorecard evidence team members to pose second-level questions about why access gaps exist, but this exercise is not transformative if participants do not recall the root causes of segregation. The idea that a college has an ethical obligation to extend the opportunity to enroll in a local program to (seemingly) far-flung urban Black students is a radical one until the history of discrimination is put squarely into focus in this discussion.

In our experience, using artwork is a productive way to talk about racism in higher education. Viewing and discussing this piece with a variety of groups has not led to recriminations and defensiveness among our participants. Instead the image pulls open the blinds on our past, which otherwise tend to remain closed. Memories and understanding of historical discrimination differ based on participants' racial and ethnic background. What is forgotten history for some is family history for others—acutely painful memories of social, legal, and political disenfranchisement and violence. To acknowledge this is productive because it creates the foundations to ask "Why" questions in a new light. The answer to "Why are there so few African Americans (or Latinos, or American Indians, or Vietnamese) in this program (or major, or department, or college)?" traces back to "Why are there no African Americans in this town? (or zip code)?" When the answer is that legalized racial discrimination kept that group of people from this town, place, and college, then the responsibility of colleges located at a distance from a population that has experienced discrimination takes on a new dimension.

Structural racism exists absent interpersonal malice and individual acts of racism. Yet structural racism, the structuring of higher education opportunities in stratified and segregated systems, still reproduces racial inequities. Action research enables us to move past historical amnesia and apathy to address higher education's role in segregation.

Distinguishing "Diversities"

It is important to recognize that the majority of practitioners in institutions of higher education do not have a strong sense of expertise to address racial equity issues. Remembering our history and inviting conversations about race provide the opportunity to improve practitioner knowledge about the root causes of racial inequities in education. The impulse to equalize and celebrate all forms of difference under the "umbrella of diversity" disregards the existence of White privilege and racial discrimination in America. Organizational change theorists in academia and business emphasize the importance of identifying the root causes of problems in order to find workable solutions (Argyris, 1977, 1982; Dyer et al., 2011; Sawyer, 2007).

The causes of social disadvantage and racially minoritized status among communities of color in the United States differ. Enslavement brought Africans to the United States as "three-fifths a person," deprived them of their personal liberties, subjected them to violence, and deprived them of the right to vote, hold office, or inherit property. The rights of American Indians and Mexicans on U.S. soil were also severely curtailed. Little attempt was made by the White dominant society to educate any of these groups in quality schools until the second half of the 20th century. American Indians and Mexican Americans experienced political subjugation and annexation, in effect becoming strangers in their own land, their language and culture ridiculed through harsh negative stereotypes.

Puerto Ricans experienced similar treatment through American colonization in the Caribbean. The Cuban and Central American immigrant experience is marked by American sponsorship of wars and corporate imperialism in developing socialist countries. Their experience bears resemblance to that of Filipinos, Vietnamese, Cambodians, and Hmong who came to the United States as political and economic refugees. Refugees do not embark on their journey with the same sense of opportunity as voluntary immigrants, whose material, social, or financial resources, no matter how meager, may be just enough to realize the "up by your bootstraps" immigration experience. The myth of the Asian "model minority" harms Asian Americans by continuing to "other" them as foreigners, even when they are intergenerational American citizens.

Through it all, skin tone continues to matter. For generations, those with lighter skin have experienced benefits of assimilation into the U.S. economic mainstream. Those with darker skin are subject to racial stereotyping in popular culture and microaggressions that articulate uninformed cultural assumptions. Interesectionality among racial, gender, and class characteristics certainly does matter. Women, like minoritized groups, were for many generations kept from owning property, voting, or expressing their aspirations for participation in all-male fields of endeavor, including science and engineering, where that history of gender discrimination has not yet been overcome. For this reason, participants in the Equity Scorecard sometimes wish to give equal focus to gender, sexuality, and class in the action research process. When this shift in focus serves to silence the discussion about race, it is not productive to racial equity goals. Racially minoritized groups were uniquely kept from accumulating intergenerational wealth whereas over time women benefited from their fathers' and husbands' assets. Racially minoritized groups were uniquely subjected to negative stereotypes about their moral values, personal habits, and aptitude for education, with many harmful theories of racial inferiority promulgated by seemingly scientific endeavors such as IQ testing.

Acknowledging these differences in the ways that different racial and ethnic groups have been ascribed minority status is an essential step to move from an agenda focused on diversity to one focused on racial equity. Colleges that make a commitment to a racial equity agenda must educate their faculty, administrators, boards, and students about the root causes that have produced racially minoritized groups, distinguishing among the histories of enslavement, colonization, political and cultural annexation, and political disenfranchisement.

Building Capacity for Equity Work

As we highlighted in Chapter 2 and Chapter 3, drawing on activity theory, all activities have historicity and multivoicedness (Engeström, 2001, 2008), but whether the voices and views of minoritized groups are heard depends on community norms. Discussions of race and racism in professional settings do carry risk. Practitioners risk being viewed as troublemakers if they speak or act outside the norm too often, for example by introducing a racial lens into a conversation when others would not think to do so.

To mitigate the risk of imposing greater social harm at the very point when a college is striving to address the race question with wisdom, we recommend that colleges build their leadership and facilitation capacity. Building the leadership capacity involves having conversations about race that are authentic and purposeful prior to planned remarks.

In addition, we recommend that leadership teams regularly involve a professional facilitator with training in interpersonal racial dynamics as well as knowledge of structural racism. An external facilitator can take advantage of his or her outsider status to point out habits of interaction that are counterproductive to racial equity work, for example the habit of quickly referencing other forms of "diversities" when the topic of racial equity is discussed, or of not mentioning race at all. Such "interaction scripts" are so engrained in professional culture that they are taken as a given. Creating new forms of interaction will require creativity and, like any creative endeavor, a willingness to engage in trial and error. In-house training programs typically do not tolerate error well because managers too often view their role as evaluating rather than assisting the performance of those who report to them. Where encouragement for experimentation is needed, an immediate emphasis on evaluation is counterproductive (Tharp & Gallimore, 1988). Practitioners, too, wish to demonstrate their expertise and are trained to act from positions of knowledge , making them hesitant to engage in activities that involve a great deal of uncertainty. If someone says or does "the wrong thing" in the process of trying to identify local manifestations of institutional racism, it is important to have a leadership group that is willing to tolerate mistakes and able take the situation as an opportunity for learning.

Therefore, the key principle for designing effective professional development programs is to ensure that effective assistance occurs among peers, among managers and those they supervise, and between external facilitators and participants in the activity setting. It is important to note that participation of a facilitator does not replace the need for collaboration and authentic dialogue among leaders and practitioners. Good facilitators will help educational leaders and practitioner teams develop a deeper level of mutual engagement and commitment to equity. Higher education institutions have a moral obligation to produce knowledge about the ways in which cultural habits of domination have become part of the organizational routines of education. Its members will not be able to do so without a stronger knowledge base and the capacity to produce knowledge based on divergent perspectives and experiences.

Through the action research process of the Equity Scorecard, we have placed local data, disaggregated by race and ethnicity, in the hands of practitioners and asked them to engage together in structured inquiry to gain a deeper understanding of racial equity gaps. Based on our experience, we see that this type of guided data use is necessary to take the growing number of "data-driven" policy prescriptions for higher education accountability off shelves and put data-based insights to work.

EQUITY-ENHANCING DATA PRACTICES

Despite a dramatic increase in data availability, institutions of higher education have made only slight progress in using data to pursue racial equity goals. While it is tempting to take the proliferation of college scorecards and performance dashboards as a sign of progress in data use to promote equity, it would also be misleading.

Currently, the accountability field prioritizes the building of databases over reflective practice using data. The development of data systems will not stimulate meaningful change if practitioners do not acknowledge that their current practices are failing students and historically disenfranchised communities. Improvement in student experiences and outcomes in programs that represent only bare opportunities in higher education today, such as basic skills education, vocational education, and transfer, cannot be achieved without the buy-in of faculty members. Faculty must be willing to look at how their practices, language, and disciplinary cultures contribute to the problem of low and inequitable student success rates.

As we have shown in Chapter 3 and Chapter 4, practitioner inquiry using institutional data motivates practitioners to change their own practices, as well as institutional policies within their control. When practitioners are motived to engage in inquiry with an equity-minded stance, they open themselves up to new understandings of what is fair and unfair. Those are the very insights that accountability policies should incentivize in order to create buy-in for transformative changes in higher education.

Local data use involving reflective practice will be the source of the new knowledge that is needed to deconstruct and reconstruct higher education in more equitable ways. Inquiry using institutional data led the honors program directors at one University of Wisconsin campus to adopt more equitable admissions criteria. By reviewing the Equity Scorecard Vital Signs disaggregated by race and ethnicity, the program directors realized a contradiction between their espoused ideals and enacted practices. Asking questions about the pedagogical and ethical basis for their admissions criteria led them to a deeper commitment to equity. Through their willingness to act as change agents, a stratifying program was reformed into one that was equity-enhancing. The equity gap, which had been created by arbitrary admissions criteria that had previously gone unexamined, was closed.

College testing, selection, and admissions procedures represent some of the many "organizational routines" (Spillane, 2012) that constitute a college culture. Other organizational routines that impact equity in college participation and outcomes include program reviews (for academic programs and student services), professional development, search and hiring processes, institutional research, strategic planning, and performance reporting. Organizational routines such as these often go unexamined because they are taken for granted as "the way we do things here." Institutional self-assessment using protocols that have been designed to focus attention on racial equity issues can productively provoke "critical disturbances" (Engeström, 2008) in the activity systems of these routines.

Based on our experience conducting the Equity Scorecard, we recommend that colleges, universities, and systems adopt equity-enhancing institutional assessment practices and strategies of data use. Colleges need structures, tools, and processes to convert institutional self-assessment into an organizational learning experience that enables them to improve student success rates in equitable ways.

Identifying Equity Gaps

Equity cannot be achieved without an intentional focus on student outcomes differentiated by race and ethnicity because racially minoritized students are often those who are served least well by existing and new programs. Average rates of student progress hide racial inequities. Equity-focused institutions consistently monitor enrollments in existing and new programs using data disaggregated by race and ethnicity. They look at equity gaps in student outcomes to see if, when, and where they may be losing or segregating students of color.

There is no hard-and-fast threshold at which an equity gap is said to exist. It will be a matter of debate among participants in any inquiry process whether a difference in student participation represents an equity gap or not. (We have provided the rule of thumb to Equity Scorecard evidence teams to look at persistent gaps of over 5% variation between groups experiencing high rates of success and those experiencing low rates of success as potentially indicating systemic inequities in college performance.)

We recommend that institutions look at their data and engage in the necessary debate to identify and name racial equity gaps. Then they should set goals for improvement. Yet goal-setting will be an empty exercise without ongoing monitoring. Campuses must also design data systems to enable numerical goal-setting by race and ethnicity for specified student cohorts. The following practices should become a regular routine of data use to measure the institution's progress in closing equity gaps:

1. Disaggregate numerical institutional data by race and ethnicity.
2. Collect qualitative data with a race consciousness attuned to understanding the sources of equity gaps.

3. Adopt equity indicators of access, retention, completion, and student participation in high-value programs.
4. Report annually on the status of equity.
5. Illustrate the number of students from specific racial and ethnic groups who would need to experience success in particular programs or academic milestones in order for the college to meet equity benchmark goals.
6. Produce reports to annually monitor progress toward equity goals.
7. Collaborate with faculty, student affairs professionals, and other administrators to assess what is working and what is not working to close equity gaps.

Actionable Data

State policymakers will not always be able to communicate effectively with highly disaggregated data. However, for local uses the ability to disaggregate and to look at specific cohorts of students in specific academic pathways is essential. Data systems should be designed for maximum flexibility to allow for different data to be used in these various settings. In our experience, evidence teams are able to ask and answer meaningful accountability questions about racial equity when they are involved in selecting and refining equity indicators. Whereas rates of student success and the total number of degree or certificate holders graduated by an institution or state system are meaningful at the policy level, practitioners become engaged through discussion about particular groups and numbers of students. In fact "small Ns," which are often dismissed by institutional researchers as statistically insignificant, are the numbers that captivate attention of faculty and program administrators (Dowd, Malcom, et al., 2012). Specific, small numbers are "actionable."

In addition, the process of selecting the racial and ethnic groupings for disaggregated data analysis is productive because it involves practitioners in conversation about the educational needs of different populations of students. In the Equity Scorecard process, Vital Signs indicators vary by a college's enrollment, region, or service area. In Wisconsin, Hmong, Native Americans, and Southeast Asian groups were analyzed by Scorecard teams. In the San Francisco Bay area, colleges disaggregated among Chinese, Vietnamese, and other Asian groups, as well as by Black and Hispanic students. In Los Angeles, several colleges disaggregated by race and gender in order to focus on the different outcomes of Black males and Black females.

Figure 6.2 illustrates the type of numerical data display Equity Scorecard teams include in Equity Scorecard reports. In this case, the focus is on

Figure 6.2. Identifying Equity Gaps

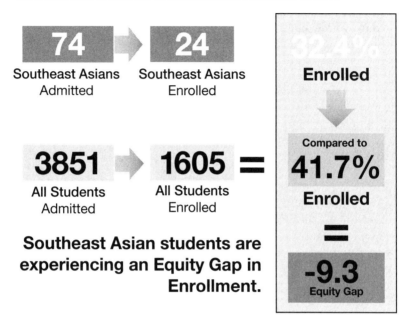

Enrollment rate for Southeast Asians in 2011

Southeast Asian student enrollment. The data show an equity gap on an indicator of access: the enrollment yield (i.e., the percentage of admitted students who enroll). The equity gap of 9.3 percentage points is identified by a comparison of the yield for Southeast Asian students (32.4%) and the yield for all students admitted to the university (41.7%). An annual "snapshot" of this type is often complemented by a multiyear trend analysis in order to see whether the equity gap is a persistent phenomenon or an unusual occurrence in a given year.

When an equity gap is identified, practitioners should then examine institutional policies and practices that may be producing the gap. Admissions officers, recruiters, and faculty all have a role to play in addressing equity gaps in access. When performance indicators point to an equity gap, the numbers need to be contextualized by asking and answering "second-level" inquiry questions. Looking at these data, an evidence team charged with examining equity in admissions might ask: "Are students from particular high schools more likely to accept our offer of admission? Are Southeast Asian students completing their financial aid applications

Figure 6.3. Locating Equity Gaps in Academic Pathways

Year-to-Year Persistence Rates for Latino/Hispanic Students who entered in 2006

Hispanic/Latino Students

296	68.9%	73.5%	95.3%	49.0%
Enrolled in 2006	Persisted to the 2nd Year	Persisted from the 2nd to 3rd Year	Persisted from the 3rd to 4th Year	Persisted from the 4th Year to Graduate in 6 Years

1711	67.9%	72.6%	91.4%	55.4%

All Students

+1.0	+0.9	+3.9	-6.4 Equity Gap

in a timely manner? Are they choosing to attend other institutions? Do our recruiters and admissions officers communicate with Southeast Asian students after they have been admitted with the same frequency as with other groups of students?"

The answers to questions like these are sometimes readily available and at other times they are not. Unanswered questions should become the basis of additional inquiry. For example, the admissions office might decide to devote a small amount of resources to contact the Southeast Asian students in the most recent cohort of admitted students who did not enroll and ask: What attracted you to apply to our university? What did you do instead of enrolling here? What factors influenced your decision?

Catalyzing Changes in Programs

Data systems and institutional researcher priorities should support local data use at the level of specific programs, majors, and courses. Most colleges and universities conduct academic program, special program, and student service reviews as part of a variety of organizational routines including accreditation self-studies at the university or degree level. Inquiry groups can be formed as subcommittees within any number of existing campus structures for program planning and assessment or be formed within specially funded grant projects. In the latter case, the group focuses on the topic of the study or project and conducts the assessments as an integral part of project planning and development.

Figure 6.3 illustrates the use of numerical data to identify equity gaps in academic pathways. This example uses the milestones of year-to-year persistence rates, culminating in a 6-year graduation rate. This type of analysis pinpoints where colleges are losing students, in this case Hispanic/Latino students. This cohort analysis reveals that in comparison to the persistence rates of all students, Latino students do not experience equity gaps in year-to-year persistence when transitioning to the second, third, and fourth years of study. The equity gap occurs on the indicator of graduation within six years. Forty-nine percent of Latino students in the cohort analyzed persisted from the fourth year to graduate in six years, which is a 6.5 percentage point gap compared to the all-student average. These data are actionable in the sense that they reveal a problem the institution can address through a number of functions such as academic advising, financial aid, and career services.

Similar data analyses should examine student success and persistence in specific curricular pathways. Course-to-course analyses often point to one or more gatekeeper courses that should be improved through targeted interventions. For example, basic skills arithmetic and introductory algebra function as gatekeepers for many community college students.

We recommend that institutional leaders adopt practitioner inquiry as a method to conduct program reviews with an expressed purpose of embedding equity goals into institutional self-assessment. Specific strategies to achieve this include:

1. Require all programs and majors to assess equity using enrollment, retention, and graduation data disaggregated by race and ethnicity.
2. Identify high-risk courses and gatekeepers for minoritized students, for example, those courses with persistent racial equity gaps in student enrollment and completion.
3. Develop a plan to have all departments collect qualitative data for institutional assessment using equity-focused inquiry tools.
4. Assess the equity of student participation in high-value special programs, such as honors programs and undergraduate research.
5. During inquiry, use assessment protocols with prompts similar to those in CUE's Equity-Minded Syllabus Review Indicators in Table 3.1 to assess the extent to which program materials validate the participation of minoritized students.

We recommend that colleges complement structural and programmatic changes with inquiry using "fine-grained" course-by-course numeric data and qualitative data collected by faculty and administrators who teach and advise students in the academic pathways that are functioning as gatekeepers.

Producing Contextualized Knowledge

Equity Scorecard teams we have worked with have conducted inquiry activities such as website reviews, peer interviews, and interviews with students. To gain a deeper understanding of the sources of racial equity gaps in basic skills math courses, for example, we recommend that

1. Observations take place in math classes and support centers.
2. Interviews be conducted with full-time and part-time math faculty who teach in the identified gatekeeper course(s).
3. Faculty conduct interviews of students who are members of groups impacted negatively by the equity gap.
4. A curriculum map be created to catalyze discussion about course alignment, pedagogies, assessment, and desired student learning outcomes.
5. Document analyses be analyzed as "artifacts of culture" to reveal what they communicate to students about the culture of math classrooms.

When the faculty and administrators involved in Equity Scorecard projects in California and Wisconsin conducted inquiry of this type, they discovered structural gaps in program alignment as well as cultural practices that imposed a "self-worth tax" on students. Documents communicated demeaning rather than validating messages to students about their potential success in college and the willingness of the faculty to support their success.

The purpose of relying on practitioner inquiry to produce contextualized knowledge is to ensure that the reforms intended to improve institutional effectiveness do not contribute to greater inequities.

Strategic Planning and Goal-Setting

Most institutions of higher education have not established standards of equity that they can use to assess their performance in improving the educational outcomes of African Americans and Latinos. Just as institutions of higher education are being expected to establish standards for learning outcomes, they should be expected to do the same for equity. Without equity standards, institutions cannot evaluate their performance; without measures of performance, institutions cannot learn; and without learning, institutional change is unlikely.

Administrators act when things go wrong. One of the ways of sensing that things are going wrong is through the analysis of data. It is also true that what gets measured is what gets attended to by campus leaders. Institutions need baseline data and benchmarks that make it possible for them to engage in a systematic and continuous self-appraisal and improvement of their efforts. The most promising strategy to bring about changes in institutional performance and improve institutional capacity to narrow the college education gap lies in more intelligent and creative ways of using evidence to understand the nature of the problem and to develop new recognitions that will impel decision-makers, faculty, leaders, and policymakers to act. Moving forward, it is necessary to locate very specifically the most critical gaps in the academic performance of institutions in educating African American and Latino students. Such a focus suggests a shift toward institutional responsibility and away from deficit-minded assumptions about the causes of racial inequities.

Strategic planning is an organizational routine that should be repurposed from a bureaucratic chore to create meaningful opportunities for organizational learning about how to achieve equity goals. When reviewing institutional data, strategic planning committees, task forces, and work groups should start by reviewing equity reports produced by the institutional research office (or, if a focus on equity has not yet been incorporated into institutional research routines, by requesting baseline data on the state of equity at the institution). Strategic planning documents should identify and prioritize specific equity gaps and describe steps that will be taken to close those gaps.

After identifying equity gaps, strategic planning groups should identify equity goals. These are publically articulated statements of purpose to close equity gaps in student access and success, expressed in percentage terms and raw numbers for each racial/ethnic group. Setting the magnitude of improvement represented in equity goals will be a matter of debate and political negotiation among inquiry team members and institutional leaders. One approach to setting equity goals that we have used in working with Equity Scorecard teams relies on external benchmarking to set that goal, comparing the college's success rates to those at a peer institution with similar student demographics but higher rates of success. This approach works well for racially segregated colleges and colleges where all student groups experience low success rates relative to peer institutions. Another approach relies on internal benchmarking, which sets the goal equal to the percentage point difference between groups experiencing low success rates and the group with the highest success rates. This approach works well for colleges with diverse student bodies and equity gaps among racial/ethnic groups enrolled at the college, as well as for systemwide comparisons among institutions of different types.

The goals set out by strategic planning committees should be reinforced through performance reporting, whether in voluntary indicators of performance adopted by the college, in a college's response to state accountability requirements, or in responding to evaluation requirements attached to federal funding for special programs. The following recommendations highlight ways to integrate equity comprehensively into strategic planning and performance reporting functions:

1. Make equity goals a priority in strategic plans.
2. Report in strategic plans on the state of equity by department (e.g., history), curriculum (e.g., general education), or unit (e.g., School of Natural and Physical Sciences).
3. Schedule quarterly or semiannual meetings and specific forums for key leadership groups to review the status of equity goals.
4. Identify the need for, and set out a process to develop, new equity indicators to fill in knowledge gaps about equity discovered through the previous year's inquiry activities.
5. Hold campuswide meetings to discuss the "State of Equity in Access, Retention, Completion, and Excellence."
6. Develop unit-level strategic plans and priorities to equity gaps.
7. Select equity indicators as optional performance-based funding or reporting metrics.
8. Develop equity indicators to incorporate into the annual evaluation of faculty, staff, and leaders.

To pursue equity goals, it is necessary for colleges to measure if student progress through key milestones and transitions in their college career supports equity goals. In addition, requiring the monitoring of students' access in moving from lower- to higher-status institutions and programs, such as in transferring from community colleges to selective public universities, will generate information needed to create incentives for institutional leaders to align curricula, learning assessment, and selection criteria.

LEADERSHIP FOR EQUITY

Many of those we have worked with over the years conducting the Equity Scorecard were motivated by a deepened understanding of racial inequities in higher education to make changes in their own educational practices. These "institutional agents" took steps to act in more just and caring ways toward their students of color. At times, consistent with the tenets of justice as fairness, their efforts led to greater vertical equity in the distribution of human and material resources within colleges, universities, or departments.

Yet these institutional agents were poorly positioned to address the stratification of quality and resources among different types of educational institutions. Institutional leaders who held the greatest capacity to create systemic change were stymied by the need for deeper structural change. It appears that leaders, due to the highly public and political nature of their work, require an even greater commitment to take action against inequities than do practitioners who work in classrooms, student support centers, and administrative offices where individuals can act independently to make changes in their own practices.

Despite decades now of attention to diversity and equity issues, a critical mass of leaders does not exist in the executive offices of colleges and universities to forcefully address racial inequality and segregation in higher education. Few leaders are compelled to risk their professional careers to challenge the status quo. Such inertia stems from privilege and is a marker of institutional racism (Haney-López, 2010). Leadership is essential to systemic change because leaders play an important role in embedding cultural norms and values. Through their actions, language, and what they pay attention to, leaders communicate priorities, values, and expectations. In many settings where we conducted the Equity Scorecard, campus leaders showed ambivalence or outright opposition to the idea of equity as a matter of institutional accountability to Black, Latino, American Indian, and marginalized Asian American groups. As one Scorecard participant at a California community college described the situation when asked why issues of racial equity were not typically mentioned at her college, "Well, I think it comes from the president. You know, the president was just saying something like, 'Let's not focus [on equity]'" (Enciso, 2009).

All communities of practice have explicit and implicit organizational routines, which leaders can focus on to bring about change. Routines "store" experiences and set expectations for behavior and appropriate speech (Spillane, 2012, p. 116). They establish what is "in bounds" and "out of bounds" in terms of language, tone, affect, and topics of discussion. Group members who have felt marginalized after violating group norms are not likely to make the mistake again, due to risk of further marginalization or "excommunication" (Schein, 1985). This is a wise strategy to protect membership in a profession because organizational routines are the medium through which "professional identity is produced, reproduced, and renegotiated" (Spillane, 2012, p. 132).

Racial equity requires justice as fairness, justice as care, and justice as transformation. Change involving the deconstruction and reconstruction of higher education to dismantle structural racism will come about through changes in the organizational routines that are expressions of, and give rise to, organizational culture. Institutional leaders must be at the forefront of these changes.

To advance equity goals, leaders must articulate equity values consistently and repeatedly. They must emphasize that being institutional agents for equity is part of the professional duties of the faculty and administrators on their campus. The objective in articulating these values is to change those aspects of the organizational culture that are reproducing racial inequities.

Routines have performative aspects, such as the tasks and activities involved in institutional research, program review, curriculum design, and strategic planning. In addition to changing the performative aspects of routines, leaders must change the ostensive aspects. Practitioners have control over the performative aspects of accountability, but educational leaders have greater control of the ostensive aspects, which Spillane (2012) describes as "the idealized and abstracted script" of organizational behaviors (p. 115). Leaders have the capacity, through their language and use of symbolic artifacts, to make race talk a routine practice. Leaders who provide a positive role model in discussing equity issues, demonstrating competence, knowledge, and moral conviction will improve the campus's capacity to address equity issues.

To articulate equity values and goals consistently and repeatedly, we recommend that presidents, provosts, deans, and other institutional leaders do the following:

1. Talk about racial equity in public speeches and meetings.
2. Talk about racial equity in private settings with diverse stakeholders to hone their capacity to articulate racial equity values "with wisdom."
3. Articulate the difference between diversity and equity and articulate the institution's commitment to diversity and equity as two different value systems.
4. Through reading and conversation with diverse stakeholders, deepen their understanding of the meanings of equity and the theories of justice that inform them.
5. Ensure that equity reports are posted on college and university websites.
6. Use social media to disseminate information about the institution's equity gaps, goals, and progress.
7. Allocate and publicize the availability of resources to support presentations about equity by their faculty and staff at professional conferences.
8. Model the importance of equity in searches for executive leaders, for example, in memoranda to committee members.

9. Give equity issues prominence in the core leadership work and groups (e.g., Provosts' Council; Presidents' Council).
10. Report equity gaps, goals, and attainments to the institution's Board of Governors and Trustee Boards.

Leaders should strive to embed attention to racial equity into the organizational routines of colleges and universities, including the routines of institutional assessment, administration, teaching, and research. Leaders must act in an intentional manner to change community norms around discussions of data, especially data that reflect racial inequities. It will not be sufficient to state, "All views are welcome" or "We want to be sure to have an open dialogue." Leaders hold the responsibility and power to articulate equity goals and to strategically embed them into the fabric of their institution.

Mobilizing the Accountability Field

Today the "college completion agenda," which has been moved forward over the past several years by a broad coalition of federal and state government agencies, philanthropic foundations, policy organizations, and academic research centers, is driving a focus on student outcomes. This agenda necessarily entails a focus on community colleges, for-profit colleges, and broad-access state universities, because selective universities and liberal arts colleges already have high graduation rates. President Obama and major higher education philanthropies such as the Gates and Lumina foundations are calling on colleges and universities to do a better job of retaining students and moving them through the credit-bearing curriculum. These efforts are mirrored at the state level in performance-based funding (PBF) policies, which aim to shift the funding incentives public colleges face from merely enrolling students to ensuring that they graduate (AASCU, 2013).

The college completion agenda could be well aligned with an emphasis on "outcome equity" (Dowd, 2003, 2008), but it has not been to date. It calls attention to the fact that providing access to college is not sufficient to provide equal opportunity. It is highly goal-oriented, as in the Lumina Foundation's Big Goal to produce millions more graduates by 2025 and the Obama Administration's goal of regaining the number-one position in the world in the proportion of citizens who are college-educated. And performance-based funding sometimes includes indicators or targets, albeit weak ones, to focus attention on the success of students of color (Dowd & Shieh, 2013).

The college completion agenda has an intense focus on academic pathways, benchmarks, and milestones toward degree completion. Tools and data systems abound to track student progress. However, the primary objec-

tive of the college completion agenda is to produce more degree and certificate holders and restore the United States to its former position at the top of
the national higher education rankings. The agenda emphasizes institutional
productivity, workforce needs for human capital, and efficient throughput
of students.

In setting goals in the aggregate and not for specific groups of students,
the college completion agenda falls short of the outcome equity agenda we
articulated over 10 years ago (Dowd, 2003). The Carnegie credit hour and
academic quarters and semesters have for decades been the core building
blocks for measuring progress toward a degree or credential. New policies
adopted at the state and federal level are embracing alternative education
delivery mechanisms such as competency-based education, stackable certificates, massive open online courses (MOOCs), portable transfer credits,
applied baccalaureate degrees (Ruud & Bragg, 2011), and accelerated curricula. These new educational structures aim to shorten "seat time," move
the locus of learning outside of college classrooms, and allow students to
earn credits and degrees through nontraditional pathways. All of this is re-
defining how and when higher education takes place and who has the right
to oversee certification and credentialing systems.

The history of tracking and stratification in the American educational
system indicates that White families with higher levels of education and cultural capital will be best positioned to take advantage of higher-status pathways (Labaree, 1997), which lead to higher earnings, employment, and social
position. Low-status credentialing systems are more likely to enroll new entrants to higher education who have less access to information to distinguish
the quality and value of educational offerings. To be equity-enhancing, the
new educational pathways that are being developed through accountability
mandates would have to break the historical pattern of ever-increasing inequality through stratification of opportunity (Posselt et al., 2012) and enroll
students of color and White students in higher- and lower-status pathways in
proportion with the demographics of a college's service area.

To accomplish this, the selection criteria for higher-status pathways
must not systematically exclude students of color. Granted, in designing
and implementing new programs administrators may not be certain which
students will enroll or whether a new pathway will lead to higher- or lower-status outcomes. But ultimately, to be equity-enhancing, new pathways
must increase the flow of students of color between lower-status and higher-
status institutions. That depends in part on the level of resources devoted
to sustaining quality in new academic pathways over time, particularly the
quality of the curriculum and of the teaching force.

The college completion agenda has focused attention on low rates of
certificate and degree completion. This focus has equity-enhancing poten-

tial, as we noted above, if it opens pathways to high-status degrees, occupations, and professions for racially minoritized groups rather than introducing further tracking and racial segregation. To know whether the academic restructuring taking place in response to the pressures of the college completion agenda is equity-enhancing or not, higher education systems and institutions will need to monitor student enrollments and outcomes using disaggregated data, adopt race-conscious action research tools and processes, and incorporate practitioner inquiry into the routines of institutional assessment and data use.

The college completion agenda will not improve racial equity unless the programs, strategies, and leading actors of this agenda strongly incorporate equity values into their public statements about the impetus for such a broad-based agenda. To implement a commitment to racial equity within the college completion agenda, in addition to experimenting with structural reforms in credentialing, accountability leaders should create incentives for colleges and universities to examine their own practices.

The accountability field has a moral obligation to ensure that programs such as basic skills education and structures such as community college to 4-year university transfer, which often represent little more than a "bare opportunity" to higher education, become more effective and equitable in their enrollment. Strong conceptions of equity demand that these bare opportunity programs be improved through investments of human, material, and financial resources to improve their quality. Such improvements might ultimately serve to desegregate programs, because they will attract students of all backgrounds, not just those whose choices are constrained by lack of money, information, or academic preparation. An equity agenda also requires a reworking of the curriculum, hiring practices for faculty and executive leaders, and selection and assessment that can only be brought about through active engagement of practitioners in a race-conscious, equity-focused inquiry process.

Weak conceptions of equity might view the existence of a stratified higher education system as a sign of equal opportunity, and therefore a sufficient response in a democratically just society, but it is clear that the current arrangements are failing.

Incentivizing Performance to Produce Equity

The objective of oversight bodies has traditionally been to gather symbols of institutional responsiveness to state goals through bureaucratic reporting procedures. Reporting was viewed as a sufficient form of compliance by regulators and educators, as the state (through elected and appointed bodies) relied primarily on the professional sense of responsibility of educators to produce satisfactory educational outcomes. Today many legislators, with the prodding of intermediaries, are looking for ways to "incentivize" performance by providing funding with market-like incentives and penalties attached for good or bad performance, for example, through performance-based funding (AASCU, 2013). These institutional logics shape discourse in a way that makes talk of institutional effectiveness, best practices, efficiency, and structural change "in bounds," and talk of racism, sociocultural dynamics, power, and privilege "out of bounds." Therefore, the accountability field's discourse of data use, accountability, and performance indicators influences whose voice is heard and viewed as authoritative and whose is not.

Just as we have provided recommendations for faculty, administrators, and institutional leaders, we recommend that members of the accountability field, including the educational foundations that have played a powerful role in shaping the discourse of the college completion agenda, develop a set of guidelines for use at meetings, symposia, and conferences that answer the following three questions:

1. To what extent does our agenda acknowledge the effects of racism in our daily lives and educational institutions?
2. What steps have we taken to support the capacity of our participant group to construct knowledge of the mechanisms and effects of institutional racism?
3. How will we elicit and engage the critical contradictions inherent in pursuing the goal of nonoppression while meeting the responsibility of our field to design effective accountability policies and practices?

Critical theory was introduced as a school of thought because scholars wanted to serve humanity by explaining how to create an "emancipated" and more "rational" society. The term *rational*, in the critical sense, refers to a society that is not weighed down by dominant groups' "technical interest in control of the world" (White, 1995, p. 6). To counteract dominant groups' interest in technical control, the accountability field must draw on philosophy and social research conducted through the lens of critical theories. Doing so will enable members of this field to use forms of reasoning and moral argumentation that would achieve a balance between technical control and other human needs. The new accountability agenda must recognize that human beings also have "practical" needs, which are met through knowledge of others, and "emancipatory" needs, which are met through knowledge of how to free oneself from the "structures of domination" (White, 1995, p. 6). Although these three "anthropologically" deep-seated interests must all be met, accountability policy in its current form tends to emphasize technical control. This is problematic because it will not be possible through technical control to address the histories of colonization, subordination, oppression, and the unjust exercise of power in domination of people of color on a global scale.

Accountability policy should first and foremost develop ways to strengthen higher education's responsibility to function as a public sphere. The public sphere refers to those venues (whether in person or in cyber-space) where citizens engage in "reasoned argument and [express] contend-ing values" (Pusser, 2006, p. 13). In order to successfully make advances on the racial equity front, members of the accountability field must recognize that: As Pusser (2011) argued,

> Creating a public sphere through higher education requires a balance of power and authority relations, one in which interests are sufficiently legitimate to hold one another in balance so that discussion, critique, and knowledge creation and dissemination . . . can take place. (p. 41)

Different theories of justice—and the scholarly ideologies that have grown up around them—produce different ideas about what counts when it comes to measuring equity in education. To eclipse these differences, higher education institutions should be held accountable as places of "unfettered critique and knowledge production . . . free from domination by any one ideology or interest" (Pusser, 2011, p. 27). From the perspective of justice as fairness, particularly as applied in positivistic research traditions involv-ing econometric designs and rational policy analysis, equity is examined in terms of inputs and outcomes, with the "black box" of the teaching and learning environments of schooling left largely unexamined. Equity indica-tors tend to be numerical. On the input side, indicators of financial and material resources include factors such as per student revenues or expendi-tures. Human resources are measured, for example, in terms of faculty sta-tus (e.g., full-time, tenured, or part-time, adjunct) and counselor-to-student ratios. Outcome indicators include degree attainment and certification rates, as well as intermediate student progress indicators such as persistence from semester to semester or year to year, credit accumulation, and completion of core classes. Intermediate student progress indicators and degree comple-tion are currently being developed.

Students are also viewed as important inputs into the educational pro-duction process. Their quality is measured by standardized test scores, grade point averages, and class ranks. Student quality, measured in this way, is a driver of perceived institutional quality, which is also ranked based on indi-cators such as research productivity and student–faculty ratios.

Justice as care calls attention to different factors. Equity from the per-spective of care is less focused on testing students' academic content knowledge. The care perspective deemphasizes student rankings, sorting, and tracking (Noddings, 1999, p. 14). It is more concerned that all students receive a quality education free from oppression and from the demeaning messages that are directed at nondominant students through discourse about "at risk" students who are creating an "achievement gap." An important indicator of the quality of care is the pedagogical relationship between teacher and student, which when marked by reciprocal relationships and attention to the growth and well-being of the student as a whole person, becomes the "authentic caring" of validating educational practices (Valenzuela, 1999).

Research on educational equity from the perspective of care tends to use qualitative data and interpretive methods rather than quantitative data and analysis. Conceptualizations of the quality of care in postsecondary settings, such as notions of "belonging" and "validation" discussed in earlier chapters, have been incorporated into survey measures of student perceptions of campus climate. Survey results are then used as part of the institutional assessment, which is a form of campus-based professional accountability. Institutional assessment has typically avoided the prospect that campuses are racialized places that can cause social harm to students of color (Dowd, Sawatzky, et al., 2011; Harper, 2012; Museus & Quaye, 2009). More recent survey items and assessment tools are introducing measures of "diverse learning environments" in order to broaden the focus of attention on student outcomes such as identity development and capacity for civic participation in a multicultural, pluralistic society (Hurtado et al., 2012). These outcomes depend on the quality of relationships among students, faculty, and staff, as well as the capacity of colleges and universities to create inclusive curricula, promote cultural competencies among faculty and staff, and institute culturally sustaining pedagogies.

The principles of justice as care and justice as transformation highlight the importance of culturally inclusive pedagogies and curricula, which are alternatively referred to as culturally responsive or culturally sustaining (Paris, 2012). However, the unit of analysis in institutional assessment tends to be students, whose behaviors, perceptions, attitudes, and beliefs are surveyed to hold up a mirror in which to see campus climate and practices. The beliefs, attitudes, experiences, and capabilities of faculty, counselors, and staff in regard to the demands they face to develop cultural competencies are hardly measured at all (Bensimon, 2007; Dowd, Sawatzky, et al., 2011). This represents a shortcoming that will inhibit efforts to gauge institutional capacity to carry out a program of justice as transformation.

A primary contribution of critical race studies in postsecondary education has been to call attention to the color blindness and race muteness of institutional assessment. Liberal programs and policies must be critiqued when they fail to produce the stated goals of justice as fairness, namely equal opportunity and meritocracy. In the absence of critique, the "embeddedness" of race in all aspects of society and education will not become apparent (Ladson-Billings, 2009, p. 19). Well-meaning liberal programs rooted in the belief that the civil rights struggle is progressive and incrementally successful may only serve to repeat past failures. We have been motivated by this concern to develop self-assessment indicators of practitioner agency and beliefs about their role in empowering students of color. The strategy of self-assessment, rather than external measurement by outside researchers, is incorporated into action research and practitioner inquiry with a focus on racial equity (Dowd, Sawatzky, et al., 2012). Although self-assessment informed by critical perspectives is uncommon (Dowd, 2008), it is needed to address the root causes of racialized inequities.

Higher education must have equal participation by members of different racial and ethnic groups in reconstituting the unjust social arrangements that exist today in educational institutions, as these are the legacy and contemporary expressions of racial discrimination. Those who have experienced racism have knowledge of systemic oppression that is not expendable—their experiential knowledge and scholarly work are necessary to counter master narratives of equal opportunity and civil progress in race relations. Knowledge about education that is not produced through experimental and quasi-experimental research designs is too often devalued (Dowd & Tong, 2007; Grant, 2009; Ladson-Billings, 2009; Lather, 2004; Noddings, 1999; Rodriguez, 2013; Taylor, 2009b).

The hard-fought battles over affirmative action, which have been the signature effort to improve diversity and equity in higher education, have overshadowed the equally important problem of racial segregation between and within colleges and universities of all types. Students of color are disproportionately found in open-access, less selective institutions, but just as problematically they are disproportionately clustered in less desirable academic pathways within colleges and universities.

American politics is so dramatically polarized along racial and ideological lines today that in President Obama's two terms, America's first Black president has risked a media maelstrom at even the merest mention of race. The political climate does not bode well for intelligent or productive conversations about racial equity. The term *diversity*, used under the "umbrella of inclusiveness," is the unsatisfactory and ineffective proxy for the discussions that are needed. It is for that very reason that colleges and universities must function as a public sphere for informed discourse about racism and race relations.

Higher education is a quasi-public good, meaning that the benefits accrue to society as a whole, to individuals, and to profit-making entities such as corporations that depend on an educated work force. Colleges and universities have always operated in the tension between these public and private interests, but their leadership in communicating the importance of the public good to the American public has diminished. This has occurred through the constant reiteration of the benefits of higher education strictly from the perspective of and "embedded in political economic logic" (Pusser, 2011, p. 40). Over time, economic interests have shaped the understanding of the general public and social elites alike that the purpose of universities is the production of private goods. This in turn has shifted understanding as to who should pay for postsecondary education, with an increasing weight placed on the private sector and private citizens—and away from taxpayers—in a shift so thorough as to depress the prospects of revenue generation through the government's power of taxation.

A similar shift has occurred in the public perception of community colleges, which are the traditional gateways to postsecondary education for the social actors who are engaged in less formal and less powerful civic associations. Unlike the graduates of selective and elite universities, the lives of students enrolled at broad-access "opportunity colleges" unfold at a considerable distance from the political–economic networks of the elite (Pusser, 2011, p. 28). This separation and the self-interested attention of elite actors to their own autonomy, resources, and prestige have left opportunity colleges, such as community colleges and less selective state universities, vulnerable.

Elite actors in the accountability field have adopted technical solutions over humane solutions. The diminishment of higher education's role in the public sphere is a loss. Although other social institutions contribute to the public good, postsecondary education contributes in unique ways by promoting "the agency of self-determining citizens" (Marginson, 2011, p. 9). It cannot fulfill this role if the accountability field maintains a position of race blindness.

Throughout this book we examined the tensions raised by differing perspectives on racism and inequality as we have involved practitioners and policymakers in the inquiry processes of the Equity Scorecard. We shared what we have learned about using participatory critical action research to create a more equitable postsecondary educational system. Action research tools and processes, including the Equity Scorecard, are not always effective. However, in our view, action research, in combination with political accountability pressures, is the most promising strategy to bring about racial equity in higher education. Action research, which is a process of knowledge production and collective action, is necessary because society currently lacks the knowledge and practical experience to effectively reduce educational disparities. Before we will see systemic reforms, a deeper, more sustained conversation is needed about what constitutes fairness in a society where racial discrimination and segregation are still prevalent.

What is fair, when it comes to creating racial equity in higher education, remains a challenging question because people arrive at very different
answers with equal degrees of conviction. Many people who have worked
their way up in society through the U.S. educational system, seemingly by
their own brains and brawn, naturally view the existing system as fair—it
worked for them. But those who view the system as a meritocracy often do
not realize that Black poverty is not the same as White poverty. Not only
were slaves kept from property ownership, but unjust debts were imposed
relentlessly on subsequent generations, for example through federal housing
policy in the 1960s and by unscrupulous mortgage lending in the years leading up the Great Recession (Coates, 2014).

The Native American, Puerto Rican, Native Hawaiian, and Mexican
American experience of colonization and dispossession of lands and language is not the same as the experience of the voluntary immigrant. Though
immigrants who have dark skin and speak languages other than English
are also subject to racial discrimination, they immigrate in search of a new
home. For those with adequate means to persist through difficult transitions, that search is often rewarded. Immigrants, the poor, and individuals who are White yet differently abled or gendered from the norm have
experienced discrimination. However, the way in which higher educational
institutions have acted to discriminate or to provide access to U.S. society
has differed for each of these groups. Producing knowledge of the historical
roots of contemporary racial inequities in higher education may fuel a sense
of urgency to do more and to do better. Then there will be a critical role
for accountability metrics, like those of the Equity Scorecard, to target and
monitor progress to close equity gaps. In constructing these new accountability policies and practices, we have an opportunity to garner a collective
sense of fairness that motivates transformative change.

References

AASCU State Relations and Policy Analysis Team. (2013, January). Top 10 higher education state policy issues for 2013. *Policy Matters*. Retrieved from www.aascu.org/policy/publications/policy-matters

Academic Senate for California Community Colleges. (2007, March 17). Basic skills as the foundation for student success in California community colleges. Basic Skills Initiative. Sacramento, CA: Academic Senate for California Community Colleges. Available on the Basic Skills Initiative website at basicskills.publishpath.com/publications

Adelman, C. (2005). *Moving into town—and moving on: The community college in the lives of traditional-age students*. Washington, DC: U.S. Department of Education.

Aguirre, T. (2012). *Evaluating the impact of CUE's Equity Scorecard tools on practitioner beliefs and practices* (Doctoral dissertation). University of Southern California, Los Angeles.

Altheide, D., Coyle, M., DeVriese, K., & Schneider, C. (2008). Emergent qualitative document analysis. In S. N. Hesse-Biber (Ed.), *Handbook of emergent methods* (pp. 127–151). New York, NY: Guilford Press.

Anderson, G. M. (2012). Equity and critical policy analysis in higher education: A bridge still too far. *Review of Higher Education, 36*(1), 133–142.

Argyris, C. (1977, September-October). Double loop learning in organizations. *Harvard Business Review, 55*, 115–125.

Argyris, C. (1982, Autumn). The executive mind and double-loop learning. *Organizational Dynamics, 11*, 5–22.

Argyris, C., & Schön, D. A. (1971). Organizational learning. In D. S. Pugh (Ed.), *Organizational theory* (pp. 352–371). New York, NY: Penguin Books.

Argyris, C., & Schön, D. A. (1996). *Organizational learning II: Theory, method, and practice*. Reading, MA: Addison-Wesley.

Attewell, P., Lavin, D., Domina, T., & Levey, T. (2006). New evidence on college remediation. *Journal of Higher Education, 77*(5), 887–924.

Ayers, W. (2006). Trudge toward freedom: Educational research in the public interest. In G. Ladson-Billings & W. F. Tate (Eds.), *Education research in the public interest: Social justice, action, and policy* (pp. 81–97). New York, NY: Teachers College Press.

Baez, B. (2000). Race-related service and faculty of color: Conceptualizing critical agency in academe. *Higher Education, 39*, 363–391.

Bahr, P. R. (2010). Preparing the underprepared: An analysis of racial disparities in postsecondary mathematics remediation. *Journal of Higher Education, 81*(2), 209–237.

Baldwin, J. (1964a). *The fire next time.* London, United Kingdom: Penguin Books. (Original work published 1962 by Michael Joseph)

Baldwin, J. (1964b). *Nobody knows my name: More notes of a native son.* London, United Kingdom: Michael Joseph. (Original work published 1961 by Dial Press)

Ball, A. F. (2009). Toward a theory of generative change in culturally and linguistically complex classrooms. *American Educational Research Journal, 46*(1), 45–72.

Barak, R. J., & Kniker, C. R. (2002). Benchmarking by state higher education boards. In B. E. Bender & J. H. Schuh (Eds.), *Using benchmarking to inform practices in higher education* [Special issue]. *New Directions for Higher Education, 2002* (118, pp. 93–102). San Francisco, CA: Jossey Bass.

Bartolomé, L. I. (2008). Introduction: Beyond the fog of ideology. In L. I. Bartolomé (Ed.), *Ideologies in education: Unmasking the trap of teacher neutrality* (pp. ix–xxix). New York, NY: Peter Lang.

Battilana, J. (2006). Agency and institutions: The enabling role of individuals' social position. *Organization Articles, 13*(5), 653–676.

Baum, S., & Kurose, C. (2013). Community colleges in context: Exploring financing of two- and four-year institutions. In Century Foundation Task Force on Preventing Community Colleges from Becoming Separate and Unequal, *Bridging the higher education divide: Strengthening community colleges and restoring the American Dream* (pp. 73–108). New York, NY: Century Foundation Press.

Bauman, G. L. (2002). *Developing a culture of evidence: Using institutional data to identify inequitable educational outcomes* (Doctoral dissertation). University of Southern California, Los Angeles.

Bauman, G. L. (2005). Promoting organizational learning in higher education to achieve equity in educational outcomes In A. Kezar (Ed.), *Organizational learning in higher education* [Special issue]. *New Directions for Higher Education, 131,* 23–35. San Francisco, CA: Jossey Bass.

Bell, D. A., Jr. (2009a). *Brown v. Board of Education* and the interest convergence dilemma. In E. Taylor, D. Gillborn, & G. Ladson-Billings (Eds.), *Foundations of critical race theory in education* (pp. 73–84). New York, NY: Routledge.

Bell, D. A., Jr. (2009b). Who's afraid of critical race theory? In E. Taylor, D. Gillborn, & G. Ladson-Billings (Eds.), *Foundations of critical race theory in education* (pp. 1–13). New York, NY: Routledge.

Bender, B. E., & Schuh, J. H. (Eds.). (2002). *Using benchmarking to inform practice in higher education* [Special issue]. *New Directions for Higher Education, 118.* San Francisco, CA: Jossey-Bass.

Bensimon, E. M. (2005a). Closing the achievement gap in higher education: An organizational learning perspective. In A. Kezar (Ed.), *Organizational learning in higher education* [Special issue]. *New Directions for Higher Education, 131,* 99–111. San Francisco, CA: Jossey-Bass.

Bensimon, E. M. (2005b). *Equality as a fact, equality as a result: A matter of institutional accountability.* Washington, DC: American Council on Education.

Bensimon, E. M. (2006). Learning equity-mindedness: Equality in educational outcomes. *The Academic Workplace, 1*(17), 2–21.

Bensimon, E. M. (2007). The underestimated significance of practitioner knowledge in the scholarship of student success. *Review of Higher Education, 30*(4),
441–469.

Bensimon, F. M., & Bishop, R. (2012). Introduction: Why "critical"? The need for
new ways of knowing. *Review of Higher Education, 36*(1, supplement), 1–7.

Bensimon, E. M., & Dowd, A. C. (2012). *Developing the capacity of faculty to
become institutional agents for Latinos in STEM.* Los Angeles, CA: University
of Southern California.

Bensimon, E. M., Dowd, A. C., Alford, H., & Trapp, F. (2007*). Missing 87: A study
of the "transfer gap" and "choice gap."* Long Beach and Los Angeles: Long
Beach City College and the Center for Urban Education, University of Southern
California.

Bensimon, E. M., Dowd, A. C., Chase, M. M., Sawatzky, M., Shieh, L. T., Rall, R.
M., & Jones, T. (2012). *Community college change agents at HSIs: Stewarding
HSI-STEM funds for Latino student success in STEM.* Los Angeles, CA: Uni-
versity of Southern California.

Bensimon, E. M., Dowd, A. C., Longanecker, D., & Witham, K. (2012). We have
goals: Now what? *Change: The Magazine of Higher Learning, 44,* 14–25.

Bensimon, E. M., Hao, L., & Bustillos, L. T. (2006). Measuring the state of equity
in public higher education. In P. Gandara, G. Orfield, & C. L. Horn (Eds.), *Expanding opportunity in higher education: Leveraging promise* (pp. 143–165).
Albany: State University of New York Press.

Bensimon, E. M., & Malcom, L. E. (2012). *Confronting equity issues on campus:
Implementing the Equity Scorecard in theory and practice.* Sterling, VA: Stylus.

Bensimon, E. M., & Neumann, A. (1993). *Redesigning collegiate leadership: Teams
and teamwork in higher education.* Baltimore, MD: Johns Hopkins University
Press.

Bensimon, E. M., Polkinghorne, D. E., Bauman, G. L., & Vallejo, E. (2004). Doing
research that makes a difference. *Journal of Higher Education, 75*(1), 104–126.

Bensimon, E. M., Rueda, R., Dowd, A. C., & Harris, F., III. (2007). Accountability,
equity, and practitioner learning and change. *Metropolitan, 18*(3), 28–45.

Bergerson, A. A. (2003). Critical race theory and White racism: Is there room for
White scholars in fighting racism in education? *Qualitative Studies in Education, 16*(1), 51–63.

Bettinger, E., & Long, B. (2007). Institutional responses to reduce inequalities in
college outcomes: Remedial and developmental courses in higher education.
In S. Dickert-Conlin & R. Rubenstein (Eds.), *Economic inequality and higher
education: Access, persistence, and success* (pp. 69–100). New York, NY: Rus-
sell Sage Foundation.

Bishop, M. (2014). *Language and identity in critical sensegiving: Journeys of higher
education equity agents* (Doctoral dissertation). University of Southern California, Los Angeles.

Blow, C. M. (2013, August 23). 50 years later. *New York Times.* Retrieved from
www.nytimes.com/2013/08/24/opinion/blow-50-years-later.html?_r=0

Board of Governors of the California Community Colleges, Academic Affairs Division, System Office. (2008). Report on the System's current programs in English as a second language (ESL) and basic skills. Sacramento, CA: Author. Retrieved September 9, 2014, from https://www.skylinecollege.edu/collegesuccessinitiative/assets/documents/resources/08CCC_BSI_Report.pdf

Bobo, L. D., & Charles, C. Z. (2009). Race in the American mind: From the Moynihan Report to the Obama candidacy. The Moynihan Report revisited: Lessons and reflections after four decades [Special issue]. *The Annals of the American Academy of Political and Social Science, 621*(1), 243–259.

Bragg, D. D., & Durham, B. (2012). Perspectives on access and equity in the era of (community) college completion. *Community College Review, 40*(2), 93–116.

Brown, R. S., & Niemi, D. N. (2007). *Investigating the alignment of high school and community college assessment in California.* San Jose, CA: National Center for Public Policy and Higher Education.

Brown, R. Z. (2012). *Equity for students of color through practitioner accountability* (Doctoral dissertation). University of Southern California, Los Angeles.

Bruning, M. (2006). *Beyond access: An evaluation of attitudes and learning towards achieving equitable educational outcomes in higher education* (Doctoral dissertation). University of Southern California, Los Angeles.

Bustillos, L. T. (2007). *Exploring faculty beliefs about remedial mathematics students: A collaborative inquiry approach* (Doctoral dissertation). University of Southern California, Los Angeles.

Bustillos, L. T., Rueda, R., & Bensimon, E. M. (2011). Faculty views of underrepresented students in community college settings. In P. R. Portes & S. Salas (Eds.), *Vygotsky in 21st century society.* New York, NY: Peter Lang.

California Community Colleges (n.d.). Education and the economy: Shaping California's future today. (System strategic plan, executive summary). Sacramento, CA: Author. Retrieved September 6, 2014 from http://www.gavilan.edu/research/spd/ccc_strategic_plan_es_low_res.pdf

Carnevale, A. P., & Strohl, J. (2013). *Separate & unequal: How higher education reinforces the intergenerational reproduction of White racial privilege.* Washington, DC: Georgetown Public Policy Institute, Georgetown University.

Carter-Andrews, D.J., & Tuitt, F. (2013). Racism as the environmental hazard in educational spaces: An overview and introduction. In D.J. Carter-Andrews & F. Tuitt (Ed.), *Contesting the myth of a "post racial" era: The continued significance of race in U.S. Education* (pp. 1-9). New York, NY: Peter Lang.

Century Foundation Task Force on Preventing Community Colleges from Becoming Separate and Unequal. (2013). *Bridging the higher education divide: Strengthening community colleges and restoring the American Dream.* New York, NY: Century Foundation Press.

Chase, M. M. (2013). *Culture, politics, and policy implementation: How practitioners interpret and implement transfer policy in a technical college environment* (Doctoral dissertation). University of Southern California, Los Angeles.

Chase, M. M., Dowd, A. C., Pazich, L. B., & Bensimon, E. M. (2014). Transfer equity for "minoritized" students: A critical policy analysis of seven states. *Educational Policy, 28*(5), 669–717.

Chesler, M. A., & Crowfoot, J. (1989). An organizational analysis of racism in higher education. In M. Peterson (Ed.), *ASHE Reader on organization and governance in higher education* (4th ed.) (pp. 436–469). Lexington, MA: Ginn Press.

Clune, W. H. (1994). The shift from equity to adequacy in school finance reform.
Educational Policy, 8(4), 376–395.

Coates, T. (2014). The case for reparations. *The Atlantic, 313*(5). Retrieved from
http://www.theatlantic.com/features/archive/2014/05/the-case-for-repara-
tions/361631/

Cochran-Smith, M., & Lytle, S. L. (2009). *Inquiry as stance: Practitioner research
for the next generation.* New York, NY: Teachers College Press.

Contreras, F. E., Malcom, L. E., & Bensimon, E. M. (2008). Hispanic-serving institutions: Closeted identity and the production of equitable outcomes for
Latino/a students. In M. Gasman, B. Baez, & C. Turner (Eds.), *Interdisciplinary
approaches to understanding minority serving institutions* (pp. 71–90). Albany:
State University of New York Press.

Cornell, L. A. (2012). *Action research as a strategy for improving equity and diversity: Implementation, constraints, outcomes* (Doctoral dissertation). University
of Southern California, Los Angeles.

Delgado, R. (2009). Affirmative action as majoritarian device: Or, do you really
want to be a role model? In E. Taylor, D. Gillborn, & G. Ladson-Billings (Eds.),
Foundations of critical race theory in education (pp. 109–116). New York, NY:
Routledge.

Denning, S. (2004, May). Telling tales. *Harvard Business Review, (82)*5, 122–129.

DesJardins, S. L. (2003). Understanding and using efficiency and equity criteria in
the study of higher education policy. In J. C. Smart & W. G. Tierney (Eds.),
Higher education: Handbook of theory and research (Vol. 17, pp. 173–219).
New York, NY: Agathon Press.

Dewey, J. (1989). The underlying philosophy of education. In J. A. Boydston (Ed.),
John Dewey: The later works, 1925–1953 (Vol. 8, 1933). Carbondale, IL:
Southern Illinois University Press. (Original work published 1933)

Dowd, A. C. (2003, March). From access to outcome equity: Revitalizing the democratic mission of the community college. *Annals of the American Academy of
Political and Social Science, 586*(1), 92–119.

Dowd, A. C. (2004). Community college revenue disparities: What accounts for an
urban college deficit? *Urban Review, 36*(4), 251–270.

Dowd, A. C. (2008). The community college as gateway and gatekeeper: Moving beyond the access "saga" to outcome equity. *Harvard Educational Review, 77*(4),
407–419.

Dowd, A. C., Bishop, R. M., & Bensimon, E. M. (in press). Critical action research
on race and equity in higher education. In A. M. Martínez-Alemán, E. M. Bensimon, & B. Pusser (Eds.), *Critical approaches to the study of higher education.*
Baltimore, MD: Johns Hopkins University Press.

Dowd, A. C., Bishop, R., Bensimon, E. M., & Witham, K. (2012). Accountability
for equity in postsecondary education. In K. S. Gallagher, R. Goodyear, D. J.
Brewer, & R. Rueda (Eds.), *Urban education: A model for leadership and policy*
(pp. 170–185). New York, NY: Routledge.

Dowd, A. C., Cheslock, J. J., & Melguizo, T. (2008). Transfer access from community colleges and the distribution of elite higher education. *Journal of Higher Education, 79*(4), 442–472.

Dowd, A. C., Malcom, L. E., Nakamoto, J., & Bensimon, E. M. (2012). Institutional researchers as teachers and equity advocates: Facilitating organizational learning and change. In E. M. Bensimon & L. Malcom (Eds.), *Confronting equity issues on campus: Implementing the Equity Scorecard in theory and practice* (pp. 191–215). Sterling, VA: Stylus.

Dowd, A. C., & Melguizo, T. (2008). Socioeconomic stratification of community college transfer access in the 1980s and 1990s: Evidence from HS&B and NELS. *Review of Higher Education, 31*(4), 377–400.

Dowd, A. C., Pak, J. H., & Bensimon, E. M. (2013). The role of institutional agents in promoting transfer. *Education Policy Analysis Archives, 21*(15), 1–44.

Dowd, A. C., Sawatzky, M., & Korn, R. (2011). Theoretical foundations and a research agenda to validate measures of intercultural effort. *Review of Higher Education, 35*(1), 17–44.

Dowd, A. C., Sawatzky, M., Rall, R. M., & Bensimon, E. M. (2012). Action research: An essential practice for twenty-first century assessment. In R. T. Palmer, D. C. Maramba, & M. Gasman (Eds.), *Fostering success of ethnic and racial minorities in STEM: The role of minority serving institutions* (pp. 149–167). New York, NY: Routledge.

Dowd, A. C., & Shieh, L. T. (2013). Community college financing: Equity, efficiency, and accountability. In *The NEA 2013 almanac of higher eucation* (pp. 37–65). Washington, DC: National Education Association.

Dowd, A. C., & Tong, V. P. (2007). Accountability, assessment, and the scholarship of "best practice." In J. C. Smart (Ed.), *Handbook of higher education* (Vol. 22, pp. 57–119). New York, NY: Springer.

Dyer, J., Gregersen, H., & Christensen, C. M. (2011). *The innovator's DNA: Mastering the five skills of disruptive innovators.* Boston, MA: Harvard Business Review Press.

Ellis, V. (2011). Reenergising professional creativity from a CHAT perspective: Seeing knowledge and history in practice. *Mind, Culture, and Activity, 18*(2), 181–193.

Enciso, M. (2009). *The influence of organizational learning on inquiry group participants in promoting equity at a community college* (Doctoral dissertation). University of Southern California, Los Angeles.

Engeström, Y. (2001). Expansive learning at work: Toward an activity theoretical reconceptualization. *Journal of Education and Work, 14*(1), 133–156.

Engeström, Y. (2008). *From teams to knots: Activity-theoretical studies of collaboration and learning at work.* Cambridge, United Kingdom: Cambridge University Press.

Espino, M. M. (2012). Seeking the "truth" in the stories we tell: The role of critical race epistemology in higher education research. *Review of Higher Education, 36*(1), 31–67.

Fulks, J., & Alancraig, M. (Eds). (2008). *Constructing a framework for success: A holistic approach to basic skills.* Sacramento, CA: Academic Senate for California Community Colleges. Retrieved 30 April 2011, from http://www.cccbsi.org/basic-skills-handbook

Gándara, P., & Contreras, F. (2009). *The Latino education crisis: The consequences of failed social policies.* Cambridge, MA: Harvard University Press.

Gasman, M. (2002). W.E.B. Du Bois and Charles S. Johnson: Differing views on the role of philanthropy in higher education. *History of Education Quarterly, 42*(4), 493–516.

Gaur, S. (2009). *An examination of collaboration amongst student affairs and academic affairs professionals in an action research project* (Doctoral dissertation). University of Southern California, Los Angeles.

Gillborn, D. (2005). Education policy as an act of White supremacy: Whiteness, critical race theory, and education reform. *Journal of Education Policy, 20*(4), 485–505.

Goldrick-Rab, S., & Kinsley, P. (2013). School integration and the open door philosophy: Rethinking the economic and racial composition of commuity colleges. In Century Foundation Task Force on Preventing Community Colleges from Becoming Separate and Unequal, *Bridging the higher education divide: Strengthening community colleges and restoring the American dream* (pp. 109–136). New York, NY: Century Foundation Press.

González, N., Moll, L. C., & Amanti, C. (Eds.). (2005). *Funds of knowledge: Theorizing practices in households, communities, and classrooms.* Mahwah, NJ: Lawrence Erlbaum.

Gonzalez, R. (2009). *Achieving equity in educational outcomes through organizational learning: Enhancing the institutional effectiveness of community colleges* (Doctoral dissertation). University of Southern California, Los Angeles.

Grant, C. A. (2009). Multiculturalism, race, and the public interest: Hanging on to great-great-granddaddy's legacy. In G. Ladson-Billings & W. F. Tate (Eds.), *Education research in the public interest: Social justice, action, and policy* (pp. 158–172). New York, NY: Teachers College Press.

Greene, M. (1988). *The dialectic of freedom.* New York, NY: Teachers College Press.

Greenwood, D. J., & Levin, M. (2005). Reform of the social sciences and of universities through action research. In N. K. Denzin & Y. S. Lincoln (Eds.), *Handbook of qualitative research* (3rd ed., pp. 43–64). Thousand Oaks, CA: Sage.

Groundwater-Smith, S. (2009). Co-operative change management through practitioner inquiry. In S. E. Noffke & B. Somekh (Eds.), *The SAGE handbook of educational action research* (pp. 238–248). Los Angeles, CA: Sage.

Grubb, W. N. (2006). "Like, what do I do now?" The dilemmas of guidance counseling. In T. Bailey & V. Smith Morest (Eds.), *Defending the community college equity agenda* (pp. 195–222). Baltimore, MD: Johns Hopkins University Press.

Grubb, W. N., Boner, E., Frankel, K., Parker, L., Patterson, D., Gabriner, R., . . . Wilson, S. (2011). *Understanding the "crisis" in basic skills: Framing the issue in community colleges* (Basic Skills Instruction in California Community Colleges No. 1). Berkeley, CA: Policy Analysis for California Education.

Grubb, W. N., & Gabriner, R. (2013). *Basic skills education in community colleges: Inside and outside of classrooms.* New York, NY: Routledge.

Gutierrez, K. D., Morales, P. Z., & Martinez, D. C. (2009). Remediating literacy: Culture, difference, and learning for students from nondominant communities. *Review of Research in Education, 33*, 212–245. doi:10.3102/0091732x08328267

Gutierrez, K. D., & Vossoughi, S. (2010). Lifting off the ground to return anew: Mediated praxis, transformative learning, and social design experiments. *Journal of Teacher Education, 61*(1–2), 100–117. doi:10.1177/0022487109347877

Haney-López, I. F. (2010). Is the "post" in post-racial the "blind" in colorblind? *Cardozo Law Review, 32*, 807–831.

Hao, L. (2006). *Assessing equitable postsecondary educational outcomes for Hispanics in California and Texas* (Doctoral dissertation). University of Southern California, Los Angeles.

Harper, S. R. (2012). Race without racism: How higher education researchers minimize racist institutional norms. *Review of Higher Education, 36*(1), 9–29.

Harper, S. R., & Hurtado, S. (2011). Nine themes in campus racial climates and implications for institutional transformation. In S. R. Harper & S. Hurtado (Eds.), *Racial and ethnic diversity in higher education* (ASHE Reader Series, 3rd ed., pp. 204–216). Boston, MA: Pearson.

Harper, S. R., & Patton, L. D. (Eds.). (2007). *Responding to the realities of race on campus* (New Directions for Student Services ed., Vol. 120). San Francisco, CA: Jossey-Bass.

Harper, S. R., Patton, L. D., & Wooden, O. S. (2009). Access and equity for African American students in higher education: A critical race historical analysis of policy efforts. *Journal of Higher Education, 80*(4), 389–414.

Hill, E. G. (2008). *Back to basics: Improving college readiness of community college students.* Sacramento, CA: California Legislative Analyst's Office.

Howard, G. R. (2006). *We can't teach what we don't know: White teachers, multiracial schools.* New York, NY: Teachers College Press.

Howe, K. R. (1992). Liberal democracy, equal educational opportunity, and the challenge of multiculturalism. *American Educational Research Journal, 29*(3), 455–470.

Howe, K. R. (1997). *Understanding equal opportunity: Social justice, democracy, and schooling.* New York, NY: Teachers College Press.

Hurtado, S., Alvarez, C. L., Guillermo-Wann, C., Cuellar, M., & Arellano, L. (2012). A model for diverse learning environments: The scholarship on creating and assessing conditions for student success. In J. C. Smart (Ed.), *Handbook of higher education* (Vol. 27, pp. 41–122). New York, NY: Springer.

Hurtado, S., & Carter, D. F. (1997). Effects of college transition and perceptions of the campus racial climate on Latino college students' sense of belonging. *Sociology of Education, 70*(4), 324–345.

Iverson, S. V. (2007). Camouflaging power and privilege: A critical race analysis of university diversity policies. *Educational Administration Quarterly, 43*, 586–611.

James, K. (2008). *Changing the landscape of institutional assessment on transfer: The impact of action research methods on community college faculty and counselors* (Doctoral dissertation). University of Southern California, Los Angeles.

Javier, M. G. (2009). *Math faculty as institutional agents: Role reflection through inquiry-based activities* (Doctoral dissertation). University of Southern California, Los Angeles.

Jenkins, D., & Boswell, K. (2002). *State policies on community college remedial education: Findings from a national survey.* Denver, CO: Education Commission of the States.

Jones, T., Bensimon, E. M., McNair, T. B., & Dowd, A. C. (2011). *Using data and inquiry to build equity-focused college-going cultures.* Washington, DC: National College Access Network.

Jones, T. (2013). *Addressing a historical mission in a performance driven system: A case study of a public historically Black university engaged in the Equity Scorecard processes* (Doctoral dissertation). University of Southern California, Los Angeles.

Kemmis, S., & McTaggart, R. (2000). Participatory action research. In N. K. Denzin & Y. S. Lincoln (Eds.), *Handbook of qualitative research* (2nd ed., pp. 567–605). Thousand Oaks, CA: Sage.

Kemmis, S., & McTaggart, R. (2005). Participatory action research: Communicative action and the public sphere. In N. K. Denzin & Y. S. Lincoln (Eds.), *Handbook of qualitative research* (3rd ed., pp. 559–603). Thousand Oaks, CA: Sage Publications.

Kezar, A. (2011). What is the best way to achieve broader reach of improved practices in higher education? *Innovative Higher Education, 36*, 235–247.

Kirst, M. (2007, Winter). Who needs it?: Identifying the proportion of students who require postsecondary remedial education is virtually impossible. *National Crosstalk, 15*, 11–12.

Kleinman, S., & Copp, M. (2009). Denying social harm: Students' resistance to lessons about inequality. *Teaching Sociology, 37*(3), 283–293.

Kuh, G. D., & Vesper, N. (1997). A comparison of student experiences with good practices in undergraduate education between 1990 and 1994. *The Review of Higher Education, 21*(1).

Labaree, D. F. (1997). *How to succeed in school without really learning: The credentials race in American education.* New Haven: Yale University Press.

Ladson-Billings, G. (1995). Toward a theory of culturally relevant pedagogy. *American Educational Research Journal, 32*(3), 465–491.

Ladson-Billings, G. (2009). Just what is critical race theory and what's it doing in a *nice* field like education? In E. Taylor, D. Gillborn, & G. Ladson-Billings (Eds.), *Foundations of critical race theory in education* (pp. 17–36). New York, NY: Routledge.

Ladson-Billings, G., & Tate, B. (1995). Toward a critical race theory of education. *Teachers College Record, 97*(1), 47–67.

Ladson-Billings, G., & Tate, W. F. (Eds.). (2006). *Education research in the public interest: Social justice, action, and policy.* New York, NY: Teachers College Press.

Lather, P. (2004). This IS your father's paradigm: Government intrusion and the case of qualitative research in education. *Qualitative Inquiry, 10*(1), 15–34.

Laughter, J. (2013). "I am my brother's keeper; I am my sister's keeper": Rejecting meritocracy and embracing relational pluralism. In D.J. Carter-Andrews & F. Tuitt (Ed.), *Contesting the myth of a "post racial" era: The continued significance of race in U.S. Education* (pp. 1-9). New York, NY: Peter Lang.

LBJ Presidential Library Online. (1965, 4 June) President Lyndon B. Johnson's commencement address at Howard University: "To fulfill these rights." Retrieved from http://www.lbjlib.utexas.edu/johnson/archives.hom/speeches.hom/650604.asp

Lee, Y.-J. (2011). More than just story-telling: Cultural–historical activity theory as an under-utilized methodology for educational change research. *Journal of Curriculum Studies, 43*(3), 403–424.

Lee, Y.-J., & Roth, W.-M. (2007). The individual collective dialectical in the learning organization. *The Learning Organization, 14*(2), 92–107.

Levin, H. L. (1994). The necessary and sufficient conditions for achieving educational equity. In R. Berne & L. O. Picus (Eds.), *Equity outcomes in education* (pp. 167–190). Thousand Oaks, CA: Corwin Press.

Loewen, J. W. (2005) *Sundown towns: A hidden dimension of American racism.* New York: Touchstone.

Levonisova, S. V. (2012). *Evaluating the impact of CUE's action research processes and tools on practitioners' beliefs and practices* (Doctoral dissertation). University of Southern California, Los Angeles.

Little, J. W. (2012). Understanding data use practice among teachers: The contribution of micro-process studies. *American Journal of Education, 118*(2), 143–166.

Lucas, J. R. (1980). *On justice.* Oxford, United Kingdom: Clarendon Press.

Marginson, S. (2011). The "public" contribution of universities in an increasingly global world. In B. Pusser, S. Marginson, I. Ordorika, & K. Kempner (Eds.), *Universities and the public sphere: Knowledge creation and state building in the era of globalization* (pp. 7–25). New York, NY: Routledge/Taylor & Francis.

Marsh, J. A. (2012). Interventions promoting educators' use of data: Research insights and gaps. *Teachers College Record, 114*(11), 1–48.

Martínez-Alemán, A. M. (2012). *Accountability, pragmatic aims, and the American University.* New York: Routledge.

Matias, C. E., & Zembylas, M. (2014, June 10). When saying you care is not really caring: Emotions of disgust, whiteness ideology, and teacher education. *Critical Studies in Education.* doi:10.1080/17508487.2014.922489.

Mazzeo, C. (2002). Stakes for students: Agenda-setting and remedial education. *Review of Higher Education, 26*(1), 19–39.

McClaren, P. L., & Giarelli, J. M. (1995). Introduction: Critical theory and educational research. In P. L. McClaren & J. M. Giarelli (Eds.), *Critical theory and educational research* (pp. 1–22). Albany: State University of New York Press.

McLaughlin, M. W., & Mitra, D. (2001). Theory-based change and change-based theory: Going deeper, going broader. *Journal of Educational Change, 2*, 301–323.

McTaggart, R. (1997). Guiding principles for participatory action research. In R. McTaggart (Ed.), *Participatory action research: International contexts and consequences* (pp. 25–43). Albany: State University of New York Press.

Melguizo, T., & Kosiewicz, H. (2013). The role of race, income, and funding on student success: An institutional level analysis of California community colleges. In Century Foundation Task Force on Preventing Community Colleges from Becoming Separate and Unequal, *Bridging the higher education divide: Strengthening community colleges and restoring the American dream* (pp. 137–155). New York, NY: Century Foundation Press.

Merisotis, J. P., & Phipps, R. A. (2000). Remedial education in colleges and universities: What's really going on? *Review of Higher Education, 24*(1), 67–85.

Metcalfe, A. S. (2009). The geography of access and excellence: Spatial diversity in higher education system design. *Higher Education, 58,* 205–220.

Milner, H. R., IV. (2007). Race, culture, and researcher positionality: Working through dangers seen, unseen, and unforeseen. *Educational Researcher, 36*(7), 388–400.

Minor, J. A. (2008). Segregation residual in higher education: A tale of two states. *American Educational Research Journal, 45*(4), 861–885.

Mmeje, K.C. (2012). *The Transfer Academy: Providing community college students with the informational, structural, relational, and cultural resources to transfer successfully to a four-year college* (Doctoral dissertation). University of Southern California, Los Angeles.

Moore, C., & Shulock, N. (2005). *Variations on a theme: Higher education performance in California by region and race.* Sacramento: Institute for Higher Education Leadership and Policy, California State University.

Museus, S. D., & Neville, K. M. (2012). Delineating the ways that key institutional agents provide racial minority students with access to social capital in college. *Journal of College Student Development, 53*(3), 436–452.

Museus, S. D., & Quaye, S. J. (2009). Toward an intercultural perspective of racial and ethnic minority college student persistence. *Review of Higher Education, 33*(1), 67–94.

Nasir, N. S., & Hand, V. M. (2006). Exploring sociocultural perspectives on race, culture, and learning. *Review of Educational Research, 76*(4), 449–475.

Neumann, A. (1991). The thinking team: Toward a cognitive model of administrative teamwork in higher education. *Journal of Higher Education, 62*(5), 485–513.

Noddings, N. (1992). *The challenge to care in schools.* New York, NY: Teachers College Press.

Noddings, N. (1999). Care, justice, and equity. In M. S. Katz, N. Noddings, & K. A. Strike (Eds.), *Justice and caring: The search for common ground in education* (pp. 7–20). New York, NY: Teachers College Press.

Noffke, S. E. (1997). Professional, personal, and political dimensions of action research. *Review of Educational Research, 22,* 305–343.

Noffke, S. E. (2009). Revisiting the professional, personal, and political dimension of action research. In S. E. Noffke & B. Somekh (Eds.), *The SAGE handbook of educational action research* (pp. 6–23). Los Angeles, CA: Sage.

Noffke, S. E., & Somekh, B. (Eds.). (2009). *The SAGE handbook of educational action research.* Los Angeles: Sage.

Odden, A. R., & Picus, L. O. (2008). *School finance: A policy perspective* (4th ed.). New York, NY: McGraw-Hill.

Ogawa, R., Crain, R., Loomis, M., & Ball, T. (2008). CHAT-IT: Toward conceptualizing learning in the context of formal organizations. *Educational Researcher, 37*(2), 83–95.

Olivas, M. A. (2005a). Brown and the desegregative ideal: Location, race, and college attendance policies. *Cornell Law Review, 90*, 391–417.

Olivas, M. A. (2005b). Higher education as "place": Location, race, and college attendance policies. *Review of Higher Education, 28*(2), 169–189.

Orfield, G., Bachmeier, M. D., James, D. R., & Eitle, T. (1997). Deepening segregation in American public schools: A special report from the Harvard Project on School Desegregation. *Equity and Excellence in Education, 30*(2), 5–24.

Padilla, A. M. (1994). Ethnic minority scholars, research, and mentoring: Current and future issues. *Educational Researcher, 23*(24–27).

Paris, D. C. (2012). Culturally sustaining pedagogy: A needed change in stance, terminology, and practice. *Educational Researcher, 41*, 93–97.

Patton, L. (2014). *Practitioner reflections and agency in fostering African American and Latino student outcomes in STEM* (Doctoral dissertation). University of Southern California, Los Angeles.

Paulsen, M. B., & Toutkoushian, R. K. (2008). Economic models and policy analysis in higher education: A diagrammatic exposition. In J. C. Smart (Ed.), *Higher education: Handbook of theory and research* (Vol. 23, pp. 1–49). New York, NY: Springer.

Peña, E. V. (2007). *The responsive academic practitioner: Using inquiry methods for self-change* (Doctoral dissertation). University of Southern California, Los Angeles.

Peña, E. V. (2012). Inquiry methods for critical consciousness and self-change in faculty. *The Review of Higher Education, 36*(1).

Peña, E. V., Bensimon, E. M., & Coylar, J. (2006). Contextual problem defining: Learning to think and act. *Liberal Education, 92*(2), 50–55.

Perna, L. W., & Finney, J. E. (2014). *The attainment agenda: State policy leadership in higher education*. Baltimore: Johns Hopkins University Press.

Pickens, A. M. (2012). *Creating an equity state of mind: A learning process* (Doctoral dissertation). University of Southern California, Los Angeles.

Polkinghorne, D. E. (2004). *Practice and the human sciences: The case for a judgment-based practice of care*. Albany: State University of New York Press.

Pollock, M. (2001). How the question we ask most about race in education is the very question we most suppress. *Educational Researcher, 30*(9), 2–12.

Posselt, J. R., Jacquet, O., Bielby, R., & Bastedo, M. (2012). Access without equity: Longitudinal analyses of institutional stratification by race and ethnicity, 1972–2004. *American Educational Research Journal, 49*(6), 1074–1111.

Post, D. (2007). *An evaluation of individual learning among members of a diversity scorecard project evidence team* (Doctoral dissertation). University of Southern California, Los Angeles.

Prior, L. (2008). Researching documents: Emergent methods. In S. N. Hesse-Biber (Ed.), *Handbook of emergent methods* (pp. 111–126). New York, NY: Guilford Press.

Pruitt, C., & Smith, B. (2005). *Expanding access to baccalaureate education in Wis-*

consin. Madison, WI: University of Wisconsin.

Pusser, B. (2006). Reconsidering higher education and the public good: The role of public spheres. In W. G. Tierney (Ed.), *Governance and the public good* (pp. 11–28). Albany: State University of New York Press.

Pusser, B. (2011). Power and authority in the creation of a public sphere through higher education. In B. Pusser, S. Marginson, I. Ordorika, & K. Kempner (Eds.), *Universities and the public sphere* (pp. 27–45). New York, NY: Routledge/Taylor & Francis.

Raudenbush, S. W. (2005). Learning from attempts to improve schooling: The contribution of methodological diversity. *Educational Researcher, 34*(5), 25–31.

Rawls, J. (1971). *A theory of justice.* Cambridge, MA: Harvard University Press.

Reason, P. (1994). Three approaches to participative inquiry. In N. K. Denzin & Y. S. Lincoln (Eds.), *Handbook of qualitative research* (pp. 324–339). Thousand Oaks, CA: Sage.

Rendón, L. I. (1994). Validating culturally diverse students: Toward a new model of learning and student development. *Innovative Higher Education, 19*(1), 33–51.

Rendón, L. I., Jalomo, R. E., & Nora, A. (2000). Theoretical considerations in the study of minority student retention in higher education. In J. M. Braxton (Ed.), *Reworking the student departure puzzle* (pp. 127–156). Nashville, TN: Vanderbilt University Press.

Rendón Linares, L. I., & Muñoz, S. M. (2011, Summer). Revisiting validation theory: Theoretical foundations, applications, and extensions. *Enrollment Management Journal, 5*(2), 12–33.

Research and Planning Group for California Community Colleges (RP Group). (2007). *Basic skills as a foundation for student success in California Community Colleges.* Sacramento, CA: California Community Colleges System Office.

Rivas, S. (2008). *Reframing the role of transfer facilitators: Using action research methods for new knowledge development* (Doctoral dissertation). University of Southern California, Los Angeles.

Rodgers, C. R. (2002a). Defining reflection: Another look at John Dewey and reflective thinking. *Teachers College Record, 104*(4), 842–866.

Rodgers, C. R. (2002b). Voices inside schools: Seeing student learning: Teacher change and the role of reflection. *Harvard Educational Review, 72*(2), 230–253.

Rodriguez, A. J. (2013). Epilogue: Moving the equity agenda forward requires transformative action. In J. A. Bianchini, V. L. Akerson, A. C. Barton, O. Lee, & A. J. Rodriguez (Eds.), *Moving the equity agenda forward: Equity research, practice, and policy in science education* (pp. 355–363). Dordrecht, The Netherlands: Springer.

Rogoff, B., Baker-Sennett, J., Lacasa, P., & Goldsmith, D. (1995). Development through participation in sociocultural activity. In J. Goodnow, P. Miller, & F. Kessel (Eds.), *Cultural practices as contexts for development* [Special issue]. *New Directions for Child Development, 67,* 45–65.

Ross, J. (2007). *Sundown Town* [Photograph]. Retrieved on September 1, 2014 from http://pleasechaseme.com/sundown.php

Roth, W.-M., & Lee, Y.-J. (2007). "Vygotsky's neglected legacy": Cultural–historical activity theory. *Review of Educational Research, 77*(2), 186–232.

RP Group (Research and Planning Group for California Community Colleges). (2007). *Basic skills as a foundation for student success in California community colleges*. Sacramento, CA: California Community Colleges System Office.

Ruud, C. M., & Bragg, D. D. (2011). *The applied baccalaureate: What we know, what we learned, and what we need to know*. Champaign: University of Illinois at Urbana-Champaign, Office of Community College Research and Leadership.

Salazar-Romo, C. (2009). *Remediating artifacts: Facilitating a culture of inquiry among community college faculty to address issues of student equity and access* (Doctoral dissertation). University of Southern California, Los Angeles.

Säljö, R. (2003). Epilogue: From transfer to boundary-crossing. In T. Tuomi-Gröhn & Y. Engeström (Eds.), *Between school and work: new perspectives on transfer and boundary-crossing* (pp. 311–321). Amsterdam: Pergamon.

Satz, D. (2007, (July). Equality, adequacy, and education for citizenship. *Ethics, 117*, 623–648.

Saunders, L., & Somekh, B. (2009). Action research and educational change: Teachers as innovators. In S. E. Noffke & B. Somekh (Eds.), *The SAGE handbook of educational action research* (pp. 190–201). Los Angeles, CA: Sage.

Sawyer, R. (2007). *Group genius: The creative power of collaboration*. Philadelphia: Basic Books.

Schein, E. H. (1985). *Organizational culture and leadership*. San Francisco, CA: Jossey-Bass.

Schön, D. A. (1983). *The reflective practitioner*. New York, NY: Basic Books.

Schön, D. A. (1987). *Educating the reflective practitioner*. San Francisco, CA: Jossey-Bass.

Schön, D. A. (2010). From technical rationality to reflection-in-action. In A. Campbell & S. Groundwater-Smith (Eds.), *Action research in education: Distinctive methodologies employed in action research in schools* (Vol. II, pp. 337–370). Los Angeles, CA: Sage.

Seo, M. G., & Creed, W.E.D. (2002). Institutional contradictions, praxis, and institutional change: A dialectical perspective. *Academy of Management Review, 27*(2), 222–247.

Smith, P. (2012). *Encouraging student success: Turning attention to practitioners and institutions* (Doctoral dissertation). University of Southern California, Los Angeles.

Somekh, B., & Nissen, M. (2011). Cultural–historical activity theory and action research. *Mind, Culture, and Activity, 18*(2), 93–97.

Spillane, J. P. (2012). Data in practice: Conceptualizing the data-based decision-making phenomena. *American Journal of Education, 118*(2), 113–141.

St. John, E. P. (2013). *Research, actionable knowledge, and social change: Reclaiming social responsibility through research partnerships*. Sterling, Virginia: Stylus.

Stanton-Salazar, R. D. (1997). A social capital framework for understanding the socialization of racial minority children and youths. *Harvard Educational Review, 67*(1), 1–40.

Stanton-Salazar, R. D. (2001). *Manufacturing hope and despair: The school and kin support networks of U.S.–Mexican youth*. New York, NY: Teachers College Press.

Stanton-Salazar, R. D. (2011). A social capital framework for the study of institutional agents and their role in the empowerment of low-status youth. *Youth &
Society, 43*(3), 1066–1109

Subramaniam, T. (2012). *A developmental evaluation of action research as a process for organizational change* (Doctoral dissertation). University of Southern
California, Los Angeles.

Sue, D. W., Capodilupo, C. M., Torino, G. C., Bucceri, J. M., Holder, A. M. B.,
Nadal, K. L., & Esquilin, M. (2007). Racial microaggressions in everyday life:
Implications for clinical practice. *American Psychologist, 62*(4), 271–286. doi:
10.1037/0003-066x.62.4.271

Sue, D. W., Nadal, K. L., Capodilupo, C. M., Lin, A. I., Torino, G. C., & Rivera, D.
P. (2008). Racial microaggressions against Black Americans: Implications for
counseling. *Journal of Counseling and Development, 86*(3), 330–338.

Swain, S. (2013). *Diversity education goals in higher education: A policy discourse
analysis* (Doctoral dissertation). University of Maine, Orono.

Tanaka, G. (2002). Higher education's self-reflexive turn: Toward an intercultural
theory of student development. *Journal of Higher Education, 73*(2), 263–296.

Taylor, E. (2009a). CRT and interest convergence in the backlash against affirmative action: Washington State and Initiative 200. In E. Taylor, D. Gillborn, &
G. Ladson-Billings (Eds.), *Foundations of critical race theory in education* (pp.
117–128). New York, NY: Routledge.

Taylor, E. (2009b). Foundations of critical race theory in education: An introduction. In E. Taylor, D. Gillborn, & G. Ladson-Billings (Eds.), *Foundations of
critical race theory in education* (pp. 1–13). New York, NY: Routledge.

Taylor, E., Gillborn, D., & Ladson-Billings, G. (Eds.). (2009). *Foundations of critical
race theory in education.* New York, NY: Routledge.

Teranishi, R., & Briscoe, K. (2006). Social capital and racial stratification in higher
education. In J. C. Smart & M. B. Paulsen (Eds.), *Higher education: Handbook
of theory and research* (Vol. 21, pp. 591–614). New York, NY: Springer.

Tharp, R. G. (1993). Institutional and social context of educational practice and re-
form. In E. A. Forman, N. Minick, & C. A. Stone (Eds.), *Contexts for learning:
Sociocultural dynamics in children's development* (pp. 269–282). New York,
NY: Oxford University Press.

Tharp, R. G. (1997). *From at-risk to excellence: Research, theory, and principles
for practice.* Washington, DC: Center for Research on Education, Diversity &
Excellence.

Tharp, R. G., & Gallimore, R. (1988). *Rousing minds to life: Teaching, learning,
and schooling in social context.* Cambridge, United Kingdom: Cambridge University Press.

Thompson, K. D. (2013). Is separate always unequal? A philosophical examination
of ideas of equality in key cases regarding racial and linguistic minorities in
education. *American Educational Research Journal, 50*(6), 1249–1278.

Titus, M. A. (2006). Understanding college degree completion of students with low
socioeconomic status: The influence of the institutional financial context. *Research in Higher Education, 47*(4), 371–398.

Tschetter, S. (2009). *Developing adaptive expertise among community college faculty through action inquiry as a form of assessment* (Doctoral dissertation). University of Southern California, Los Angeles.

Tuomi-Gröhn, T., & Engeström, Y. (2003). *Between school and work: New perspectives on transfer and boundary-crossing.* Amsterdam: Pergamon.

Tuomi-Gröhn, T., Engeström, Y., & Young, M. (2003). From transfer to boundary-crossing between school and work as a tool for developing vocational education: An introduction. *Between school and work: New perspectives on transfer and boundary-crossing* (pp. 1–15). Amsterdam: Pergamon.

U.S. Census Bureau. (2000). *Profile of general demographic characteristics: 2000. Geographic area: Wisconsin. Table DP-1.* Retrieved from www.census.gov.

University of Wisconsin Extension & Applied Population Laboratory. (2001). *Wisconsin's racial and ethnic diversity: Census 2000 population & percentages.* Madison, WI.

University of Wisconsin, Office of Policy Analysis and Research. (2012). *Student Enrollment Fall 2010* [Data]. Retrieved August 2012 from www.uwsa.edu/opar/ssb/

University of Wisconsin, Office of Policy Analysis and Research. (2008a). UW College New First Year Students in need of English or Math Remediation, 1999–2007, by Race. Unpublished raw data.

University of Wisconsin, Office of Policy Analysis and Research. (2008b). Student Transfer, 1999–2007, by Race. Unpublished raw data.

University of Wisconsin, Office of Policy Analysis and Research. (2014). Headcount enrollment 2006–2007. Retrieved August 18, 2014, from http://www.uwsa.edu/opar/ssb/2013-14/pdf/r_a100_tot.pdf

Valenzuela, A. (1999). *Subtractive schooling.* Albany: State University of New York Press.

Verstegen, D. A. (1998, Summer). Judicial analysis during the new wave of school finance litigation: The new adequacy in education. *Journal of Education Finance, 24,* 51–68.

Viesca, K. M. (2013). Linguicism and racism in Massachusetts education policy. *Education Policy Analysis Archives, 21*(52), 1–37. Retrieved from epaa.asu.edu/ojs/article/view/977

Vines, E. (2012). *Re-mediating practitioners' practice for equity in higher education: Evaluating the effectiveness of action research* (Doctoral dissertation). University of Southern California, Los Angeles.

Wells, A. (2014). *Seeing past the "colorblind" myth of education policy: Addressing racial and ethnic inequality and supporting culturally diverse schools.* Boulder, CO: National Education Policy Center.

Wells, G. (2009). Dialogic inquiry as collaborative action research. In S. E. Noffke & B. Somekh (Eds.), *The SAGE handbook of educational action research* (pp. 50–61). Los Angeles, CA: Sage.

Wells, G. (2011). Integrating CHAT and action research. *Mind, Culture, and Activity, 18*(2), 161–180.

What Works Clearinghouse: A trusted source of scientific evidence of what works in education. (2006). Retrieved July 19, 2006, from w-w-c.org/

White, S. (1995). Reason, modernity, and democracy. In S. White (Ed.), *The Cambridge companion to Habermas* (pp. 3–18). Cambridge, United Kingdom: Cambridge University Press.

Wisconsin Technical College System. (2010). System-wide enrollment by sex and race/ethnicity. Retrieved May 25, 2010, from www.wtcsystem.edu/reports/data/factbook/index.htm

Wisconsin Technical College System. (2012). *Student Enrollment Fall 2010.* Unpublished raw data.

Wisconsin Technical College System. (2014). *Fact Book 2014.* Retrieved August 18, 2014 from www.wtcsystem.edu/reports/data/factbook/pdf/headcount.pdf

Witham, K., & Bensimon, E. M. (2012). Creating a culture of inquiry around equity and student success. In S. D. Museus & U. M. Jayakumar (Eds.), *Creating campus cultures: Fostering success among racially diverse student populations* (pp. 46–67). New York, NY: Routledge.

Woerner, C. R. (2013). *Designing equity-focused action research: Benefits and challenges to sustained collaboration and organizational change* (Doctoral dissertation). University of Southern California, Los Angeles.

Yamagata-Lynch, L. C. (2007). Confronting the dilemmas for understanding complex human interactions in design-based research from a cultural–historical activity theory framework. *Journal of the Learning Sciences, 16*(4), 451–484.

Yosso, T. J., Parker, L., Solórzano, D. G., & Lynn, M. (2004). From Jim Crow to affirmative action and back again: A critical race discussion of racialized rationales and access to higher education. *Review of Research in Education, 28,* 1–25.

Yosso, T. J., Smith, W. A., Ceja, M., & Solórzano, D. G. (2009). Critical race theory, racial microaggressions, and campus racial climate for Latina/o undergraduates. *Harvard Educational Review, 79*(4), 659–691.

Zembylas, M. (2011). Investigating the emotional geographies of exclusion at a multicultural school. *Emotion, Space and Society, 4,* 151–159.

Index

INDEX

203

About the Authors

Alicia C. Dowd, Ph.D., is an associate professor of higher education at the University of Southern California's Rossier School of Education and codirector of the Center for Urban Education (CUE). Her research focuses on political–economic issues of racial/ethnic equity in postsecondary outcomes, organizational learning and effectiveness, accountability, and the factors affecting student attainment in higher education. Since joining CUE in 2006, she has been instrumental in developing the Equity Scorecard, CUE's signature action research process.

Dowd is currently the principal investigator of a study of organizational learning through data use under conditions of accountability in higher education, which is funded by the Spencer Foundation. Previously, she was the principal investigator of several national studies of institutional effectiveness, equity, community college transfer, benchmarking, and assessment, including a multiyear National Science Foundation–funded study of *Pathways to STEM Bachelor's and Graduate Degrees for Hispanic Students and the Role of Hispanic Serving Institutions.* The results of these studies have been published in numerous journals including the *Review of Educational Research, Harvard Educational Review, Review of Higher Education, Research in Higher Education,* and *Teacher's College Record.*

Dowd is a frequent speaker on the topics of diversity and equity. She has provided Congressional testimony on diversity in STEM to the House subcommittee on Research and Science Education and addressed the topic of "Developing supportive STEM community college to 4-year college and university transfer ecosystems" at a convening of the National Academies of Sciences. Dowd was awarded her doctorate by Cornell University, where she studied the social foundations of education, labor economics, and curriculum and instruction.

Estela Mara Bensimon, Ed.D., is a professor of higher education at the University of Southern California's Rossier School of Education and codirector of the Center for Urban Education, which she founded in 1999. Bensimon applies her knowledge on organizational learning, leadership, and

207

equity at colleges and universities in several states. With a singular focus on increasing equity in higher education outcomes for students of color, she developed the Equity Scorecard—a process for using inquiry to drive changes in institutional practice and culture.

She is the principal investigator of Equity in Excellence in Colorado, a place-based project funded by the Ford Foundation and Bill and Melinda Gates Foundation. She was also the principal investigator for the Equity Scorecard Initiative in the Pennsylvania State System of Higher Education. In 2007 Professor Bensimon received a grant from the Ford Foundation to organize a series of institutes on the use of critical research methods for over 100 young scholars of equity in higher education.

Bensimon has published extensively about equity, organizational learning, practitioner inquiry, and change; and her articles have appeared in journals such as the *Review of Higher Education, Journal of Higher Education, Liberal Education,* and *Harvard Educational Review.* Her most recent publications include a coedited book, *Confronting Equity Issues on Campus: Implementing the Equity Scorecard in Theory and Practice.* She is also the coeditor of *Critical Perspectives on Race and Equity,* a special issue of the *Review of Higher Education.*

Bensimon was president of the Association for the Study of Higher Education in 2005–2006, and vice-president of the American Education Research Association, Division on Postsecondary Education in 1992–1994. She has served on the boards of the American Association for Higher Education and the Association of American Colleges and Universities. She is the current chair of AERA's Social Justice and Action Committee. In 2011, she was inducted as an AERA Fellow in recognition of excellence in research. She is a recipient of the USC Mellon Mentoring Award for faculty and Distinguished Service Award from the Association for the Study of Higher Education.

Bensimon was associate dean of the USC Rossier School of Education from 1996 to 2000 and was a Fulbright Scholar to Mexico in 2002. She earned her doctorate in higher education from Teachers College, Columbia University.